DEADLY FORCE
The Lure of Violence

DEADLY FORCE

The Lure of Violence

By

ROBERT S. CLARK, PH.D.

CHARLES C THOMAS • PUBLISHER

Springfield • Illinois • U.S.A.

Published and Distributed Throughout the World by

CHARLES C THOMAS • PUBLISHER
2600 South First Street
Springfield, Illinois 62717

© *1988 by* CHARLES C THOMAS • PUBLISHER

ISBN 0-398-05462-2

Library of Congress Catalog Card Number: 88-2113

With THOMAS BOOKS *careful attention is given to all details of manufacturing
and design. It is the Publisher's desire to present books that are satisfactory as to their
physical qualities and artistic possibilities and appropriate for their particular use.*
THOMAS BOOKS *will be true to those laws of quality that assure a good name
and good will.*

Printed in the United States of America
SC-R-3

Library of Congress Cataloging-in-Publication Data

Clark, Robert S., 1916-
    Deadly force.

    Bibliography: p.
    Includes index.
    1. Violence — United States. 2. Nonviolence.
3. Violent crimes — United States. 4. Liberty. I. Title.
HN90.V5C57 1988   303.6'2   88-2113
ISBN 0-398-05462-2

To all deadly killers and violent criminals—
And the innocent children they once were.

FOREWORD

The same quirk in the human psyche which urges man to defend his fellows, or his God, at the cost of his life, if necessary, has other consequences. It renders him helpless at the command of his belief, driven to commit cruel evils. In fact, whatever foolish fancy is tendered him under certain conditions, rules his mind, his heart and his action.

When these conditions exist, free will is nonexistent, the human spirit takes whatever shape is fostered by that circumstance.

As Professor Stanley Milgrim[1] discovered, and reported, people will obey commands to punish, without understanding, logic or reason, simply in response to covert stimuli, unrecognized by the automatic robots people become when under certain mental states. People will also believe and have faith in doctrines and ideologies without foundation in fact or truth, supported by nothing more than responses built into their nerve cells, by the phylogeny of evolution.

We have found in this study that Man has Heaven and Hell within his own soul. Do they exist elsewhere? The irrationality which commits him to maniacal sadism and masochism also impels him toward an unthinking love and altruism which spiritualizes his being and raises him to god-like compassion and purity.

It is not religion which is the opiate of the people, it is Man's tendency toward suspension of reason, in blind suppression of his identity as a freely thinking being. Man thinks, and therefore is. But is his thought free? Aristotle commented that unless a man thinks and dreams of a future he can command he can be little other than a slave.[2]

When his thoughts are subject to another's command, he has lost his freedom.

Man can learn—he must learn, he is built that way. But what he learns is largely beyond his control. He has evolved as a social being. Whatever

---

1. Stanley Milgrim, *Obedience to Authority: An Experimental View* (Harper and Row, 1974)

2. Aristotle, *Politics* (Harvard University Press, 1932).

he is to become, depends hugely on specific social experiences which shape and mold him into an urban criminal, or a sports announcer who later becomes president of a great nation. Both very probably could have started with equivalent genetic endowment.

"Man is born free, but is everywhere in chains," said Rousseau.[3] True, but the chains are of our own making. It would be grand if we could simply strike off the chains to attain liberty. It cannot be so, for the quivering fingers of our private experience write our fate upon our soul, for better or worse. These traces do restrain us from evil, as well as bind us to do good, but the reverse is equally true: We can be, and often are, locked into patterns of self-punishing violence and crime.

If we are deadly, we have been taught to be so. Those teachings bind us, chained to the deeds we have commited, and must commit in the future. Thus the violence becomes not evil to us, but useful, necessary, even beneficial in the chartered vision of our worldly eyes. As peace and cooperation are programmed into us, so is violence and deadly hate.

Can we be taught otherwise? The conclusion of this study is, "Yes." Just as we learn to be violent, we can learn to be nonviolent. In both cases, we must start early enough, and work at it hard enough. Does that mean we would become a nation of programmed robots, mindlessly acting "nice," like idiot children, smiling peacefully and ingratiatingly at our programmers, our masters?

That is: If this could be done.

Looking beyond that question, the next questions are: Would we would be a wealthier, happier nation if focused effort were given to guide our children along nonviolent routes? Would we be wealthier, happier as individuals?

We cannot pretend to know the answer to any of these questions, except the first one. We do know that it can be done.[4]

The method is implicit in the provable thesis, "Poverty does not cause crime. Rather, crime causes poverty!"

That requires some explanation of the empirical foundation for the statement. The following chapters try to do this.

_____

3. Jean Jacques Rousseau, *Social Contract* (Penguin, 1968)

4. The literature on human behavior is enormous, with perhaps a good starting point: B.F. Skinner, *Contingencies of Reinforcement* (Prentice-Hall, 1969, his *Beyond Freedom and Dignity* (Bantam, 1972) and continuing with the many citations in Chapter 3 of this book.

CONTENTS

PART FOUR: RIGHTS OF A FREE PEOPLE

PART FIVE: TOWARD REAL PERSONAL LIBERTY

LIST OF FIGURES AND TABLES

DEADLY FORCE
The Lure of Violence

PART ONE
THE CASE FOR VIOLENCE

Chapter 1

THE LURE OF VIOLENCE

*"How wonderful it is to crush
your enemies and watch them
bleeding in the dust...*

Ghenghis Khan

"It's really terrible," my wife turned the pages of the evening newspaper, scanning the headlines.

"What's up now?" I asked. "Bad news, Ciel?"

"This violence! That's all you read in the papers."

"Yes." How can one respond to a cliché? I switched on the television.

The PBS channel had "An Evening with Pops," and I listened for a moment to the familiar tune.

Ciel turned to the movie reviews and read the caption aloud. "A remake of Rambo, with more machine guns and blood!"

I shrugged and turned the knob to another channel, a street scene flickered into view, with a man leaping into a pistol-marksman's crouch to pump three fast slugs into a the body of a man, a villainous type, who fired vainly into the air. The bad-guy's partner ran to his escape car, slammed it into gear, and burned rubber. I settled down to enjoy the picture.

"Oh, come," said Ciel. "You're crowding up against the screen. Come back here on the sofa so I can see it too."

I stood up, my eyes still glued to the tv-window, slowly backing up to the sofa so I wouldn't miss a single moment. The hero ran to his own car, a sleek racing type, backed it out of the parking space, crashing into two other cars in doing so, and streaked off in pursuit of the escaping bad-guy, leaving the other culprit's dead body on the paving of the parking lot. I settled back with my wife to enjoy the show. We loved it.

Typical? Apparently so, for violence is now used to sell almost anything. Unless all of Madison Avenue is cooperating in the most colossal fraud in history, people want—they demand—to see violence more than almost any other thing. They want it, and it is provided for them. Of course, the "they" is you and me . . . just about all of us. We are lured by violence, enchanted by it, while some of us, myself included, rail against it, and feel, not so privately, ashamed.

We can ask ourselves a question: If we are attracted by violence, why do we feel ashamed about it? Shame about love and sex has been just about eliminated from public and private life. The human body is seen *au naturel* everywhere, on beach and boulevard, with non-prurient pleasure by almost all of us. We have extended sex and nudity tolerance very far.

While decrying violence at every opportunity, we actually enjoy the depiction, the exibition and practice, of violence. Are we pretending to be something we are not?

With withering comment, film critics downgrade macho, violent film stars. The more violent, the more devastating the comment: *Rambo* . . . ugh! *Conan the Barbarian* . . . even worse! They call the actors, untalented, stupid, even comically inadequate, but we spend hundreds of millions to see Sylvester Stallone in his many transmogrifications, we quote Clint Eastwood's, "Make my day!" at every opportunity. At the repeated revivals of *Death Wish* we stand up in our living rooms and cheer when Charles Bronson turns on the muggers and murders them out of hand. We love it, indeed we do.

In common with most ordinary Americans I believe in the infinite perfectability of people, and I am not satisfied with my own imperfect state. I am a man who deplores violence in all my public utterances and writings. Nevertheless I am enthralled by it in every form. I have not fallen so far as to subscribe to the magazine, *Soldier of Fortune,* but I must confess that I assiduously thumb it in my local 7-Eleven Store, before I reluctantly return it to the rack.

Recently they have removed *Playboy* and *Penthouse* from many newsstands in my county, in response to local pressure in the community for a return to a stricter moral standard. Too much sex, they claim. But we can't get enough violence to please us.

We read about it, talk about, "No. I don't go for walks at night any more. You *know* why . . . " We are surrounded by violence, and can't help be mired in it.

But that's not really true, is it? There are many other things I could do, from time to time: touch up the new scratches on the car paint, fix the bathroom faucet drip. . . . But those are chores, of transient interest, monotonous, even while we do them. If we have our druthers, we opt for violence.

For instance: Yesterday I stopped working on my car to run down the street to watch two kids whaling away at each other. Nor was I the only one. The fathers of the two boys soon became involved, and the whole neighborhood was treated to the sight of fully grown men shouting and threatening each other. This led to pushing, and—most satisfying of all—eventually knocking the tar out of each other.

It was only when the women started to scream for someone to separate them that we (me) got between the huffing and cursing combatants. Finally, sweating and breathing hard, they subsided.

My wife was scornful. "Full-grown men . . . actually fighting!"

I agreed with her. "Yeah. It was stupid."

Come to think of it, it *was* ridiculous. I had been there, nevertheless, savoring the excitement.

Afterwards we went back to our house. Nothing to do—the car was forgotten—I turned to the fights on television. I remember feeling my shoulders move with the punches, and my feet, inside my slippers, danced around the ring.

Does a mugger get the same satisfaction out of violence that I do? Does a soldier enjoy combat? Well, he enjoys the idea of combat, that's what makes a good soldier. Looking back, I remember being scared as hell in a firefight. But my diary records my elation at first hearing gunfire, in the distance. The occasional louder "bang!" made me jump in elation as I rode in a jeep toward it, then. I am afraid I would feel the same, if it happened again. . . . afraid I would feel the same . . . ? I *hope* I would feel the same! I feel the seed of it, as I write this down today.

Wasn't I really more ridiculous than the prime actors in the street fight between the two fathers? Without any personal stake of concern for my child, or for my prestige. . . . I, by my presence, encouraged and instigated explosive tempers and violence. I confess, I was lured by the sure knowledge that violence is interesting. It opens possibilities. It promises change from the hum-drum, from the status quo. I do not like the status quo, though I am better off in every way today, than ever before in my life. I have been programmed by parents, school, by my whole culture to be impatient with the status quo. I want change, and the way to reach for change is: Violence.

It is quite obvious that violence is the most frequent cause of change. It is the preferred means, the most convenient means, and often the only available means. It is sanctioned by every revolutionary movement since the world began. The example of our own American Revolution is today hailed as the herald of violent resistance in every Third World country, in every underground movement, in every terrorist organization. "Violence, as Rapp Brown said it,[1] "is as American as cherry pie." He would have said an even larger truth if he had said violence is as human as eating and breathing.

I am still fascinated by stories about World War II, the Korean War, and about 'Nam. Newsstories about violence, such as the bombing of our Marines in Lebanon, and the recurrent hostage-taking violence, sends me down to the newsstand, to buy the latest edition of the paper, to discover the details I can't get on the television screen.

I admit, like so many, most of the time we don't bother to buy the paper. We get enough "news" from the big tube at the 11 o'clock roundup. But a really juicy story of violence in the Middle East, a death-dealing earthquake in Mexico, or a skyjacking with great savagery will send even my wife out at odd hours to review all the brutal facts. That's interesting!

Is it because we are truly concerned? I doubt it. I, for one, practically never do anything about it. I just glory in the story. It is only occasionally, such as now, that I make excuses for my macabre taste in contemporary literature.

If all there is to this matter of violent force is that a lot of people use violence, and a lot of people enjoy the spectacle of outrageous brutality, it would not be important, except to strict moralists and philosophers. It goes beyond that, however.

We Are Under Siege.

It means that the world has come to be under siege. It has come to be that we expect violence, actual and symbolic, in some form every day. Each shocking scene inures us, hardens us, so that even more vivid stimulation is demanded to arouse our excitement the next time around. It takes quite a vicious breaking of the peace to attract even nominal notice. We casually dismiss daily disasters affecting other people as routine.

This violent onslaught on our perceptions occupies our mind and our efforts, preempting our individual and national attention. Terrorism has become institutionalized, with a "Chief Terrorism Analyst," employed by Rand Corporation, the California think-tank. Nor are they the only example of organized submission to the ethos of terror and violence.

Some governments not only provide logistical backing and sanctuary, but designate an agency to oversee relations with terrorists.[2] These agencies compete for influence and budget, and resist dismantling, as do all bureaucracies, and seek ever wider areas to which their powers can be extended. These bureaucratic institutions, in effect, become planning and research departments for the ever more widely extended terrorist networks.[3]

Subcultures of Violence.

On the international scene a permanent subculture of violence and terrorism is already in place. Of course, locally, in countless neighborhoods and byways, we have long ago institutionalized violence and terror not only as entertainment, but also with "survival" training which somehow has evolved into large scale paramilitary idolization of actual and symbolic violence.[4]

Whether the media respond to the market, or create the market, is a chicken-and-egg-argument. No doubt, media and market interact, each responding to, and creating each other. Experts repeatedly describe the condition, but few prescribe credible treatment. The circumstances has become too splintered, nationally and locally. We are all part of it, now. Violence is an accepted fact of life — "commonplace, ordinary, banal, and therefore somehow tolerable."[5]

Chapter 2

IRRESISTABLE URGES TO DEADLY FORCE

"The best lack all conviction,
while the worst
Are full of passionate intensity"

William Butler Yeats

When Should You Shoot An Intruder?

"In the middle of the night," reads a newspaper feature story[1], "lying fast asleep in a bedroom, you're awakened by a sharp noise: A burglar is in the house. You have an expensive set of sterling flatware in the dining room—and a gun in the night table. Should you use it?"

The impulse to do so is almost irresistible. You are defending your home. If your loved ones are present, you *must* take action! Could you restrain yourself? Should you restrain yourself?

Isn't this a case in which you could legally, ethically and tactically shoot to kill? Many people would say the criminal deserves it. In any case, you feel you must do so, to protect your home and family. We anticipate this emergency, as shown by the statistic indicating one out of every four registered voters owns a gun and keeps it in his home. In many urban areas the percentage is over 50 percent of householders.

The armed burglar knows this, and has already decided to use his weapon, "In my own defense if I have to," is his rationalization. He, too, feels that he is a victim of the situation, merely defending himself. His urge to use deadly force is as irresistible as that of the homeowner.

We're not making a brief for the utterly unjustified urge to aggression rising in the veins of the armed burglar—we speak simply of the fact that the urge to violence is there. The "Law of the Situation" takes over.[2]

Such confrontations make up the materials which are later reported in annual statistics of the use of deadly force. Handguns are built with such one-on-one situations in mind. Simply put: To shoot at people.

10

The Mystique of the Killing Arts.

We make an art form of handgun shooting, simulating the killing of humans. Public pistol and rifle ranges throughout the country provide sites for practice in combat shooting. Fast-draw competitions are compelling attractions, and popular practice for police and criminals, adults and little boys. An innovation in police training films now shows women and young girls entering the hot race to take combat handgun positions, demonstrating improved domestic skills in the use of deadly weapons.[3]

The mystique is irresistible; can we deny it? To look at a finely fashioned pistol is to feel the desire to hold it. The butt fits snugly, satisfyingly in the palm. Fingers naturally curl around it, index finger automatically going to the trigger. Holding it brings on a rush of desire to point it at someone. "Bang! You're dead," says the child. Too often it becomes fact, not acting-out. For self-defense is a daily fact of life for many people today. Especially is this so in poor neighborhoods.

The laws against concealed weapons must be ignored by ghetto youths, as a statement of personal reality. If a gun cannot be obtained, a knife will have to do. If not a knife, then one must practice various deadly martial arts, kung-fu, kendo, and become skilled in use of devilishly clever weapons. Each has accompanying appropriate techniques to commit instant death. All this is needed for personal survival in a violent world. But you know this.

We deplore the violent attitudes that are mandated on ghetto children. But even those better off cannot resist the urge to send young children to schools to learn how to deal in violence. We lose the gambit by participating in it. "Youngsters even in the upper middle-class must learn to survive, too," say mothers. Children's registration in martial arts schools has risen 3000 percent in ten years.[4] Instruction to children in deadly arts is truly a growth industry.[5]

Americans Export Violence.

One might think that Americans would decry bloodshed overseas, but the terrorist raids in Northern Ireland are hugely funded by Americans who vicariously share in that deadly force. The equally bloody suppressive actions of the British military are supported by other Americans, and the United States government. Everyone weeps that both sides lose, but the lure is too great, and the killings continue.

The Contagion Spreads.

Flashes of terrorism criss-cross the world, as we get the news. One is from Lebanon, then Germany; next Puerto Rico, then back across the Atlantic we hear of bombs in Athens, Greece and then Turkey. Omit the genocidal Iran-Iraq war, when a government does it, is it terrorism? Skip across the ocean again to Nicaragua and San Salvador. All present their irresistible attractions to people, . . . and their particular anguish. Periodicals addressed to militants, radicals, conservatives, soldiers of fortune are filled with ads calling for recruits and financial aid. Officially and unofficially we participate in the worldwide terrorism we hypocritically deplore. We call our own violence: "Defense." But our statements are more a defense of violence, than of ourselves.

Moral Burnout.

Our children are born into a world that has been weakened with ethical burnout. The *tabula rasa* of a young mind is especially susceptible to incitement to violence. Children, today, exhibit moral burnout long before their teens. After a particularly horrible murder of a mother, by her fourteen-year-old daughter, the California prosecutor said, "They sank into this morass of listening to this music of sex and violence."[6]

To the jury it must have sounded like a poem to pain. The girl and her boy friend beat the mother with a wrench, and stabbed her with a kitchen knife. Absorbed in Satanism and heavy metal rock music, said the prosecutor, they willingly responded to the suggestions of irresistable need for violence and death as a solution to all problems.

This is not to say that it has been proved beyond doubt that such music is actually an incitement to murder. The basic problem is that we are willing to ascribe our problems to such causes, accept them as explanation, and then do nothing about it.

Some research indicates that youngsters may not even be aware of the meaning of the words of songs calling for sadistic killing and sexual aberrations, but the violence and black morality projects its message across emotional channels which are perceived by prosecutors and the rest of us, as certainly as children and dogs perceive hostility between adults.

The Cult of Liberty.

Since 1776 Americans have luxuriated in a cult of liberty for all. We have bathed in it, and gloried in it, attributing to it our economic success, our political mobility, our world prestige, and our standing as the haven of choice for persecuted people overseas. Blindly, we cling to this cult as the solution to all our lingering enclaves of minority dissatisfaction. We think we've solved the problem: One person, one vote. Numerical majority to rule. It has become a shibboleth, our panacea, needing no other recourse, for every social ill.

Has this social ideology so overcome our minds that we must use it as a universal cure? Is there no way to look upon the face of a violent ogre that on occasion lyingly calls himself "Freedom" but is more truly seen as, "To Hell with you?"

Louis XV's pompous comment, "After me the Deluge!" is echoed in deed and word, by every spoiled, grasping, demanding child, and we dote upon the little ingrate as merely, "expressing himself." We dare not tread upon his freedom. Why should we? When we see our highest officers, our wealthiest citizens, practicing the same credo.[7]

Editorialists cripple their complaints in the media by their phrasing: "Where are the limits of freedom?"[8]

It is not freedom that is the problem, it is the cultish, mindless use of that word, to describe what is simply uninhibited greed and hate.

Crossed Signals.

Not everyone sees the matter so clearly; particularly not our public towncriers, our politicians and leaders. Certainly our commentators in print and electronic media send crossed signals. The issues presented are mixed, in confused sequence. Every police and citizen confrontation provokes this general confusion and disagreement among the survivors, witnesses, bystanders, and outsiders.

It is without dispute that police policies and training in the use of force in life-threatening situations require massive reevaluation. Such reevaluation, however, is seriously, if not impossibly, handicapped because the dogmas of our society interfere with rational police policies.

Is Self-Defense Vigilantism?

With self-defense on everyone's mind, the police are forced by their roles to deplore the possession and use of weapons by civilians. "Leave it to us," they say. They must say that, because that is their job. But due to no necessary fault of theirs, they do not, and cannot do their job. There is violence out there that must be defended against.

The laws of most states permit deadly force in defense of one's life and limb. Here we have another divisive factor wrenching our society. Is Bernard Goetz a Subway Killer, or a distraught, imposed-upon victim of our failure to protect him?[9] A New York jury called him victim. Hundreds protested the decision in the streets of the city. But thousands throughout the country silently applauded.

Police or Home Invaders?

Repeatedly, there are instances where police are charged with not having identified themselves so as to allay fear on the part of citizens, when the police act in pursuit of an investigation. Often youths who resist with force will claim they feared being mugged by men brandishing guns—who were only later discovered to be police on a lawful mission. This seems reasonable under current conditions, where it can commonly be assumed that the next fellow is armed. How to resolve this dilemma?

"Protect Yourself At All Times!"

Modern police street tactics call for officers to minimize their own risk in threatening situations. But that ignores the prime function of the police: To protect the public. Thus we have a reversal of roles. The protectors become the first protected, and in many cases, the only ones protected. Is this easily resolved?

To minimize the officer's risk is a goal that to police, and their instructors, seems eminently reasonable. Consequently they must recognize that weapons and the intent to use them are widely present in the community. The logic follows: Police concentrate on training in instantaneous response in "Shoot/Don't Shoot" situations.[10]

Events are complicated in the field, by fluctuating emotions and erratic behavior. Neither can be predicted or taught precisely. It follows that such tactical training, and its implementation under conditions of uncertainty on our city streets forces "police patrol" to become a macabre hunting sport of kill or be killed. As is well known to military psychologists,[11] the morale and interest of both adversaries—cops and robbers—rises to high levels, to meet these challenges.

In the backrooms of police stations, and in the ranks of the street people, the stories of derry-do reach high pitches of excited retelling.

Prisoners Practice Pistol-Shooting Too.

Gloomily looming over police academy and stationhouse gun training, however, is the information returned from prisons that inmates practice quick-draw action in their "recreation" hours. Another course in their informal curriculum is the art and science of disarming police officers. Bravo for education, and upward mobility!

Both sides, theirs and ours, constantly update their procedures, revise their "game-plans" and reinforce the lessons with rigorous training.

Tension in the police increases when news broadcasts excitedly report five officers are shot in a single county in five days.[12]

As can be expected, the police reaction is to arm themselves even more thoroughly.[13] It is now recommended by experts in police tactics that officers carry, in addition to their service revolver on duty, another revolver in an ankle holster, and still a third pistol in a pocket in their trousers. Thus, even if the officer is disarmed in a struggle, he will have these backup guns to maintain firepower. Ancient Romans restricted their gladiteorial contests to the Colesseum. We, more democratically, use the streets of our crowded cities, with audience participation.

Of course, it is recommended that all officers on duty wear bullet-proof vests or shields.[14] Query: Why not off duty, too?

Why not all of us?

We Pay the Consequence.

What the effect of all this is on the strained relationship between officers and community has not been fully comprehended. It is clear, however, that we are in a bind from which we do not know how to extricate ourselves. Recruiting teams, trying to induce young men to apply for positions with the police, tend to emphasize the hazard and glamor of the job, with thrilling street battles by over-armed police officers prevailing television-style, over all odds. Reality thereafter patterns itself after art, as police academy graduates eagerly watch television's heroic performances for clues to proper style. Experienced police executives describe the police-style promoted by the boob tube as: "Pandemonium."[15]

The few lone voices that object to the heightening of the level of violence and deadly force deplore the facts, but offer few practical remedies. Juries react by releasing survivors of the frequent shoot-outs, impressed as they are with the reality of the defensive roles played by all concerned.

A License to Commit Crime.

America symbolizes a free country, true, but the symbol has come to mean: A land where if expected upward mobility does not occur easily enough, well, . . . guns are simple to obtain and easily used to expedite the upward mobility that has been promised without conditions of tedious labor, habits of savings, or technical education. That is to say, to commit crime.

Haitians, landing one way or another, on our shores as timid, friendly refugees from political or economic persecution, soon become violent resisters of assaults upon themselves, and shortly acquire new moods and attitudes, toward the use of deadly force and crime against others.[16] There is no hint of blame intended in this statement. It is clearly Hobbesian personal defense.

No longer do we have watchful neighbors to monitor behavior, raise alarms, and bring on immediate aid to suppress the first signs of violence in children and adults as it was in tightly knit communities of long ago. When teenagers fight among themselves or with their elders, we continue to walk straight ahead, as if we wear blinders. We go uneasily about our own business, not wanting to be involved, "Watch out, John, he may have a knife . . . " or a gun, for that matter.

Only the constant presence of a police officer sets some damper on overt violence. The police, however, mostly pass at thirty-five miles an hour, sealed within their air-conditioned, or heated cars. They see not, and hear not—listening only to distant drum-commands from radio-central. Violence on the streets proceeds unchecked.

The general process of growing up in urban America fosters a personal dynamic tending to increase the use of deadly force. An often cited grand jury report states:[17]

Delinquency, crime and urban violence should not be mysterious if we take the time to try to understand.

The data suggest a direct and causal relationship between failure and alienation, as experienced by our children when in school. Eighty percent of adjudged delinquents read at the three lowest levels of ability.

Schools are the dumping grounds of society's problems. Closely linked as they are with other key elements of a child's life, we try to place on the school the burden which they have never been able to carry: Build motivation to be nonviolent.

Most credible research indicates that unless a child develops the motivation, before school age, to react nonviolently, he will never learn it. That is to say, not in school, nor in later life. The only reliable inhibitory influence will be the youth's ultimately slowing responses. The drying up of passionate juices that middle-age brings, that will let violence begin to seep away from his personal responses to life's agonies.

What schools can do, fostering small lessons in cooperation, is founded on a child's success in schoolwork. But success in school, as presently conducted, is dependent on coping with a highly competitive environment. The raw competition of school-work alienates and depresses the sense of success of most children. It is only with constant support, and insistent aid of parents and relatives that a child can survive to reach the grail of becoming a happy problem-solving adult. Unfortunately, the seeds of pupil failures are often planted before the child is three years old, when he first clearly learns that there other people in the world who can, and often do, frustrate and oppose him.

That sense of failure does not occur late, or suddenly. In large measure it is the destiny of a child brought into a world he never knew. Depending on the child's family situation, it occurs early and gradually. With incompetent parents inconsistent in their guidance and discipline, it grows malignantly, with increasing certainty of failure, disenchantment, and alienation. With angry punishing parents, the child outwardly surrenders, in defense of his own soul, he turns off, as the phrase has it, first to idleness, then to ignorance and violence. The raging anger of a three year old is impressive in its abandonment to sheer emotion. Ahead lies only more alienation, unless there is a turnabout.

What happens when the child reaches school age? Empirical research implies that condemnation of the school for egregious errors is an exaggeration, for the school does not start with raw material. On the contrary, it is burdened with the product of home environment. Further, the home and neighborhood influence persists even during the few hours of the school day. Long after-school hours, holidays, and vacations further encroach on the time of school exposure. Continuation of preexisting home-grown errors, if any, is almost certain. It is not difficult to forecast the extremes of either failure or success in school. Much of that is foreordained. For the school can do only so much, granted its present structure and constraints.

It is not a lack of money for the schools that seems to be called for. More money could possibly increase the obstinacy of the problem. Unfortunately the route we have been using to improve is loaded with erroneous assumptions, that infect even reform ideas.

And the multiplication table! What pain we inflict on our children before that instrument of torture becomes a part of our instinctive response: "Eight times seven is fifty-six!"

As adults we often experience the exciting inspiration of learning new things. That does happen for children, too. Not, however, as often as we'd like to remember. Schooling, in particular, is unutterably boring, a series of annoying misfortunes for most kids—especially for those who become deadly problems as they grow older. They learn to seek any avenue out of the enraging burdens set upon them.

Permissive Parenting.

Ghetto parents who lovingly try to ease this burden by permitting absence from school, instantly gratify their happy children. Accepting these offers to escape from obligation, a child can appreciate a parent who finds fault with teacher or school system. Both parent and child are irresistibly impelled to downgrade the importance of learning pesky school subjects. Naturally the child feels completely justified in refusing to learn the tedious unrewarding three R's. How much more thrilling and immediately useful it is to learn to terrorize a younger child into surrendering his lunchmoney! Much more. It is exciting to learn that with other kids in a gang you become free from individual guilt. The other kids did it! It is even more exciting to learn that with the help of bigger kids one can confuse and frighten adult motorists stopped at a red light, and make off with purses. This is a *good life*. It satisfies.

Self-Actualization.

This discovery, that crime is fun, is a revelation that refuses to consent to confinement and drudgery in school. Violent resistance is manifested by defiant graffiti, broken school windows and assaults on the goody-two-shoes children whose parents insist on school success.

We have not found a way for either teachers or school system to command the attention and respect needed for the weary travail of schoolwork. Despairingly, we search for better teachers who will be able to eliminate the toil and trouble of learning basic skills. Somehow we hope they might be able to make it all an "adventure in learning." For the average child that is a nauseating metaphor. School is a drag. If there is a chance that boredom and drudgery can be escaped by violence, that chance will be taken, as a lesser evil.

History shows few examples of ways to insulate our children from the deadly monotony and labor of learning how to become civilized. Permitting 'natural' childish violent resistance to express itself, without a return to dedication to the tasks themselves, has only germinated seeds for further violent reaction to frustration and deprivation.

Until we invent a world without frustration and impotence we must train our children to bear the present pain for hope of future gain.

In Pain Are We Born . . .

Our community leaders, and school bureaucrats, acting in good faith, develop their own illogic of blaming the school and society for what may well be a natural condition of mankind: "In pain are we born, in labor do we live, and in sorrow do we die."

An executive's schedule that features eleven-hour office stints, mandatory social activities, endless meetings, as well as nights and Saturdays devoted to business, accepts it all only because he has become inured to it over a long learning period. We have found no way to make a childhood utterly free and without obligation, that can train an individual for responsible conscientious adulthood. Child-psychologist Bruno Bettelheim's[18] indulgent view of children and the "need to play," has come only with his advancing years as a loving grandfather. As we grow older we become, we are sure, wiser. We envy the lost hours of play . . . hours that many of us never had, and we want to indulge our children and grandchildren. That is quite well-intentioned, right enough, but what has that got to do with bringing up children who will perform well, and will avoid violence?

Why should we ever have expected to find such a nirvana...one without hard study and boring drills for our lovely children? In insisting on fumbling attempts to provide a heaven for children when they are young, we have driven many of them, especially those without rich families to subsidize them, to the fringes of a hell of brutal existence, because they never learned to deal with small hardships. Too easily they fall into patterns that provide them with a world where violence becomes a desirable resolution of all problems.

Commercial Exploitation of Violence.

The hypnotic fascination deadly force has on our consciousness is catered to by the proliferating firms which sell weapons in a vast array of styles and prices. They are displayed attractively in the most unexpected places, each offering stimulating another incitement to become part of the violence-system. Each rerun of films such as *Platoon, Dirty Harry, Full Metal Jacket,* and countless others, prods a rush to the local gun store for pistols, rifles, and shotguns. Flea markets are a favorite outlet, clandestinely, or openly, vending brass knuckles, ninja sticks and chains, 'stars of steel,' designed to be thrown at offending victims. The urge is not merely toward defense, it is clearly meant to attack.

The Female of the Species.

Female street gangs are so numerous and aggressive they have attracted serious study by academic criminologists at Rutgers and other universities. As Professor Anne Campbell has stated, these girls, "get involved in quick, dramatic, exciting soap-opera events in order to give their lives some meaning."

The squalid reaches of these studies do not prevent the researchers from romanticizing the roles involved. "Getting down," that is, to fight with firearms is considered an initiation, or rite of passage among such girl-gangs. They are not denied "equal rights" with the young male gangs.

The only thing that seems to hold such youth gangs under control is the fear of escalating violence by other gangs. There never seems to be a lack of violent youth gangs using abandoned buildings of the urban ghettoes. For girls, coming from hostile, one-parent families, lonely, illiterate, unemployed, and often saddled with one or two babies by age fifteen or sixteen, life is a personal West Side story. Like other youth, they are irresistably urged to violence.

Glamorized by the media, the horror of it all escapes us . . . most of the time.

Chapter 3

WHAT CAN BE DONE NOW?

> *"Whatsoever thy hand*
> *findeth to do, do it."*
>
> Ecclesiastes, IX, 10

Faced with rising rates of violence locally and on the international scene we are offered a gamut of cures. The cures proposed have ranged from mild, even peaceful, efforts to channel self-interest along nonviolent paths, to more aggressive opposition to violent groups with force, applied robustly, by state and federal police and the military. Nevertheless, what to do remains a puzzle because we have tried both ends of that spectrum, without much success. We have not been able to reduce the use of deadly force, either locally, nationally, or on the international scene. Paraphrasing Eccliastes, what our hand has found to do, has not been sufficient.

The questions devolve on, "Where is the source of the legitimate and credible authority that could command peace and social order?"[1] The world has searched for this for millenia. Many are the routes that have been taken, seeking the answer.[2] Of the thousands of devices and systems tried, those that have offered promise clearly reveal two basic modes:

1. *Internalized Controls:* Various forms of moral suasion, founded on religion or reason; passion or prejudice; conscience or consequence.

2. *Externalized Controls:* Rigorous use of deadly force and fear of immediate physical pain, extended punishment or penal servitude.

In actual practice, combinations of these controls have been quite usual. The external brutalities of Ancient Rome were supported by a large number of ethical and patriotic guides to internalizing conscience.[3] To leap ahead in history, the Founding Fathers of this country, properly suspicious of man's propensity to mischief, based their efforts on the moral sentiments of the Declaration of Independence, and the complex fabric of the Constitution, with its many checks and balances. Underlaying these, however, were the restraints of religious consciousness, which elicited respect.

Respect, it has been remarked, was one of the themes of the Declaration itself, claiming as it did, a "decent respect for the opinions of mankind."

Violence: Problem or Solution?

Violence, we must note, is not inevitably a problem. On many occasions it is a tempting solution to individual and group predicaments. Most countries show a history of moralist defense of preferred lines of violence. A common excuse is: to suppress even greater violence. Or, as in our Declaration of Independence, to right great wrongs.

As to the control of violence, however, over the years from the dawn of history, we have let much old experience and wisdom become lost, washed away in an orgy of revulsion, contrition, and horror at the overwhelming disaster of World War II. Modern imagination appears to conceive of only one way to have a nonviolent citizenry. That is: Government use of overwhelming violence.

Europeans, having had their fill of government violence in the years of World War II, prefer a mild reaction to criminal violence. Thus, most of Europe has eliminated capital punishment.[4] Penal sentences are short compared to the United States.

The United States is almost as reluctant to use government violence to suppress crime. Organizationally and emotionally, our reactions tend to think of rehabilitation, humaneness, and even forgiveness. We cling to parole, community treatment and probation, despite statistical proof that they, and other gentle measures are not really working. We have become politically incompetent to deal with violence in our cities to the point where a backlash of opposing sentiment is developing. Although avoidance of violence to suppress violence never became persuasive to some of the world's governments, today, more nations are beginning, once again, to see violence as an attractive and productive solution to problems of personal and political violence that will not go away.

Controlling Violence Through Conscience.

We can omit describing the almost endless list of past methods of dealing with crime, violence, and disorder. Instead, let us go directly into peaceful human groups, and even inside the individual member's consciousness and awareness of that group. That is, from the position of the individual member's subjective experience of social life. What does *membership* in different groups really mean to him?

There are groups which we can call, "Hyperorthodox."[5] This rather unusual word denotes a group with extremely rigorous demands on its members in terms of acceptable behavior and thought. Forms of behavior are ritualized. Thoughts and consciences of members are repeatedly examined for adherence to strict standards.

It helps to remember examples of such groups, which include any of the more fervid religions, even false religions or cults, or any group which elicits extremely passionate and devoted compliance with detailed tenets of belief and action. During wartime, many a nation has reached such a high pitch of patriotic devotion and partisanship as to fit this category.[6]

When an individual is conscious of his membership in such a group, and fully accepts its dogma, doctrine and duties, several interesting phenomena are demonstrated.[7]

Skepticism and criticism appear to be suspended. Faith becomes the only acceptable credo, and disbelief in the smallest measure becomes sinful, even criminal and detestable. A great mutual love and support among members arises. Respect, even adoration for the leaders and outstanding exponents of that group becomes usual, even mandatory. Fanatical, rabid protestations of faith and willingness to sacrifice even one's life to advance the cause of the group become the norm.

In recent years we have seen reports of such devotion to various and quite different creeds. The boysoldiers of the Iranian military show these characteristics, as do their mothers.[8] Willingness to self-sacrifice is outstanding. Many terrorists engaged in holy war against Israel, the United States, and other "Satans," have shown a similar disregard for their own safety and lives.

The reaction shown by victims of such dedicated violence often rises to equal intensity. Over time, often a mirror image of the initiating hyperorthodoxy is created. Both hyperorthodox groups develop in each of its members a consciousness of spiritual identity with his own group. There is an obverse side to the faith: As part of the piety, there arises a spiritually inspired opposition to the other group, as the enemy. Often the obverse side goes so far as to identify all other groups as "devils," nonpersons, . . . as enemies.

In each individual, the passionate identification with one group, and the ineradicable sense of opposition to the other, become mutually reinforcing doctrines, which then tend to merge and come to identify that individual in his consciousness, more certainly than his own name.

By whatever term, doctrine, ideology, or movement, a large part of the personality of a member is submerged into his group. The group's dogmas become his morality, his conscience. Of course, when this level of indoctrination is reached all violence in support of the movement becomes virtue.[9]

The special point of all this is that members of these groups attain a very high level of strict observance of the particular laws of these organizations. However complex and arduous the rules of behavior may be, obedience is expected, and given. In fact, research suggests that the complexity and arduous nature of the practices demanded by the ideology is a powerful factor in reinforcing obedience.[10]

Law observance under such conditions is just about universal. If nonviolence becomes the law of such a hyperorthodox group, it exists not only as the expected norm, it becomes the reality as well. Such a person will remain nonviolent, even at peril to his own life.

Social Groups and Bonding.

Societies ruled by such hyperorthodox methods have frequently built virtually crimeless communities.[11] Other groups less demanding of their members, try to control less, and thus exhibit less control. The range of this control is wide, varying between each group, although all hyperorthodox groups try to internalize bonding with other members, with the leadership and with the basic dogma. If monitoring constraints on thought, conscience and behavior are less, and threatened spiritual punishments are less, no doubt spiritual rewards promised and granted, are less as well.

Some of these associations consist of adults only. The prime nonreligious examples of such organizations that reach for hyperorthodoxy of attitudes, emotions, and behavior are military forces. But less publicized examples are found in unions, political campaign organizations, and some public interest groups, such as pro- or antiabortion, environmental task forces, an other dedicated associations.

Religious groups, however, and families, impose their training on children, as well as adults. Their rules and rites generally are severe in demands of internalization of control of conscience and mind. In Freudian terms, they impose a superego of moral precepts mandated by the family or congregation, and leave few basic value judgments to random individual development.[12]

We Claim to Forbid Hyperorthodox Methods.

Our U.S. Constitution, with its ban on intermingling of secular and religious matters would seem to prohibit imposition of hyperorthodox processes to inculcate internalized controls. The idea smacks of religion, and the First Amendment forbids government to make any law "respecting an establishment of religion, or prohibiting the free exercise thereof."

Thus many people are under the impression that we labor under a general prohibition against using hyperorthodox methods of indoctrination and teaching. Even if what is proposed to be taught is nonviolent behavior, a purpose that is undeniably good, there are many that would protest on the ground of constitutional barriers.[13]

This, however, may not necessarily be a truly valid position.[14] That is, if hyperorthodox methods can be implemented by nonreligious groups, if the technique can be modified so as not to intrude on essential privacy, if it can be conducted in a humane style. That may be where we have to search. If religion can be excluded from consideration by a hyperorthodox process, if all pretensions of divine guidance or appeal are eliminated, perhaps the constitutional objections can be surmounted. Let us look at some examples.

Patriotism As a Base for Hyperorthox Motivation.

History shows love of country, patriotism even without religious overtones, has on occasion, been a strong influence on groups and their members. Self-sacrifice in war is no stranger to anecdote or the chronicles of heroes.

Deeply felt belief-systems of many human associations have aroused their members to dedicated commitment. Family commitments, parental, filial, and marital devotions have often reached great heights of loyalty, and devotion to performance. Friends, closely-knit groups reaching mutual fraternal love, combat teams, have repeatedly shown such altruism. Highly motivated peace movements have drawn upon an emotional and psychic energy that has, in ideal situations suppressed violence in themselves, and in others.

Criminal Justice Has Always Been Punitive.

The route taken by our criminal justice system has uniformly been punitive. There are few, if any instances to cite of high motivation toward law compliance being discovered and used by any criminal justice system. We use force in the form of police or military units, using the same powers such forces have used in past centuries against subject populations: physical pain, incarceration, threats, and death.

Today, however, we are not subject populations. Unlike former centuries, we must now take a gentler, approach. Corporations and businesses, for instance, use money as a motivator, in the form of: salaries, wages, and pensions, as basic inducements to comply with rules. These and other organizations also use fringe benefits and symbolic rewards: symbols of prestige, badges, medals, ribbons, and gold keys and watches. Of course, promotions, social acceptance and honors of all kinds are inducements to bring us together in norm-performance. But none of these rewards, nor the punishments of jail, fines, or public notoriety seem to have anything like the efficiency and effectiveness exhibited by the hyperorthodox methods.

Particularly inadequate are ordinary reward and punishment methods to control violence. Police and all their clientele are violent. The same is true of corrections people and the people with whom they deal. Both are equally unsuccessful in suppressing violence.

Fundamentals of Hyperorthodox Methods.

It appears that hyperorthodox methods are much more efficient than all the others. More effective than pain or punishment, reward or pleasure, hyperorthodox methods are not being used to control violence, as once they were. However, it is possible to adapt these techniques to promoting non-violence and peace. One way to do this could be put this way:[15]

1. Strong early identification by an individual with a peaceful group and that group's ideals,
2. ... buttressed by a belief-system which grants a spiritual foundation (if divine support for those beliefs is forbidden)
3. ... together with assiduous monitoring of performance,
4. ... with universal strong condemnation by that group for any unforgiven transgression,

5. . . . will result in maximum suppression of violence and violations against the rules of that group.

Analysis of several hundreds of organizations, associations, and other human groups indicates that almost any reward or punishment will have some influence on the belief and behavior of members. The greatest influence, however, invariably appears when the elements of hyperorthodoxy are the basic influences, and reward and punishment are merely auxiliary.

The Battle Is the Payoff.

An old saw regarding competition between groups is, "The battle is the payoff." It refers to a practical, if risky, way to determine which organization is "better." It is interesting that military organizations which are outstanding in performance in war, invariably concentrate to an amazing degree on hyperorthodox methods, for their internal discipline.

The list is extensive: Alexander's Companions; Roman Legionnaires; Turkish Janissaries, World War II Russian attack battalions, and their opponents, the Waffen SS. Nor can we overlook Japanese Kamakaze Suicide pilots; or the dedicated North Viet infiltrators. The current Arab and Iranian zeolots have been mentioned before. But what has all that to do with peacetime community performance?

The question ignores the fact that people remain people, whether in peace or war. The political fact of war does not appear to be the critical variable, for high performance, we find similar high devotion to duty in contemporary religious orders and cults. The Roman Catholic Church has received high marks for efficiency from professional administrative analysts. It has prevailed for some 2,000 years with more than reasonable compliance with dogma, tenets, and strictures against violence between communicants.

Other hyperorthodox groups have manifested equally high adherence to their rules of nonviolence in their internal relations with their each other: The Jews, Quakers, Mennonites, Amish, Buddhists are only a few examples.[16]

It is interesting to examine the interactional levels of subjective experience of people joined in different relationships. Figure 3-1 is an attempt to indicate the subjective experience sensed by individuals in various types of groups.

GROUPS

Subjective Experience

TYPE	Spiritual Identity	Dominance or Submission (Hierarchical)	Pleasure	Contract	Consciousness of Kind
A. Hyperorthodox (Cults, Religions, Movements)	Yes	Yes	Yes	Yes	Yes
B. Bureaucracy/Association (Corporations; Clubs, etc.)	No	Yes	Yes	Yes	Yes
C. Families Friends Neighbors	No	No	Yes	Yes	Yes
D. Trading Groups Negotiators Sellers-Buyers	No	No	No	Yes	Yes
E. Societal Groups (Age; Sex; Height; Ethnicity, etc.)	No	No	No	No	Yes
F. Statistical (All Capricorns; People born on Sunday; etc.)	No	No	No	No	No

Figure 3-1.

Multi-Group Membership.

Of course, any one person can be, and almost invariably is, a member of more than one group-type. Also, the urge to action provided by one type of group may be in opposition to the impulses created by one of the other types of the individual's membership. Finally, an individual often is a member of several groups within a single type. We are all members of several different clubs, associations, and even corporations, in one role or another.

Which of these types of groups is likely to have the deepest influence on our beliefs and actions? There is no doubt the type named "hyperorthodox," fits that description best. This is the type of organization that seems to be losing its former ubiquity in American life.

Not only is the hyperorthodox organization becoming less commonly a part of the average person's life, but also, those hyperorthodox groups we do encounter, are not community-wide, but cross community lines, and tend to add to the hostility between communities.

It may be that we are too skeptical, too sophisticated a people today to accept a Universal Faith, as it was in Europe of the 12th and 13th century. But it is something to think about. Are there things we all can believe in, can join in, can agree on? Is one of those things, possibly . . . denial of deadly force in daily life? Can we agree that children should not be brought up thinking that force is an acceptable way to resolve personal problems? If we can, . . . that may be a start!

PART TWO
A BILL OF WRONGS

Chapter 4

BACKGROUND TO DEATH

*"During the time men live without a
common power to keep them in awe, they
are in that condition which is called war;
and such a war as is of every man
against every man."*

Thomas Hobbes
(1588–1679)

The Hobbesian nightmare of brutal, natural man, "in continual fear and danger of death," was avoided by grouping into communities of mutual interest and protection. Many such communities must have been formed. But not every such community survived. If the processes of evolution applied, one can imagine that those that survived tended to perpetuate the members who, from early training and familiarity, continued the kinds of social and behavioral patterns they had learned as children and had contributed to that community's survival. The methods they had learned worked—therefore they did not change them. In primitive times social patterns persisted for many generations with relatively little change, according to the cuniform and stellae records we have. Today we say, "If it works, don't fix it!" The concept is so simple, so basic, and so true there is no doubt people used it then as well as we do now.

Primitive Society From the Inside.[1]

These primitive societies, and even the few primitive cultures existing today, exhibit the full array of techniques of social management listed in the previous chapter as "hyperorthodox." Each child, from birth is made to understand "who he is, and what he is expected to do." These controls become almost completely internalized. He comes to comply with the norms and rules because at bottom, he has learned to *want* to comply. It's natural to him. To him, it's the only normal and proper way to believe

33

and to behave. His control has been internalized: He feels overpoweringly guilty if he violates the code he has accepted, as we used to say, "with heart and soul."

The Peaceful Society.[2]

An individual born into such a culturally primitive group finds the enforced peace and support of the hyperorthodox society a haven of brotherhood, nonviolence, and comfort. Obedience and compliance bring low levels of anxiety in daily life. Universal rejection of all those not within that society binds the member ever tighter into the warm circle of "his own people." If violence is not an acceptable type of behavior in that society, the thought of violence never occurs to him.

Is the solution to deadly force really so simple? If so, why don't we just do it?

Difficulties in Implementation.[3]

Unfortunately, in this century, as well as in prior millenia, Man has not been able to make it work for large populations, or over great areas. Communication between distant places is and has always been difficult. To know personally, and have a direct effect on more than say, fifty or one hundred people is unusual. On special occasions, there were great public meetings. If properly orchestrated, with sometimes thousands of people in rapt attendance, massive crowds could be influenced at the hyperorthodox level by talented orators, whose speeches almost invariably would continue for hours. Apparently the fatigue, and prolonged fixation of the listeners' interest on the orator's face and figure were a part of the necessary technique.[4]

In times past, great military leaders would make a special point, especially before a great battle, of exhorting the troops.[5] Reaching a high emotional level, these harangues were intended to raise the fighting spirit of the warriors, and bring their emotional level and dedication to the point where the danger of facing the sharp swords of the enemy would be seen as of little consequence compared with the great upsurge of positive feelings unleashed. *In hoc signe victus!*[6]

Electronic Communication.

Radio and television media enormously extend this range, to cover literally millions of individuals in a one-way communication that has brought careers and millions of dollars to particularly expert or well-situated individuals.

Generally however, today, as in ancient times, the basic managerial device, is a tabled organization of agents, in hierarchal arrangement. Of course, many different organizational patterns have been experimented with. In exceptional circumstances variant patterns of communication, command, and influence have been successful, but the hierarchy has survived as the most effective way to extend the reach of influence of a single leader, or small leading group.

It has been the social arrangement of choice to maintain hyperorthodox controls over large populations, through time and space. Dedicated agents, issuing orders to equally devoted lower-level agents who report back receipt of commands, and information about success in obeying those commands. This has been the mode chosen by successful leaders trying to extend their influence in monarchies, religions, nations, their military and naval affairs, city departments including police and even business firms. The hierarchy is well adapted to apply the efficient techniques of hyperorthodoxy with maximum effectiveness.[7] It is also adaptable to using less powerful techniques, such as issuing reward and punishment, either alone, or in combination with hyperorthodoxy. The awesome effectiveness of all of them in combination has been known and used for thousands of years. Most of written history, despite this, details how low-intensity motivations, particularly punishment, caused human events to happen.

We do have, however, convincing accounts of the pervasive power of the Universal Church of the period between about 500 A.D. and 1500 A.D. with its Christian injunctions to "love thy brother as thyself."[8] The peace thus enforced was broken by violence among the faithful of small communities relatively infrequently. Since then, however, "without a common power to keep them in awe," there has been a steadily increasing rate of violence and deadly force in Europe, until the peak of violence was reached with World War II.

The factors implicated in the increasing violence have been variously stated to be rising nationalism, technological advancements which made killing easier, the lessening of the influence of religion and others.

Actually, however, those influences could have had a beneficial effect, had they been differently directed. A tool can be used to build or destroy, depending on the mind of the one who holds it.

Now we have available the most wonderful tool of all, electronic communication. Perfectly adapted to provide lines of communication to influence people, it has been used with magical effect on hundreds of millions of people. However, that tool has not been directed to build peace and harmony. On the contrary, it has been used to instill in us an acceptance of violence in all its forms, to the point where we seek to make combat and the tactics of killing ever more accessible.

It is said[9] that the way we have used electronic communication, with its known power of behavior control, has been to increase our level of violence. Electronic communication, however, is just a tool, it could instead be turned to a different use of its manifest power, to lower the level of violence, and improve the quality of real life. There have been some efforts in that direction lately,[10] but not nearly enough.

Even when a strong influence-network has been established which instills and maintains peace and nonviolence, the trace of human history has been to succumb to the lure of violence, and find, or make, breaks in that network of peaceful confinement. Strangely, despite the apparently overwhelming power of these methods of behavior control even before the advent of electronic communication there has appeared inevitable breaks in the lines of communication necessary to maintain them messages of harmony and peace. Our Founding Fathers fell victim to the lure of violence, too.

"When In the Course of Human Events."

We have often said, "Events forced us into it." Thomas Jefferson phrased it to the approval of thirteen English Colonies, "When in the course of human events," such a schism occurs within an existing hyperorthodox society, ranks close against former brothers. Differences between erstwhile brethren are acutely examined to justify reprisals and estrangement. The break becomes wider and permanent, ranging people against each other in formal roles of opposition on every conceivable basis of differentiation. Eventually, almost any basis has been sufficient to prevent mutual acceptance of membership in the same community of hyperorthoxy. Then, in line with the strictures of the hyperorthodox process, hate for the Outsider becomes not only a strong integrative factor for one group, but a bitter ban on any peaceful communication with the Outsiders, who are automatically defined as Hobbesian enemies, deserving only of the most brutal treatment, and exclusion. Killing these utterly worthless people is sanctified by every tenet believed worthy of blessing and divine reward. Whether the actors in these tragedies massacred women and their babies, in 1645 at Drogheda and Wexford, or in 1987 in Sri Lanka, the sacredness of the killing is all the same.

Civil War and Other Types of Fratricide.

History has shown that when two separate hyperorthodox groups merely hear about each other, they often detest each other's practices. This easily leads to detestation of the other group entire. Doubts immediately arise that they are worthy of being called "human." Many primitive tribes have had only one word for "People," and that word is synonymous with, "We." They have only one word for others outside their group, these have been noted as:[11] "Animals," "Outsiders," "Enemies," "Gentiles," "Goyem," "Infidels," "Devils," "Heathen," "Alien," "Pagan," "Heretic," "Giaour."

When these groups additionally are rivals for economic benefits, and later come into contact in any way, the most extreme forms of deadly force and torture can be exerted with mindless cruelty.[12]

The maddened hate between two contemporary branches of Islam, the Sunni and the Shiite sects, has brought forth war that has been matched by equal violence between Moslem and Christian religionists in the Middle East. Cruelty beyond imagining becomes reality between hyperorthodox groups when emotions rage and hate blinds both sides forgetting they claim they worship the same God, have much the same ethical standards, and claim brotherhood as a basic tenet of dogma.

Though not of the same scale, the bitterness between Catholic and Protestant in Northern Ireland is comparable in depth of hate and incidence of personal violence.

The Heaven and Hell Within Us.

Thus it is that the quirk in human psyche that can create the maximum of peace within a group, sustains and fosters a contentious adversarial conflict without regard for the ecumenists among us, and exacerbates violence between opposing factions.

Returning to the epigraph at the beginning of this chapter, "During the time men live without a common power to keep them in awe, . . . " implies Hobbes' conviction that such a common consent is required lest we have a "war . . . of every man against every man." The National Lawyers Guild puts it another way, "Our society simply lacks the elementary social cohesiveness, sense of shared purpose, and fundamental social and economic fairness to make possible a solution of the problem of crime . . . "[13]

We Often Choose Hell.

If the above represents today's reality in any substantial way, our society, specifically the United States of this century, expects police to perform an impossible task: We encourage hyperorthodox organizations to proliferate. We expect them to be nonviolent. We forbid citizens to use significant self-help against personal violence, proscribing it as vigilantism. We restrict use of deadly force under severe constraints even to lawful authorities, and expect them to resolve all disputes with minimum or no physical force monitored by severe internal supervision, citizen watchers, and heavy fines even for inadvertent violations under the United States Code. Our federal law even grants substantial attorney fees to plaintiffs who win a case against a police officer, his department, and his municipality, for civil rights violations. One might think it more a reward for successful litigation, than a damper on violent force. For ultimately the individual officer is not held personally accountable either in monetary or other fashion. The charge is laid on the taxpayers, who have only diluted control over any individual police officer, who may violate civil rights.

Violence and Hyperorthodox Organizations.

As it has happened, formally organized hyperorthodox groups have been fairly rare in exhibitions of deadly force. There have been some cults that were major protagonists in cases of recurring deadly force in Philadelphia, in Miami, in Los Angeles, San Francisco, and New York. As frightening as those exceptional events were, they pale before our national statistics of thousands killed every year by people who are not members of formal hyperorthodox organizations.

In fact, when we examine the matter more intently we discover that active members of formal hyperorthodox organizations in this country are outstandingly crime-free, rarely committing deadly force. This is in line with the fact that practically every formal hyperorthodox organization in this country has accepted as part of its faith the doctrine of nonviolence, at least between members, and enforces it.[14]

Where does that lead us? Well, for one thing, it confirms our finding that hyperorthodoxy, if it teaches nonviolence, is successful in such preachments. Going only a bit further it brings our attention directly to the source of our most pernicious violence, ghettoes. In urban ghettoes we can find all the essential elements of the hyperorthodox process[15] in the life-scenarios of individuals who have been repeatedly arrested and convicted for use of deadly force. These beknighted people have internalized patterns of behavior and attitude, founded on powerful beliefs in the value and justice of violence.[16] They exhibit:[17]

1. Strong early identification by an individual with a group and with that group's ideals,
2. ... buttressed by a belief system which grants peer group, community spirit, even, in some cases claims divine support for those beliefs,
3. ... together with assiduous monitoring of performance,
4. ... with universal strong condemnation by that group for any unforgiven transgression. All of which ...
5. ... will result in maximum suppression of acts against the rules, and maximum performance of all approved actions and beliefs.

Indoctrination Into Violence.

Repeated research with violent youth, recidivist criminals and maximum-security prison inmates reveals that the vast majority of violent youth have life experiences that correspond almost exactly with the above sequence. They are indoctrinated.

Early in life they identify with the mores of the violent life style of the ghetto streets. Often they accept the credo that they have been disadvantaged by an evil conspiracy of the White System. School and other institutions provided by The Man are scorned and derided, and the way to local prestige is by rebellion and a macho exhibition of fearless aggressiveness in style and substance.[18]

The most violent and aggressive of the youths become leaders of their age-group. They are called in on criminal capers schemed or contrived by other members. They learn to call the shots on further violence. If they are arrested, they acquire even greater reputations, with more opportunities for profit and renown.

Reprogramming the Indoctrinated.

There is nothing in our criminal justice system that is prepared to cope with this indoctrination-process of violence and criminalization. We have few capable reprogramming technicians. In the attempt to be effective in the roles assigned to them police have been tempted to excesses, which break law, transgress the Constitution and aggravate community tensions. These are not tensions of simple poverty. Money is only one of the lacks, and not the most important one. Many of the ghettoes in New York, Miami, Chicago, Los Angeles, San Antonio, and other urban centers are complete catastrophes, exhibiting total social as well as material destitution. Beyond poverty,[19] the mind-numbing addiction to violence is the critical variable.

By Seven Years They Are Already Lost.

"They're coming in younger now, off meaner streets; hooked on crack at age 9, commiting crimes of opportunity—burglary, purse-snatchings, male prostitution—even before adolescence.

"In the streets they grow like weeds, unattended, unwanted, often the children of children, hardened to a world of harsh codes and sudden violence."

"... hating the world and wanting to get even ... "[20]

Taking it all together, violence in our streets is simply what we have taught our children. Children, thus programmed to violence, give and receive violence at the hands of their peers, the adult community, the police and jailors, all as part of the psycholegal system with we we are burdened, which reinforces the mode of violence.

Changing the System.

Changing the system is very difficult, because of segmentalized vested interests. The efforts of organized religion are thwarted because of differences in faith, and bitter opposition for turfs and talent. There are loosely organized groups devoted to practicing and preaching peace, harmony, and love, whose efforts are subverted by violence around them, and peculation within. We have powerful groups with strong sympathies for individual rights and privacy, but have been persuaded that protection from crime requires repeated invasions of privacy and individual dignity. Still other groups confirmed in their admiration for constitutional freedoms insist that the most dangerous source of violence can be the police themselves.[21]

There are people opposed to police abuse of power, who remain silent, or even strongly support the police in small tyrannies, for fear of weakening law enforcement's hand in dealing with crime.[22] We find groups who support even illegal tactics of police to enhance and preserve their special social and political privileges. This injures and infuriates those who identify with the victims subject to the illegal tactics. It can reasonably be judged that condoning even technical police illegalities incites to further illegalities, even violence, by those who should and could be our protectors from the violent.

We have not discovered ways to satisfactorily dispose of these grievances either on the international or the local scene. We are reduced, perforce, to recurrent use of government violence in an already too violent world. Each contender accuses another of unwarranted use of violence, as each wallows in violence to the hilt.

Political Victims, or Urban Killers?

Urban killers, today, explain their development into human time bombs of death by saying, "I had to become violent to survive in my neighborhood."[23]

This is a claim that they are political victims of a system which gave them no choice. Even Thomas Hobbes condoned self-defense. There is no denying, becoming violent personalities before the age of seven, their lives easily extrapolated to childish assaults on classmates for petty change, to night burglaries, and eventually to major roles as deadly robbers and hired killers.

We can with only a bit of difficulty comprehend the depth of feeling and profound intensity of dedication involved on both sides of religious war and terrorism. The same can be said of rival patriots who war with bombs and biological poisons. It may be more profitable to us as a nation to apply the same degree of understanding to members of our national groups. Dealing with our common problems calls for understanding the conscious and unconscious purposes of those who become violent criminals, and then we must cope with those purposes at *their* level of perception and comprehension.

In general it appears that belief precedes action and becomes confirmed by it. The devoted member of a violent cult starts with firm beliefs, and piously acts as he knows he should. In the course of his action it comes to his attention that a law forbids a certain act. Since his intended action is in conformity with his values, even mandated by his belief in a higher, more important and just rule, he must break that law. Confirmed by action, breaking the law becomes fair, just, and essentially right.

A Universal Phenomenon.

The sequence is not uncommon. It is found in the actions of our nation's Founding Fathers, the Southern States of the Civil War and present-day ministers of the gospel who smuggle San Salvadorans into the United States, and give them sanctuary.

Today we have countless laws and regulations on the books which are often unenforced because in the mass they are unenforceable. Whole areas of personal conduct are placed under bans that were rarely, if ever, the subject of legal constraint within the memory of many alive today. When we add the new mores and usages that have developed in recent years, the use of recreational drugs; sexual practices and employments; pornographic literature and devices; the conflicts of belief-systems tending to law-breaking are almost as numerous as the laws. If it is true, as recent research indicates, that there is a strong connection between exploitive pornography and violence, we add a new incitement to violent solutions to events.

Laws that are not enforced by effective external and internal compulsion are just not obeyed. Too, they feed a growing disrespect and rebellious rage at the society which irrationally both condemns and condones. Laws to protect the weakest from their own folly, make prisoners of us all. The process of the law thus devours its purpose. We are left, then, with endless rounds of crimes, simulated enforcement and ultimately national ennui.

Causes and Consequences.

"Causes go deeper than poverty.[24] Poverty denotes something you can cure with money, something undernourished. What we are seeing is the failure to nurture children. Some people think money will solve the problem. Money buys nourishment, but it won't nurture. That's an emotional process of relationships and love."

We are talking about kids who are serious offenders before 12 years old, the product of a hyperorthodox process in the slum which teaches violence, hate, ignorance, and crime.

One finds little disagreement among those knowledgeable of the situation: We need an emotional process. We do not need another agency, another bureaucracy. We need to manage the normal hyperorthodox processes of actual living, aimed to different goals than the present ends of violence, hate, and crime. About 80 percent of the most delinquent kids come from such areas. Most have no fathers at home, or live with a female relative. That, in itself, does not necessitate accepting the dogmas of violence, there may be ways of even handling that family scene. New philosophies do not come easily. It takes patience and effort and an accurate dream of what can be.

New Hazards, and How to Handle Them.

In the meantime, new drugs are hitting the street. There are always new dangers—we must anticipate that—we need ways to cope with them. That may take a revolutionary reversal of thought, or a new twist that at first may seem incongruous, if not worse. Sometimes doing what has seemed, incrementally, to be the next logical step, has turned out to have hidden traps and unbidden consequences.

There are many examples, but taking as one, the designation of drug abuse as a crime, as terrible as that vicious practice may be, has not only provided the motivation for a vast criminal drug traffic and large-scale murder, but also provides powerful motivation for hosts of other crimes, by addicts trying to pay for their habit.

It also provides cash for underworld operations in fields other than drugs. The flow of funds that corrupts elected and appointed officials, bankers, and even entire government administrations, would dry up without constant infusion from crime.

It is said that marihuana is the most valuable cash crop in California.

Illegal drugs add some five billion dollars annually to the economy of South Florida—much of it in nonessential and wasteful luxuries. People close to the heads of government in Cuba, Mexico, Bolivia, Colombia, Iran, and Iraq have been charged with mulcting the drug trade, and ultimately the citizens of the United States, the best customers for drugs at the retail level. Why do we contribute to all this? By the articulation of our laws and our justice agencies, we have created an apocalyptic beast that threatens to consume us.

There is no doubt that drugs are physically, mentally, and emotionally harmful. Practically every foreign substance taken into the human body has damaging effects. This is true even for medications from aspirin and bicarbonate of soda, to zeolite. Conservative opinion is firm that any chemical invasion of the body is harmful. But we do not have to create crimogenic conditions which spawn world-wide criminal conspiracies if we really want to prevent crime and harm to people. Nor should we. The fact that we have done so is convincing evidence that misguided belief-systems have once again led us astray.

Avoiding Crimogenic Patterns.

Law prohibiting behavior must be founded on consent of the governed. Without acquiescence of mind and body of the controlled, the purpose intended cannot be attained. As a people we have not consented to the follies of a justice system that has been captured by a few ideologues, politicians, and administrators for their special self-conceived interests.

Only Consent Legitimizes Authority.

True, consent can sometimes be extorted by threat or punishment. It can be seduced by persuasion and charisma. But to suppress abuse of drugs, crime in general, or violence in particular, apparently takes more mental effort than we are ready to exert. We are heirs to a Rousseau-like confidence that other people are as "good" as we would like them to be. If left alone, we are sure eventually they will come around to our way of thinking and doing. This, however, is an illusion.

Human personality, as it develops from birth appears to be able to take any of many diverse forms. To expect this nascent psyche to react to the innumerable influences that bear upon it in any anticipatable way shows supreme confidence in a most chancy result. After the fact pseudoscience often "explains" how a person developed into the being he has become. Rarely can we predict, and even more rarely can we control or prevent the most unexpected consequences. All parents are Pygmalion to some degree, but the child-Galateas they gestate, birth, nurture and care for . . . develop into quite unique and unexpected personalities.

We cannot predict the outcome of a single child's development. But in the mass, of large groups, and on a statistical view we can detect the influences which predictably mold our children into monsters of violence, to grow up to waste their lives and to waste the lives of others.

Chapter 5

MAN'S DAILY BREAD

That's the American way.
If little kids don't aspire to
make money like I did, what the hell good is
this country?

Lee Iaccoca

The Workers vs. the Shakers of the World.

When Lee Iaccoca was queried by the press how he excused his receiving $20 million for one year's management of the Chrysler Corporation, he responded as is shown in the epigraph, above.

There is a world of difference between the working philosophy of this corporation president and his many admirers, and that of some other political figures in the land. At the 1982 Presidential Democratic Convention, one of the candidates, Jesse Jackson, proclaimed, "my constituency is the damned, the disinherited, the disrespected and the despised," These contemporary economic losers do not aspire to $20 million a year. They don't aspire. They know they lost, they believe they never had a chance in Lee Iaccoca's America.

Thus we have two directly opposing doctrines being proclaimed, by opposing groups. If they are adhered to with cultish determination we shall have a direct confrontation. Certainly this will encourage hostility. Even if they do not come to open warfare, with overt violence we have the solid bones of a continuous antagonism. The two public statements, alone, are the seeds of hostility, the more we speak of them, the more of a social reality such a confrontation must become.

We often speak of vigorous, but fair and open competition. That is a euphemism, applicable only to a few prosperous businessmen in special situations. Most businessmen are not so sporting.

Laborers have often shown bitter enmity to rivals in the workplace, particularly against those culturally or ethnically different from a ruling

46

majority. They have constantly sought every available advantage in the sometimes desperate struggle for daily bread. In trying to combat their employer-corporations they have formed unions. These highly integrated organizations, both unions and corporations have used every known cultish, hyperorthodox device to intensify their group loyalty and solidarity. In common with all groups urged to maximum performance, they have angrily defined their own group in large part by defining those who were not of their group.

In structured assembly, new members, nonconformists, those who are "different," are regularly placed under disability, or excluded. One tendency has been to coordinate internal cohesion by using the psychosocial forces of ethnic identification. But it has not only been a black and white matter.

Our Kind and Their Kind.

Asians, too, have felt discrimination, although in recent decades not to the high levels of the 19th century. Nevertheless, in 1986, a report by the Commission on Civil Rights concluded, "Anti-Asian activity in the form of violence, vandalism, harassment and intimidation continues to occur across the nation."

Discrimination certainly is not a uniquely American phenomenon. It is extremely difficult for any foreigner to successfully undertake economic activity in Japan, or in France, or for that matter, in almost any developed country. Everywhere, each nation tends to take care of its own. It appears to be occur universally. Any group will respond to internal pressures to prefer employment for its own kind, with or without government sanction. Along with the preference for one group, arrives discrimination against others.

Often, to notice the difference that another ethnic group exhibits is to detest it. This, too, is a world-wide phenomenon, rarely controlled and then only by coordinated government effort, with either material or ideological rewards, for suppression of aggressive hostility. It is only when Church and State, with constant admonition, and exhortation, use all powers of persuasion, that peace is maintained. Often Church-State efforts have had to go beyond admonition and exhortation, and apply criminal and religious sanctions, to obtain reasonable coordination of labor and management toward national goals. This kind of cooperation has on occasion been reached during moments of great national crisis, such as a war. Between-times, violent clashes by rival groups for employment has been usual.

Apparently neither admiration, love nor even tolerance is earned by an outsider-group, though it may demonstrate all the virtues of the work ethic. On the contrary in America, the Asians, and East Asians, with a strong tradition of work and saving, have been denoted a "Super-minority," to be guarded against, and watched carefully. Being known as "hard-workers," has earned for them much scorn and little admiration or emulation.

Banner headlined newsstories detailing the resentment this group has aroused are frequently seen. Despite sometimes bitter discrimination, exasperatingly, Asian minorities have succeeded economically much better than the average American. The fact that this group scores much higher than average on American intelligence tests has not made the resentment any easier to bear.

Illustrative of our dysfunctional approach to this social problem: Instead of being grateful and rewarding this group, which works hard and produces for us all, we place handicaps in their path, make taunting jokes about them, and talk about the need to place a restrictive quota on their entrance into colleges and universities, lest they capture all the scholastic honors. On the Gulf Coast their fishing boats have been burned, and they have been assaulted. It is not a pretty picture.

Blacks have been smeared with the opposite accusation, that they are inferior in intelligence and lack willingness to work. They have received equal, if not more discrimination from the general public. The pattern is always the same: Difference results in discrimination. Especially so, when it affects the purse.

Religion as a Peacemaker.

It is to be noted that the discrimination noted above occurs despite the alleged integrative, loving support demanded by the dogmas and precepts of the religions of the intolerant majorities involved. Discrimination prevails, nevertheless.

When there is a difference in religion between two opposing groups, invidious discriminatory attacks are even more violent than usual. The experience of the Jews has been the classic case. Over the centuries there have been many attempts to eliminate them by banishment, death, or conversion. One might think that is long past, of historical interest only.

True, ancient sufferings are over, the forced migrations demanded by the Assyrians, in biblical times, the Inquisitions of the Middle Ages and the Early Rennaissance, and the Holocaust of the Nazi years are all long past. The phenomenon, however, persists. Even today, in this country, Jews are being accused of overly loving money, and too successful at accumulating it. The truth or falsity of the charges has little relation to the envy, rivalry, and hate engendered.

The facts of difference are not as important as the judgments. Thus it is not the skin color, religion, or the ethnicity, nor even the language that powers the hate. Those distinguishing marks are merely means to identify our rivals. If those means were not visibly at hand, we would find others to fuel our hate, as did the Jacobins and the Royalists of Revolutionary France, in 1793 who could shift from one role to the other by changing their hats, shirts, or trousers.

At root, it is the rivalry, the competition, that creates the pressures that explode in hate, and deadly force and violence. The Hatfields hated the McCoys, in Kentucky at the turn of the century. Now the Iraquis hate the Iranians, North Irish Protestants hate the North Irish Catholics, even Fiji, that South Sea paradise, and haven that used to advertise itself as "The Way the World Ought to Be," demonstrates intense economic rivalry between the native Melanesians, and the more numerous Indians.[1]

Controlling Hate.

There seems to be two major ways people have tried to control intergroup hatred. One is based on the theory that if there were no competition in the workplace hate would be lessened, thus we could create a utopian world, without rivalry, resentment, or greed over benefits.

Could it be done in the workplace, could all material goods would be equally shared, in loving brother and sisterhood? It is the stuff of the early Christian communities, and their many imitators. The Mayflower Compact of the first Pilgrims to this land in 1620, sought this early version of a Nirvana in the New World. Somehow, the happy hopes of the Pilgrims vanished under the realities of a harsh land, which reluctantly surrendered its fruits to only the hardest working, and luckiest individuals. But other utopian communities persisted, and do in small enclaves of the world today.

Idealogues, political pretenders and extortionists have used such tempting appeals for their own purposes, with great success. It is an intrinsic part of the the doctrine of communism as used to organize susceptible people, under slogans such as, "From each according to his ability, for each according to his need." In many countries this ideology has helped bind the poor into political forces to combat existing governments.

In the United States, for the most part, we have been able to avoid that kind of organized confrontation by a number of techniques starting with the relief and work programs of the New Deal in 1932–1937, which made President Franklin D. Roosevelt's voice and face a heartwarming assurance in an otherwise dreary world of economic depression.

It was not until 1941–1942, when the War and a growing war industry absorbed the time, energies and faith of the nation that economic health returned to the nation. The New Deal, nevertheless, had provided hope and sustenance to the most abjectly poor, and so defused a rising radicalism, manifested by the Veterans March on Washington, the many May Day riots, and countless strikes and sit-ins.

After World War II, employment levels were high. For the most severe cases of hardship, relief programs were continued. This blunted the edge of every effort to organize the latent tension between the haves and have-nots in this country. Presidential candidate Jesse Jackson's efforts in the campaign of 1980 were completely unsuccessful, and the opposing ideology pungently expressed by the epigraph quoting Lee Iaccoca at the beginning of this chapter captured the imagination of the politically potent majority, in 1980.

Even the oil glut, with falling prices, which ravished the Texas oil industry, and the decline in agricultural product prices, which squeezed out of the farming industry a large percentage of smaller, marginal producers, with consequent widespread hardship in the prairie states, has not changed the fundamental ethos of today which is still: Make a buck. That seems to be the prevailing doctrine today, despite the wards to which Jesse Jackson appealed.

The mood of the Reagan administration from its inception, in 1980, tended to glorify stylish wealth, with many outstanding even notorious examples that showed what can be done in this country to acquire a fortune, if one has nerve, disregards consequences, and has an idea. In some measure, that continuing American tradition of yearning for speedy, and extreme upward mobility explains much of current history from the success of organized crime, illegal drug dealing, stock manipulations, and the inevitable books and films exploiting these crimes, such as *The Godfather,* and its imitators, as well as books and news stories of making millions in business, such as Carl C. Ican, T. Boone Pickens, Ivan Boesky, Ross Perot, and others.

Competition.

Some cultures have prided themselves on demanding a leveling of individuals into a common acceptance of conformity without rivalry. Junior college courses on anthropology often cite the Hopi Indians of the American Southwest as one of many examples of noncompetitive society.[2] That really is old history, for in this generation they have absorbed the competitive ethic, and are taking a uniquely contemporary route to exhibit it: Litigation against those who they feel would take and keep their land. In any case, the Hopis of a generation ago, and the meek of the earth at any time, have not been persuasive role models to Americans. We have always been of a tough breed. We want fortunes. We will take enormous risks to get them, for success in making a fortune has become the only acceptable measure of the final value of a person's life. We are not satisfied with making daily bread. We want wealth, large masses of money and income-producing properties that will, we hope, give us the liberty to be and do whatever we want. Today, that is the freedom most of us fight for. The fight for political liberty that began in 1776, and continued through the one-man-one-vote United States Supreme Court decision has mostly been won. It's the money we want, now. That's what being a success is all about. To that end, we are completely performance oriented.

"Making It."

We are willing to take risks, and when we fail, perhaps even imprisoned for law-breaking, in the obstacle race to financial success, we still do not surrender the chase. We try to turn defeat into victory, by writing best sellers promptly on leaving prison, and giving lectures at exorbitant fees. All of which are eagerly subscribed to by other Americans who want to follow the same path, with greater care, perhaps, to avoid being caught.

Ivan Boesky, charged with having dealt in billions in illegal insider trading, is fined $100,000,000 and still has more than that left to his own use. We recognize his success. Being fined, being imprisoned wots little. Breaking those laws is not shameful, today. The laws are merely artificial walls we are challenged to climb. Boesky is still a hero of accomplishment, successful, and therefore enviable to millions of Americans.

American-style, a photographer cuts out a life-size photo of Ivan Boesky, and teeners and yuppies fight to have their picture taken with the idol.

The very term, "yuppy," young, upwardly mobile professional, implies this straining for high levels of income, consumption, and exhibitionism. What in a simpler day was scornfully called, "conspicuous consumption" is today stylish and enviable.

Would-be reformers alarmed at all the reaching and grasping, have urged recourse to the criminal law to try to control these ambitious, energetic Americans. Perhaps they are even more alarmed at the many Americans-to-be, as they still come to these shores. For the drug-dealers, smugglers, and large-scale cocaine distributors all partake of the same cultural obsession with "making it," in terms of money. This was not the vision of de Crevecoeur.[3] Nevertheless, what you see is what you get. Welcome Newest Americans! You are on your own. Make it while you can!

The Limit of the Criminal Sanction.

It's a social condition. Business people, cultists, television evangelists, stock market speculators, and our newest imports, "cocaine cowboys," all appear to have accepted the basic ideology: To make life good, get a fortune, spend, enjoy.

Belatedly, some now try to call a halt. We seek to invoke criminal laws to prevent what, we after the fact, call "excess." That decision, however, can be made hastily, without sufficient thought to whether or not that social condition is beyond the limits of the law. Police enforcement is not well adapted to suppress ideology. That is what the confrontation is all about.

The issue of whether or not to use criminal law to deal with a social problem is complex. There are many alternatives. Criminal law, above all, requires, before the formulation of legislation, being sure of the answers to some hard questions: Can we clearly state the acts that are to be prohibited? Are those acts relatively few in number? If both requirements are met, then criminal law *may* be effectively enforced. There are, however, even more matters to consider and carefully weigh before we come to a final decision to define and apply a new criminal law.

The historical development of our criminal law relied on the offender's state of mind, the *mens rea,* as first formally stated in the 12th century. Even the older Roman law required careful consideration of the mental element in crime: *dolus* (wilful deceit, fraud) and *culpa* (fault, neglect).

The canon law, insisting upon moral guilt and relying much on consciousness of guilt, as an element in blameworthiness, of course, was paramount in the development of our Anglo-American criminal law. It was church doctrine that guided the community in every aspect of criminal law.

Moral Guilt for Violence.

It is crucial to understand the doctrinal basis of criminal law. Particularly must we be concerned with the strengths and weaknesses of doctrine, as a guide to human institutions and control of human behavior.

We can note that moral guilt, the *mens rea* as anciently defined, is lacking in much of the behavior leading to violence today. In addition to all the industrial crime having to do with negligent manufacture, improper use of technology, and careless handing of pollutants, we now have deadly shootings without the community's moral objection.

"Storekeepers Blast Robbers, Set Off Vigilantism Debate," reads the headline[4] of a series of news stories of a groceryman who used a shotgun to kill a would-be robber, and another who reached under his counter, pulled out a .357 magnum and dealt out death. These hardworking local businessmen were firmly sustained in their moral position by their community. The public reaction to repeated burglaries and robberies, was enthusiastic expressions of approval and goodwill to the few who had the courage to turn against their oppressors.

Not only was there no moral guilt for the use of deadly violence held against the shopkeepers, there was high approbation. Of course, there was no prosecution.

Chapter 6

TOOLS OF DEADLY FORCE

"... any man's death diminishes me,
because I am involved with mankind."

John Donne

Self-Help as Ultimate Authority.

In the background of our lives lurks the moral sentiments of the Declaration of Independence. Americans have always debated the sources of authority, and the different ways to channel personal self-interest and violence. Inherent, too, in the Declaration is the admission that American society was always governed ostensibly by political institutions, but more deeply by a sense of individual right and worth more dependent on self-help than established government. That was our genesis, it has been our history.

Thus we have used personal weapons to make up the difference between men, to emphasize our equality in right and power of self-defense. The hallowed six-shooter of Western sagas was called "The Equalizer," for very good reasons. With it within reach, a man or woman was not only entitled to a respectful hearing, but also that right could be enforced.

Personal Tools of Deadly Force.

Personal tools of deadly force have been successively improved in power and efficiency in delivering death. Since the six-shooter, we have progressively improved the technology of death. We have invented automatically loaded pistols, machine guns, sawed-off shotguns, bombs, and grenades. We have available now what may be the ultimate small munition: A nuclear back-pack.

With what we know of deadly radiation and radioactive fallout from

54

atomic bombs, which can spread over entire countries, it is clear that the capacity for individually committing violence knows no bounds.

One truck, carrying a few tons of explosives, driven by one dedicated man, was able to destroy the United States Marine barracks in Lebanon, killing over two hundred young marines, forcing the United States to move all military forces from Lebanon, and destroying our prestige in that part of the world.

A council of representatives of Arab nations has announced its program to obtain the ability to produce atomic, and nuclear bombs. With their wealth, there is no reason to doubt that they will ultimately succeed in entering the community of nations with that capability. With their ready supply of fanatic warriors, there is little reason to suppose these weapons will not be used to terrorize all their adversaries, everywhere in the world.

From Defense to Attack.

Thus tools of convenient violence have moved from a device of protection for the individual, toward making machines that can only attack, offering death itself as the final equalizer.

Almost any device, used to build or improve can be turned into a tool of injury and death. Plowshares can be beaten into swords, as the ancients said, but rarely is the reverse true. Swords, guns, and bombs, carry the mystery of life and death; hammers, saws, and . . . bank accounts are mundane and trite. And the mystery is more enchanting when it moves from mere defense — a passive, almost cowardly thing — to splendid, noble, inspired attack. We accept defenders, but we glorify those who can and do go on the attack. Thus we, ourselves, become the tools of deadly force.

Hero-worship and Mystery.

In a dimly understood beginning, as our ancestors were becoming human, in the phylogeny of our nervous system, or perhaps in a corruption of a pre-Iceage common culture, there has grown a thread of hero-worship of the mad and mysterious.

Some of the very oldest remnants of prehuman life show evidence of individuals, buried with artifacts of practical or mystical meaning. Presumably these artifacts were to be of use after death, in another, invisible world.

In ancient times those who exhibited strange behavior, claimed to see visions, or speak to disembodied spirits, were believed to be "touched by God." In a similar vein persons who led others into orgies of violence, causing widespread death, destruction, and despair, usually were, and are, seen as heroic figures. Called conquerors, we often add the word "Great" to their name in our history books. With the passing of years a hallowed veneration attaches to their memory, their sins are forgiven, the minutiae of their lives become treasured anecdotes, artifacts used by them become sacred relics. Above all, their personalities become the subject of respectful inquiry into the mystery of who they were, and how they came to be the way they were. We love the mystery!

It has always been so. The cruelly punishing classic gods of ancient Greeks and Romans were created out of fantasies of those otherwise great peoples.

Only a few people have the talent to be wantonly cruel. The rest of us are fascinated by these uniquely endowed individuals. We see them as monsters or gods, they are the subject of wonder and awe. The savage cruelties Hannibal used to enforce discipline among his motley invading Carthaginians were "justified by military necessity," even by his troops, as well as by the Romans he massacred.

Tales of the inexorable ferocities of the barbarian hordes that completed the destruction of the Roman civilization entertained generations of armchaired audiences. Inspired by the example, occasional individuals, took up their own violent vendettas against the world, to provide fresh materials for violence-based entertainment, the fireside telling and retelling of sagas and songs of violence and death. Thus we make ourselves into tools of the self-fulfilling prophecies.

We Make the Child in Our Image.

Children are tolerant, they conform to the world we make for them. Do we really hate our children so much that we give them the tools to become violent whichever way they turn? Whatever the permissive qualities of the pedagogical theories underlying even the most progressive of educations, our basic culture accepts, condones, and admires violence, especially deadly violence. A preschool child is not yet equipped to resolve conflicts implicit in our culture. He is forced to conform to whatever he is exposed to because he cannot survive by himself. Whatever native ability the child may have to make crucial judgments, is conditioned by culturally mandated perceptions. At every economic level, even the gifted, half-educated child, reaching his teens in a middle-class or upper-class environment is exposed to the condonation, and expectation of violence at our most refined levels of culture.

The bloody stories of the Old Testament, the equally bloody tale of the scourging and crucifixion of Jesus Christ, is followed with equal zest by the Grimm Fairy tales, later the tragedies of Shakespeare. Operas, whether they be by Wagner, Puccini, Bizet, or others, touch these well-springs of emotion. Even our philosophers, from Macchiavelli, to Nietzche to Blake accept violence as one of the facts of life.

Today we submit to repeated reruns of films of the fall of Berlin to the killing machines that Nazi cruelties had taught the Russians to become. Cinema remakes of the unspeakable infamies of the Holocaust, and their copy-cat crimes in Cambodia and other parts of the world fit our idolatry of violence, under the guise of entertainment. Films and television features vie with each other, inventing ever newer instruments of torture and violence.

Not long ago, an unrealistic but delicate veil was drawn over actual pictures of an act of deadly force . . . the death blow would not be shown. Now it is customary to show the swing of the ax, the splashing of brains and blood as the blow lands, the severed head gorily fills a thirty-foot screen.

The response of the hero, as often as not, is to dismember the villain, or deliver a shotgun blast into the bad-man's face. Crimson splashes all over the screen. This too, we call entertainment.

The Media As a Death-Tool.

"The media," as it is euphemistically called, has become a tool promulgating death-force as an immediate and constant part of our environment. Their commercial advertisements promote toys and games that imitate weapons, and often are deadly themselves. With the aid of the media, successful generals run for public office and win election. A prime goal of every deadly terrorist gang is to use the media as a tool for their violent messages.

Our Reward System.

Practitioners of violence are rewarded in our system by being made the subject of best-selling books, even as they are in prison. If the violent

ones are foreign leaders, we give them our imprimatur by rewarding
them with more military arms. We sell them high-tech tools of death, or,
if they have no money, we lend or give them funds to aid in securing
their political power on an unsecured promise to help us in the future. If
violence is used against our citizens overseas, that aid is withheld, consequently we pay the kidnappers to release our hostages, and encourage what
has become the "terrorist industry." Again, we have been the tool of death.

That, however, merely reflects our own social and legal structural bent
toward worshiping violence and the violent, as we shall see in the next
chapter.

Chapter 7

SOCIAL AND LEGAL ENVIRONMENTS

"... in order to enjoy the inestimable benefits
that the liberty of the press ensures,
it is necessary to submit to the inevitable evils
that it creates."

Alexis de Tocqueville

The Gunslinger as Hero.

Claude Dallas the outlaw of the northwest, is hailed by many of our countrymen as a modern day version of the rugged individualist of the Old West.[1] Outlaws, even when fugitives from the law, have a cherished place in the mythology of America. Perhaps they represent fighters for a freedom against confining customs, rigid law, despotic government and all the strict enforcers that society has invented, police, prying neighbors, even parents.

Our ideals run to freedom of the individual, freedom from arrogant authority. Proudly we shout to the world, "This is a free country!" The cry is echoed by the newest immigrant to our land. "This is my opportunity! A free country!"

Yes, but can a free society come to understand that human personality and mentality needs an early authoritative culture if the child is to become "good," whatever the *a priori* definition of "good?" That is, individual freedom of the child must be curtailed to fit within channels of what the culture permits.

The Gentle Way to Command.

We may try to ameliorate resentment and resistance of the child against his teachers and parents by arranging events so it is "the law of the situation" that demands he confine his actions, moods and beliefs within cultural boundaries. At bottom, however, acculturization is a process of inexorably turning the wide potentials of the child into one of the recognizable patterns that are acceptable to the culture of his time and place.

Does such prescriptive treatment tend to create its own image? Without a doubt, the answer is, "Yes." But that is its purpose. It need not, however, make personal violence a part of that image. On the contrary, that is exactly what it must avoid, if we are to build a nonviolent society.

We Do It Upside Down.

What actually happens, however, is the reverse. We are permissive in school about teaching basic skills and virtues, and many students do not learn. Since the advent of Secretary of Education William Bennett we have seen a rising tide of objection to the lack of a disciplined approach to school study, and homework assignments. There has occurred a slight rise in student test scores, but the fight to retain the old permissive ways is manned by powerful interests. The influential National Education Association (NEA) opposes this kind of educational reform.[2]

The NEA opposes "parental choice" over where children are sent to school, and competency tests for teachers and students. The Congressional Budget Office has studied the matter and reported that at least some of the gain can probably be attributed to demographic and cultural changes. The Secretary of Education, however, insists that what has started the students on the correct path is the increased sensitivity of parents and textbook writers to the chaos under which the system has been operating.

There is much recent comment in opposition to the allegedly overly strict administrative interpretation of United States Supreme Court decisions which appeared to have barred the teaching of morality and values in publicly financed schools.[3] The Secretary of Education is strongly supported in this position by a variety of organized groups, ranging from church authorities, to people who simply have become dissatisfied with the present results.

The conflict has political implications but we are not concerned with that. There is no real reason for us to be embarrassed about our tradition of moral values. Although many of our beliefs have sources in biblical authority, there is no reason to take the position that if a practice is praised in the bible, it must, by that token, be avoided in secular life. If diligence in study and in work promotes the "General Welfare," as the

Constitution uses the term, quite obviously we have sufficient secular authority to support the position of promoting diligence. That would be simply common sense, phrased in legalese. Actually, of course, it seems to most observers to be common sense, even without Constitutional approval.

Thus are we are upside-down in not teaching subjects and beliefs that will be useful to children in their adult life. Another upside-down approach we have fallen into is: We do not act to prevent children from being exposed to, and learning things that will deny them success in adult life. One glaring example is that we do not intervene to prevent the learning of violence outside the school. Violence-learning comes at the whim of the individual child, and his often hostile social environment. Certainly there is a strong public interest in this, so important to the child's welfare. Who is in charge, here? The answer, often is: the child is in charge of what and how he learns.

Chaotic Learning Practices.

The child need not become literate if he decides not to. He need not learn his sums or the multiplication table. Often he will be promoted in any case. If he is passed over and 'left back,' he becomes more of a disturbance than ever, and turns off the entire class program of assigned work.

Enthusiastically learning nothing of the school assignments, his attention becomes fully involved in making trouble for the other kids and the school. Eventually, in desperation, and to protect the other children, the troublemaker quietly is permitted to leave school, not having learned basic educational skills, let alone any of the other cultural values we leave for the school curriculum to cover.

Is this enough to at least partially explain the enormously high rate of illiteracy in our country?

To learn to spell, cries for a despotism of the mind. It is the kind of discipline which we have today despaired of teaching our secretaries, typists, and clerical workers. Now the typing machines must include a built in 50,000 word dictionary which tries, by the tryanny of the machine, to do what we are not able to force down the throats of unwilling students. Instead of the burden being placed on the student to learn— that is, by creating a situation where he *must* learn, we try to devise technological bandaids, add classes for the backward, and special teachers.

The situation deteriorates to the point where we plead for him to be interested, and we beseech teachers to, "Please make it interesting, or he won't learn!"

For it is the students who are in command of the classroom. As usual the law of the situation rules. But it is a situation created at the behest of resistance to learning, and puerile consent to ignorance.

How and Why We Learn.

How is something complex and difficult really learned? There are thousands of research studies published relevant to this question.[4] It would be impossible to reduce the data, rationales and findings to fit within our space. At the risk of oversimplification, many teachers would accept, "People learn what they feel they *must* learn." One hard-working and frustrated teacher was tempted to add, " . . . and nothing more!"[5] But that last comment is clearly uttered only in despair. For children learn many things that one would be puzzled to discover the how and why.

The teacher went on to say, "It is the 'difficult' subjects that are not learned properly. The ones which encounter the most resistance. These tough subjects, however, are the ones that are so important to the child's success and feeling of accomplishment."

Such as arithmetic for instance? Were it not such a tragedy the facts would make one laugh. We have lawyers who cannot do the simple sums necessary to complete the closing statements necessary in a transfer of ownership of a small home. In the average college classroom to chalk the most elementary algebraic equation on the blackboard of a class in the humanities is as to write in Sanskrit. No one demanded that they learn algebra, in their young lives they never *needed* it. In fact they never needed to be able to figure out the cost per ounce of different breakfast cereals. Thus price comparisons are beyond them . . . some may see a conspiracy of silence here! The truth is probably simpler: Why should they bother?

We Teach the Wrong Things Well.

The meek acquiescence with which we condone illiteracy and ignorance is in sharp contrast with the authoritarian way in which we insist on exposure to violent messages. We arbitrarily condemn our children to learn all about violence every day of their lives. By approving violence, we damn our children to commit violence.

In total, the child is forced into absolute obedience to the authority of violence. He is dosed with violence from his earliest years if not in his home, by video entertainment provided, and by repeated casual play in even otherwise good homes and neighborhoods.

Most terribly of all, in countless homes violence is the *lingua franca* of communication. Violence or the threat of it, almost invariably is employed in the service of disorder and personal disaster for the child. The child is forced to obey.

With a complete reversal of logic, the authoritarian education to which he is exposed is never in the service of learning useful skills or attitudes. It is against the law to educate in school with punitive methods. But it is not against the law to condone *ad hoc* instruction in violence!

Thus the basic subjects: three R's, and the virtue of nonviolence are left to a "take-it-or-leave-it" classroom setting. Whereas violence, stealing, and harrasment of others is forcefully taught in the schoolyard and the street by other children with long prior experience in these arts.

The leadership structure and support the poor child accepts is oriented toward a violent view of life. It would only be by chance that he would learn nonviolent means to succeed, and . . . it would be quite inadequately taught.

We Learn What We Must.

When violent means of attaining desired goals are so productive, there is no good reason to learn other means. Can there be any inducement to nonviolent behavior and ideals without indoctrination by an authoritarian cultural mandate? We are horrified by use of words such as manipulation and indoctrination. We are embarrassed at the word, discipline. We would love to discover ways to make education sweet-tasting and invisible. But wouldn't that be the greatest manipulation? Must we "doublespeak" to tell the truth?

We approve words such as "education." As though the word itself has a divine import. With a Rousseauan naivete, and confidence in good intentions, we try to entice reluctant students toward hard work. Supremely confident in Maslow's[6] assurance that there are "higher levels" of learning and aspiration, we seek ever better teachers with superhuman charisma and dedication, without recognizing that life is full of the average, the ordinary person, that as Lincoln said, God loves so much.

To accomplish student learning with the teachers and the equipment we have, all we need do is provide the circumstances in which the child sees for himself that he must learn. Then he will learn, despite everything and everyone. Only then, can we safely let the "law of the situation rule."

The Rulebreakers Make the Rules.

Certainly breaking the rules is today often rewarded more than compliant action. It has become endemic in our society even on the national level. A recent example is: American government policy all unknowingly has accepted violation of law as the properly effective procedure. We exclude from immigration those men and women who have enough regard for law and order to officially apply for immigration. It is the law breakers who confront the system eyeball-to-eyeball, forcing the system to blink, and scramble to find an exception or exemption, and thus obtain legal immigrant status for the immigrant who entered illegally.[7]

How Hard-Core Criminals Escape Justice.

In ordinary municipal criminal justice, police and prosecution are on a collision course. As many as half of all felony charges result in dismissal. This is why: Police are trained to establish probable cause for arrest. Usually the officer's sense of reward and accomplishment is complete with the arrest. But to carry the case forward to successful prosecution the lawyer representing the state must obtain evidence that will meet the court's higher standard of "beyond a reasonable doubt." Some prosecuting attorney's offices have an investigating staff, but none have a staff large enough to complete all this work. This is the crack into which fall so many cases, divided responsibility.

The police officer has earned his "merit badge" for performance, he has made a "good arrest." If the prosecution fails, that is no fault of his.

The prosecution, too, looks good. After all, how can a state or district attorney successfully prosecute a case if there is insufficient evidence to prove guilt beyond a reasonable doubt? The prosecutor's office can blame the police officer for failing to have enough evidence, and the prosecutor can *nolle prosse* the case without receiving any demerits for nonfeasance. On the contrary, should the state attorney be able to bluff the arrestee, or his lawyer into plea bargaining, it is counted as a prosecution score of "guilty," a clear win for the prosecution over the defense.

Thus both of the good guys, the police and the prosecutor, almost always come out looking like roses. But it is all a fraud on the public weal, for the really bad criminal has had a field day, either getting off scot-free, or pleading to a token crime, that is merely nominal compared to the crimes he really committed. Because of the missing link in the arrest-prosecution chain he will never have to pay the appropriate penalty.

It is important to emphasize there is no need for this break in responsibility, and consequent lack of accountability.

England Closes the Crack.

England has a simple way to close the crack: Almost all cases initiated by the English police remain as their retained responsibility. Constructing a case sufficient to convict is completely in the hands of the police who even prepare the case for trial. They are responsible for providing evidence "beyond a reasonable doubt," if they are to receive credit. The responsibility never shifts. It is where it belongs.

Of course, there are historical reasons why we have this flaw in the chain of accountability. In the late 1700's the American Colonists came to distrust Crown prosecutors.

Later, county and state governments, suspicious of police corruption and incompetence, wanted to assure that a proper case would be presented to court. It is doubtful, however, if these conditions exist today. It is doubtful, too, if our solution is any longer the best way to overcome those dangers.

The net result is a legal environment that isolates the crime prevention and control function from the realities of needs of the community. We have built large police departments trained in scientific skills of detection and apprehension. We have huge staffs of lawyers trained to prosecute—some counties have more than 150 lawyers assigned. To add to that we have equally massive staffs of public defenders, all going through a charade of apprehension, prosecution, and defense, with no all-round responsibility, but with enormous cost that is almost as great as if we left criminals on the street to ply their vocations, undisturbed.

Chapter 8

PHYSICAL ENVIRONMENTS

Let us hope ... that by the best cultivation
of the physical world ... we shall
secure ... happiness ... "

A. Lincoln

Controlling Violence By Controlling Space.

Our concern here has been violence, and the factors that are related. Now we come to physical environments, and a concept that has been developed relating physical environment to crime and violence.

"Defensible space," has come to be an important topic to be studied, for it is one of the many factors related to when and where violence is committed.[1] It has been noted by researchers that physical characteristics of the space occupied by people are correlated with, and appear to influence the frequency and type of crime that will occur. It involves both space and people, and as such is termed a sociophysical phenomenon.[2]

"The physical elements that are used to create defensible space have a common goal: to release the latent sense of territoriality and community among inhabitants so as to allow these traits to be translated into inhabitants' assumption of responsibility for preserving a safe and well-maintained living environment."

As a nation we have witnessed large-scale failure of low- and moderate-income developments—a failure increasingly attributable to rising crime and vandalism rates.

The lack of security in housing has produced fear of invasion by violent criminals, high vacancy rates, and heavy financial losses. In some cases it has led to the complete abandonment of housing projects. In the periods before abandonment, residential developments that suffer high crime rates have been found to receive only minimal use by their residents. The areas outside the dwelling units go unused—whether

66

laundry rooms, lounging areas, parking lots, or playgrounds. These areas are also heavily vandalized.

Residents living in an insecure housing environment withdraw from each other and from all areas beyond the interior of their homes. They are frightened to make the trip from their homes to neighboring streets, to shopping areas, or to the transportation facilities that will take them to other parts of the city.

In a world of latently violent individuals without inhibitions against committing crime, it has been noted that one crime-prevention alternative is the *direct observation by many other people.*

It may not be the ideal solution to the problem of crime, but it ameliorates the condition somewhat to arrange space so that it has the appearance of being composed of small, defined areas controlled by specific groups of occupants. The effect is an environment that is intensively utilized and continually monitored by its inhabitants. In a world composed of opportunistic potential criminals, where darkness and secrecy tend to crime, practical experience has indicated that bright lights and the presence of many people with an interest in stability and peace, tend to repress the more violent inclinations of the few.

What Happened to Dreams of Privacy?

Experts in the field suggest that "residents and nonresidents alike should feel that they will be recognized by other residents and that their presence can be questioned."

How far we have traveled from the ideal of individual privacy, inviolate from outside inquiry, even by police officers! Our decision-law has insisted that everyone has a right to free passage in public places—without inquiry by anyone. A Harvard law professor walking on a suburban street after midnight, when queried by patrolling officers indignantly refused to answer their queries, objected to being stopped, and went to court to prove the justice of his right.

Now, it appears we have modern science reintroducing concepts universally held in primitive communities. But this is directly opposite from the path we have traveled for the past 100 years, during which our civil libertarians have fought unceasingly in the courts for protection from outside investigation and inquiry.

The Anonymity of the City.

The city is noted for the anonymity of life possible in high-rise urban residences where we can live for a generation without ever seeing, knowing, or being bothered by our next-door neighbors.

A common visual media joke, unmarked by dialogue, is the scene where the urban apartment dweller goes to the door of her apartment and laboriously unlocks four or more bars, latches and keyed knobs before she can open the door. It is a silent commentary on our times, and on the financial success of the security industry.

Much of the violent crime increase has concentrated in the low and moderate-income sections of the nation's cities, the same areas that contain most of the government-funded housing. Thus the problem of proper apartment security has come to the attention of the federal and state governments, to halt the abandonment of badly needed housing, a growing problem in many cities.

One fact is clear: Law enforcement agencies cannot preserve from violence, even our easily observed open streets, not to mention the far more difficult problem of enclosed private and public spaces.

Making Enclosed Space Safe.

Given the inherently limited role of police, various government agencies, among them the National Institute of Justice, and the United States Department of Housing and Urban Development have supported research in "defensible space," which has examined residential crime patterns and the physical and social factors that correlate most strongly with crime.[3]

Actually, the problem is an old one. Concern with the safety of jailers, prisoners, and public has always been a part of prison design and construction, but recent years have seen a new trend in design applications.

The "Big House."

Maximum security prisons were always very expensive to build, to maintain, and to keep secure. They involved a high-walled perimeter, much isolation of prisoners, regimentation of movement when not isolated, drilled routine, frequent body and cell inspections, and punishment, corporal and otherwise.

However, they were invaluable because of the security with which they restrained the prisoners from escape. There was discovered, however, additional "values." The "Big House" affected the minds of the prisoners . . . and their behavior as well. Researchers noted this, and applied this knowledge to developing a new procedure which they called, "Classification."

Half a century ago classification of prisoners came to be the very first 'treatment,' given new inmates. To gain political acceptability, the process was stated to have the purpose of determining "the best type of treatment and facility available to rehabilitate the prisoner." But that statement was merely to present a beneficent public image, the reality was not so gentle in intent.

Since correctional and police officers, and most of the professionals in the field knew that rehabilitation was not feasible, classification actually was in the first place more an analysis of the new inmates' character as a security risk, than a search to determine the specific "corrective" treatment that would be suitable.

Even more important, was to reach the minds of the prisoners, to affect their future behavior. As old-time correctional officers termed it, "It's good to give them a touch of the whip." Presumably the new inmate would be cowed by the rigid discipline, and harsh routine into a submissive mood. Further, he knew that if he was lucky enough to be sent to a less restrictive institution, he would be more likely to toe the line, lest he be sent back to the big, gray, high-walled prison, that punished the mind, as well as the body.[4]

Creating the Inmate Personality.

As far as reality of corrective treatment in prison is concerned, the development of an "inmate personality" seems to be the prime objective. To make the new prisoner submissive to prison discipline, current practice is to use the classification process to give all newcomers a taste of the despair and depression which maximum security prisons tend to induce. With that memory lingering, granted that the client submits, and is now considered less of a security risk, he will be assigned to a less secure, and less expensively constructed and maintained facility.[5] The universality of this practice is a testimony to the the belief that controlled space can change the behavior of people. It may be questionable, however, to apply the same concepts to free citizens, going about their ordinary business.

Nevertheless, the adoption of territorial attitudes and policing measures are perceived by some authorities as "the strongest deterrents to criminal and vandal activity."[6]

What is interesting is that the quoted section is from a government text advising designers of residential property, where citizens and the public at large are legally in their rights as they move freely about.

One is urged to question the authorities as to how much can we expect defensible space designed under those strictures to affect the lives and personalities of American citizens. Is the public ready to surrender the design of their lives to prison architects, and accept surveillance norms of policing and being policed?

We need not here go into the details of how correctional facilities are now designed to reduce to a minimum the passageways that are not easily kept under observation. Or how the inmates are grouped in large areas. Unarmed guards are locked into these areas with the inmates to observe. There are no partitions or columns behind which surreptitious moves can be made without being seen by the guards. Glass windows, with suitable steel grills to protect them are in strategic places to facilitate observation from outside, in addition.

Principles of Defensible Space.

In sum, the principles are: Space will be considered to be defensible and assaults reduced in that area if: The space can be kept under constant, or at least frequent, random observation; it is well occupied by a moving population of inmates or other persons who have no apparent reason to conspire with each other to cause disturbance or disorder. One notes that these guidelines are designed not only to reduce the incidence of assault, but to reduce costs.

Forcing Statistics to Prove a Case.

As expected, the new open-type prisons described above do show a lower rate of general violence than the traditional prison without open spaces for congregating prisoners. In at least one sense, however, this is deceiving.

For it must be stated that none of this really addresses planned assaults, or other crimes. General riots are not hindered to any great extent by the above principles.[7] It would appear that an entirely different set of principles should be followed, if we want to reduce conspiracies, illegal activities such as drug smuggling and dealing, and city- or prison-wide riots or mutinies.

It is only the spontaneous, or casual assault that might be prevented. Planned violence would merely more carefully choose its time and place. One theorizes that the deliberately violent would indulge their passion in passageways, staircases, in nooks and crannies, and areaways, in storerooms, or while in transit from one area to another.

Proving the theory, statistics from these new prisons confirm the guess. Place-analysis of the reported figures reveals certain areas in these new prisons manifest even higher rates of violence than any given area of most maximum security prisons. This is so, despite the fact that the populations of the newer-type prisons are preselected for less propensity to violence.

Residential Defensible Space.

In urban, and particularly residential environments, the traditional means for providing security has not come to mind until after-the-fact of commission of many crimes. Noting where and how criminals made their entrance, owners and occupants purchase and install fences, alarms, walls, hardware, and security personnel as needed.

Attention, too, has always been given to preexisting barriers and structures, such as rivers, hills, depressions, buildings, industrial facilities such as railroad yards, airports, highways, telephone and other communication structures.

Complete as that may seem, today most professionals would find intolerable the lack of focused attention to security design, in the initial planning process. They feel that many specific design features can be incorporated into a basic plan, that would be impossibly costly to add after constructions. Under the general rules regarding keeping close watch on costs we can list design criteria by the numbers:

A first consideration is the gross physical features of the location being considered, and the effect these characteristics may have on security. Physical aspects such as streets, adjoining buildings, waterways, even air approaches are part of this mix.

Second, and of prime importance for cost reasons is maximizing *function* of the space to be used by the people involved.

A third is, control of the space by dwellers, pedestrians, motorists, and other users.

A fourth could well be classification of the different types of users, and the particular use each makes of its respective environment.

A fifth naturally follows: Using the capacity of each group to contribute to its own security.

Controlling Planned Assaults.

Assaults and other violent crimes often are carefully planned in advance. A criminal will reconnoitre the future scene of his crime as carefully as a military tactician. Much of the efforts put into designing and constructing defensible space serve, at best, to send the would-be attacker on to another less well defended place. By itself, that would not reduce total crime much. Nor would it deny the fact that if the attacker wants to place his attention on a specific place, though it be well defended, he could, and likely would, prevail.

The old rules about attack and defense in war seem to be relevant: The attack always has the advantage of timing and surprise.

Summing Up On the Concept of Defensible Space.

That being the case what has happened with the concepts of defensible space as applied to urban violence was as expected by behavioral scientists: not very much. It is certainly true that assaulters, rapists, robbers, and burglars will be attracted first to nondefended areas. The essential problem of such violence, however, the desire to commit it, remains untouched.

Most violence is committed in low-income areas, and:[9]

> In low-income, anonymous, high-rise housing environment, teenage children living among families with few male heads of household, playing in areas distant from home, soon learn that there are few restraints upon their behavior. Everything is theirs for the doing or taking; they can rip off a building and its residents with little concern for possible repurcussions. If an honest cost accounting were done, the destruction wrought by children in elevator buildings would make any building economist question whether ever to put families into high rises again. Unfortunately, the men who estimate the cost of buildings for construction are not the same men who estimate the cost of their maintenance. Those in charge of developing new housing normally get credit only for the number of new units they make available; they are seldom around three to five years later to pick up the pieces.

The increased use of security design, devices, and equipment has not had a measureable effect of reducing the total incidence of violent crimes. The business of producing these items has been, and still is, brisk. The cost of modifying structures and procedures away from prime function, toward maximizing protection from crime, while tempting in the short-term, is devastingly costly in the long-term, when applied everywhere, to everyone.

In short: While very useful for a particular problem spot, the concept of defensible space does not appear to be all we would like it to be.

Granted the theoretical validity of the position that "proper design and construction in the use of space can, ideally prevents most crime," we are struck by two factors:

1) The great cost of such procedures, when fully implemented, and
2) The change in the quality of life produced.

If we are not ready to change our entire way of life, putting the emphasis on fear of crime, we must look elsewhere for amelioration of human violence.

It does not appear that the concepts of defensible space can reduce the lure of violence without unacceptable changes in rights to privacy, quality of life, and personal freedom verging not only on unconstitutionality, but against the very integrity of the human personality.

Yes, we must look elsewhere.

Chapter 9

CHANGING PATTERNS

"... to be a city ... there must be in households,
a sharing of the good life ... "

Aristotle
384-322 B.C.

"We walk by faith, not by sight."

St. Paul
57–67? A.D.

"The state of man: inconstancy,
boredom, anxiety."

Blaise Pascal
1623–1662

Discerning the Pattern of Change.

Man's living patterns have always changed over time. It is difficult to say that there is any evolutionary pattern toward an ultimate development. Rather, one is tempted to see the changes as being cyclical without any apparent end-goal in view.

When a particular circumstance seen as a "problem" appears to be within human capacity to change, often individual or joint effort is made for correction. The change, when and if it does occur, often results in unexpected new problems.

How can the present situation on the use of deadly force be described? In sum, we live in a country with a the highest rate of use of deadly force in the West. Commentators give impressions, opinions, recite political catechism, or descend to polemic accusations of the violent tendencies of Americans.

Of course, there is recourse to statistical reports and analyses. Not that these are more "true." They are not. They are merely another way of

74

trying to communicate information, in which the biases are, perhaps more identifiable, the data collection tactics are revealed. But biases do exist, nevertheless. Since rarely do we know the sample-base, or the specific interactions involved in collecting the data, it is usually difficult to locate, and estimate magnitudes of the biases implicit in every statistical presentation.

The U.S. Department of Justice, Bureau of Justice Statistics presents its latest annual, *Report to the Nation on Crime and Justice,* which summarizes much data about changing patterns. Homicide data have been compiled from death certificates filed throughout the United States[1] based on the judgments of appropriate authorities as to the causes or probable causes of death.

Homicide rates have been compiled from death certificates from the beginning of the 20th century, to date. This makes it possible to view rises and falls in the homicide rate against a backdrop of events and developments of national magnitude in order to explore the possibility that any of these events or developments have had any influence on the homicide rate.

Three major long-term trends in homicide are evident. From 1903 to 1933, the rate rose from 1.1 to 9.7 homicides per 100,000 people. Between 1934 and 1958, it fell to 4.5. From 1961 through 1980 it rose again to 11.0. Many minor, short-term trends are also evident, such as the 1945–47 rise within a long-term falling trend.

The Bureau of Justice statisticians, with the confidence typical of experts in every field, conclude:[2]

> While it is safe to say that many national events combine to contribute to affect the crime rate, some occurrences seem of such magnitude that their influence seems to be a major factor: "World War II clearly affected the homicide rate, by a sharp decline during the war years, and a short-term rise immediately after the war's end, when most of the soldiers returned home.

That, of course, merely states the obvious: the young men who might have killed at home, were deployed to wreak death overseas. Those that remained in the United States were either in military service, busy working in exempt jobs, or young, impressionably caught up in the drama of the war, and—perhaps above all, filled with the ideological fervor of national unity in the face of threatened violence from the declared enemies of the country, and so diverted from committing violence at home.

The postwar baby boom generation began to reach age 16 in the early 1960's, at the same time the homicide rate began to rise sharply.[3]

Victims or perpetrators? Possibly both, but most in-depth analyses indicate the old truth, those who commit violence are killed by violence.

Homicide rates are generally regarded as the most reliable and valid of all crime statistics. In confirmation, the F.B.I.'s Uniform Crime Reports, and the Public Health statistics both show a homicide rate that has been rising since 1961.

Except for homicide, most violent crimes do not involve the use of weapons. The data can be tabulated.[4]

Weapon Used	Homicide	Rape	Robbery	Assault[**]
Firearm	62%	7%	18%	9%
Knife	19	15	21	9
Other-type	13	1*	9	14
Unknown	0	2*	2*	1
None used	6	77	54	66
	100%	100%?	100%?	100%?

(Note: Because some crimes involved more than one type of weapon, detail may add to more than 100%.

(* Estimate is based on 10 or fewer samples-items and is statistically unreliable.)

(** Includes simple assaults, which by definition do not involve the use of a weapon.)

Deadly Weapons.

Weapons were more often used in killings of law enforcement officers than any other method of assault. Thus validating the typical alarm manifested by law enforcement officers when an incident involves a citizen exhibiting, or even possibly possessing, a gun or knife. With the increase in the number of weapons owned by the public one can expect more homicides of police officers. Many local jurisdictions have recently made it easier to own, possess, and carry sidearms, responding to public outcries for their need for self-defense. We have yet to see the effect on assaults on police and peaceful citizens.

Terrorism is unexpectedly rare in the United States, thus far. Interestingly, our bombings are overwhelmingly caused by nonterrorists. Terrorist groups claimed responsibility for only 20 of the 1,249 bombing incidents in 1985. Half of all bombings are for unknown motives. Of those where the motivation is known, the most commonly claimed were animosity, mischief, and revenge.

Fear of Strangers Justified.

Most fear of violence is centered around the fear that strangers will be the perpetrators. The fear of crime, in general, is the fear of a random unprovoked attack or robbery by a stranger. At bottom it appears to be fear of strangers who may have deadly weapons. The common apprehension appears to be well-founded, for as measured by the National Crime Survey, most violent crimes are committed by strangers. The outstanding exception is murder. More than half of all homicides are committed by someone known to the victim. Relatives, that is, commit 17 percent of all homicides, but only 7 percent of other violent crimes on related victims.

But it has always been that way, we kill our loved ones, and steal from strangers. Fair enough, at least we are warned. Relatives take your life, strangers only take your money. If we are to guard against homicide, the remedies will have to do with family relations and circumstances. In a phrase, when affection, and doctrinal feelings of personal obligation, are tested to breaking point, danger looms.

The Role of Youth.

What is the role of youth in violence? The statistics confirm common experience. Participation in crime and violence declines with age. Except for a small minority of offenders, the intensity of criminal activity slackens about the mid-twenties.

The reduction of the number of youths in the population in the 1970's accompanied a drop in the total number of violent crimes by youth.

The problem is succinctly analyzed to the two critical variables: A) Youth, and B) Belief systems.

In our country, today, youths are indoctrinated early in the values of fighting, violence, and rebellion. That, added to whatever evolutionary tendencies may exist appears to be a sufficient explanation.

Of course, we could look for more refinements in the inquiry, go farther afield, for subtle differences in individual environment. One can seek shelter, however, in the shade of Occam's Razor and accept the obvious, the simple, and, certainly in this case, the straightforward conclusion as to high correlation of youthful indoctrination into violent responses, and the actual incidence of violence.

We have university courses on deadly force which are described in newspaper headlines as, " . . . Newest Course: When to Shoot An Intruder."[5]

It is as though even the academic world has assented to the cultural mores of the day. If violence is up, let's do it scientifically, systematically, better!

Thus the indoctrination toward violence receives apparent approval from the most responsible, and prestigious institutions of the land. Strange country we live in, where the schools deny prayers for peace. Where faith and doctrine on behalf of nonviolence are frowned upon, but condoned and encouraged for violence.

Chapter 10

ADAPTING TO DEADLY FORCE

*"Human history becomes more
and more a race between
education and catastrophe"*

H.G. Wells

Revulsion Against Deadly Force.

Unrestrained horror at the devastation and death committed by national governments during World War II, resulted in a public revulsion which forced many European administrations to seek ways to erase the images of that nightmare from the collective mind.

One way Europeans came to terms with the idea of deadly force was for many countries to eliminate capital punishment for crime, even for murder.[1]

For the first twenty years after the war the rate of deadly force in Europe remained even lower than its traditionally low rate. Then a rising radicalism started to use force to make its political points.

Deadly Force Was Only Hiding.

The Mid-East always had its quota of violent death, stimulated by rivalry between Turks, Arabs, Christians, and Europeans seeking spheres of influence, and wealth. After World War II, Jews and their new state of Israel were in perpetual conflict with surrounding Islamic nations, violent incidents increased in number and ferocity. All the while, Christians fought Arabs in Lebanon, and internal Islamic schismatic differences continued.

Terrorism Becomes Big Business.

It wasn't, however, until radical political organizations acquired increased funding from foreign sources, that they were able to use more systematic methods to kill each other. Training camps were built, and tactical techniques of infiltration and escape, sabotage and bombing were taught by military veterans and specialists. The theory of psychological warfare of terror, as exploited by the Nazis, used with reverse effect by various WW II underground forces, was now modified for use by small groups, in lightning forays.

The theory held that killing, maiming and mutilation of the weak and helpless has much greater shock power than the killing of military personnel who are expendable. Wasted by terror, the theory relied on the survivors to use political pressure on their governments to submit to the terrorists' demands whatever they may be.[2] The theory worked for years. Terrorist organizations were given formal recognition in the United Nations, and in many sovereign states.

New devices were perfected, better weapons secured, with supporting staff to provide counterfeit identification, passports, foreign exchange, bills of lading as needed, traffic experts in rail, ship, and air scheduling, and information analysts were amassed with the increasing funds available. High levels of skill were developed in the arts of dealing death in small doses all around the world. A few experts became famous among their congnoscenti, able to obtain even more funding and cooperation from states extending from Libya to Bulgaria to Syria.

The Importance of Indoctrination.

The importance of indoctrination was recognized from the very beginning. Many practiced revolutionaries, guerrillas and terrorists, ranging from Hitler, Mao-Tse Tung, and Che Guevara, to Yasir Arafat and Ayatolla Khomeini have insisted that indoctrination is more important than weapons to success. Their messages were taken to heart by the international terrorists. Indoctrination-training proceeded in many countries: Japan; Turkey; the West Bank of the Jordan River, among the Palestinian Arabs; Italy; Germany; Ireland; and several of the African countries.[3]

A large cadre of radicalized displaced persons existed to provide personnel for raiding terrorist bands, particularly among the dispossessed Palestinian Arabs numbering over 800,000. Disaffected youth were actively recruited in many other nations. Training camps were established in the Fertile Crescent area of the Middle East to mould minds to appropriate belief-systems, and to give training in the methods of sabotage and assassination. Outstanding students were invited to attend the Patrice Lumumba University in Moscow for advanced education in Marxist theory and philosophy of the war between the classes.[4]

Success in early operations was met with wide media coverage, which encouraged even more generous funding from foreign sources. With substantial, international cooperation and assistance now certain, the strategy and tactics of the use of terror to unsettle, and ultimately to topple existing governments became more sophisticated, with a claim to providing the dynamics of national revolution in dozens of countries. Some countries succumbed to the powerful new revolutionary armies, which quickly reorganized as full-dress national governments and applied for admission to the United Nations.

At first tentatively, then with more sureness and skill, refined terrorist tactics were applied at great distances from the points of indoctrination, training, and supply.

Separate ideologies were custom-designed to fit the hates of each national revolutionary group. Though specific to particular national situations, these zeolots and their ideologies hung together sufficiently to provide a feeling of comity, encouraging mutual aid among the revolutionary movements.[5]

With doctrinaire hate of the great democracies, national terrorists became a force that had to be reckoned with. Money, weapons, even personnel were exchanged, borrowed, paid for in an internal mart of murder that was mostly invisible to the international press and national governments.

Most Western nations did not realize this, at first. Political assassinations by individuals, or teams of two or three terrorist expanded into larger operations, involving simultaneous attacks hundred of miles apart, evincing a level of coordination and timing worthy of national government operations. Over a dozen terrorist organizations, with covert foreign aid by several governments, became expert in hijacking, maiming, and hostage-taking in Italy, Northern Ireland, Spain, to some extent in Germany, and other places.

It wasn't until later, after the Mid-East nations could rely on huge incomes from the increased price and profits from oil flowing from their nationalized fields that the world-wide hostage-taking, air-jacking, bombings of innocent children and women began in earnest.

Soldiers of Fortune.

The pain and suffering inflicted on the innocent did not affect the bravado with which the restless or rootless of Europe and many other countries, especially the United States, enlisted as mercenaries in bloody conflicts around the world.

Calling themselves "soldiers of fortune," these generally were individuals who had not personally suffered the worst agonies of war wounds. With some military training, but having been lucky enough not to feel the personal bomb, shell, or bullet, they remained with a feeling they had missed on the glamour and excitement of "the most important event in history," as one bandoliered combat-armed American spoke of it, in Guatamala. They supplied a resource valuable to many revolutionary movements: military skill. Many of them are impressive in speech, appearance, and style. For young poverty-stricken youngsters in third-world countries they provided flesh and blood charismatic figures.

Soldiers of fortune sometimes are inspired by dedication for, or against communism or other ideology, or the relatively good pay offered mercenaries in the advertising pages of magazines filled with hair-raising stories of derring-do on foreign shores. American mercenaries were represented all over the world, and are to this day.

How the United States Adapted to Global Deadly Force.

The United States compared to Europe, has been said to have demonstrated a retarded morality. For we did not exhibit revulsion at government-inspired deadly force. Although we avoided the term "war" the United States was itself a prime mover in a bloody "police action" in Korea with token participation by the United Nations in the 1950's. Our Marines invaded Iran, during Eisenhower's administration, funded and sent officially recognized, or covertly supported military "advisors" to several local minor wars, and took on a redoubtable foe in Viet Nam in the 1960's, in a military action that lasted, in one form or another for ten years.

Although there were widespread civil demonstrations against American involvement in Viet Nam, enough to cause the withdrawal from candidacy of a sitting President, the objection in general was not against the killing, but rather against the politics of the situation. Students and other activists were indignant at the arrogance of an administration which called for free Americans to be living sacrifices, despite the lack of a formal declaration of war by Congress, as representative of the wish of the people. There were many biases and prejudices in applying the draft. There was a general absence of agreement as to why we were investing treasure and blood in Southeast Asia.

The horrors of previous wars appeared to have been mostly forgotten by the administration in Washington, and even most of the public. There was little public display of stars in the windows indicating servicemen and women killed in action.

Renunciation of Capital Punishment.

There had been, in the United States, progressive relinquishment of capital punishment in most of the states, as the ultimate sanction for crime, but that was to a great extent the product of constitutional litigation, and special-interest lobbying, to the political representatives of a disinterested public.

An observer is tempted to say that revulsion against violence did not penetrate very deeply into our national psyche. In a phrase, we were and are not indoctrinated against violence, as were the other participants of global war, and, particularly Japan, the only country to have suffered the ultimate catastrophe of atomic bombing.

Americans passively accepted a de facto pause in the pace of capital punishment. Growing numbers of condemned waited on death rows for their appeals to be completed. This was not so much because of the public's desire to avoid execution of criminals as a deterrent, but because our appellate system was overwhelmed by highly organized, legally eloquent ideologues representing the most directly concerned: Prisoners charged with capital crimes, their families and sympathizers.

American Response to Social Problems.

This was a typically American response to a social issue. The tactics are as follows:

1) Spearheading by a small core of dedicated ideologues, who provide guidance and support.

2) Phalanxes of emotionally involved families, and relatives, of those under sentence of death.

3) They are guided in forming public demonstrations, with much excited shouting against capital punishment, which is easily maneuvered into television and other news-spots.

4) The mothers, wives, and girl-friends are portrayed in grieving, sympathetic roles.

5) An important corollary is the complete avoidance of messages of contrary import. That is, information about the mutilated and killed victims of the convicted murderers is absent and ignored.

6) Under the expert legal guidance of constitutional lawyers, each case is fought at every appellate level to the Supreme Court.

7) Constant effort is made, down the line for maximum media and political impact, both locally and nationally.

The Facts of Political Bargaining.

As a people we admire sincerity. Thus devoted, emotional faith in an issue has always attracted favorable support in this country. Nevertheless, a chief feature of American political life has been a pretence of non-ideological bargaining. On the face of it, political leaders try to balance the interests of those most vigorous in presentation of their points of view.

When the courts are resorted to, an important part of the presentation is documentation of "essential fairness," for the cause espoused, particularly *vis à vis* the adversary in court.

It is not a method based on a broad view of causes and consequences. Although many of our leaders are trained in public administration, and have wide experience in public management, there is not much more than lip service given to organizational science concepts, such as "system theory," goal-oriented administration, impact analysis and others. Even cost-benefit analysis is rarely admitted to the councils forming, promoting or implementing policy and making political judgments.

One method to implement the struggle of an interest group desiring to change a political or social *status quo* is to work on the emotions of the majority. If the interest group can obtain from the majority consent to a compromise arrangement that "can be lived with," even if it only part of the way toward the interest-group's goal, the tactic is to say: "We, too, can live with that." The wait commences until the next confrontation, with a new starting base.

Hallowed by Mohandas Ghandi in the struggle he led against the British Raj, the method has been very successful against governments that rely on public support for power. Ghandi, however, conspicuously labeled his effort as "peaceful resistance," and "peaceful disobedience," weakening the moral resistance of successive Parliaments. Gathering support from the British public, Ghandi and his followers objected in sequence, to everything about the British regime, including its alleged "wanton use of force and violence." Finally, the ultimate prize was won, independence from the British Empire.

Dr. Martin Luther King, Jr. studied Ghandi's methods and used them in modified form in the United States to gain civil rights for blacks, in the 1960's. Dr. King's people, however, did not register any specific objection to deadly force, except when civil rights were involved. However, as further gains were not obtained to the satisfaction of younger, more impulsive young blacks, Dr. King's influence waned, and a call for more energetic, if not violent confrontation was made.

The Politics of Deadly Force.

There are a great number of ways human societies have organized to reduce, or virtually eliminate violence in a community. Many of them have successfully reduced violence to miniscule percentages, as they successfully adapted to the threat of deadly force by measures designed to eliminate it from their society. There were, of course, trade-offs, each technique involved a balancing of advantages and disadvantages.

Essentially, to adapt to deadly force one group of approaches is to try to accommodate to it, and reduce its most pernicious effects. Even that basic approach has its defects. Here are some examples from the past.

Victorian Morals and Mores.

One former means of adapting to deadly force has acquired a halo of nostalgia for "old-time respect for law and family, order and harmony."

One should, however, also consider the hobbling of ambition and personal dreams, that was the necessary consequence of rigid role specifications, an etiquette which enforced the old-time virtues. Women, particularly have since objected to the limited number of satisfactory roles permitted the Victorian woman. There were substantial objections even then, to the confining clothing, corsets, high-necked dresses, bustles.

Restriction to certain activities of a "lady-like" nature, exclusion from politics, from sports, sexual opportunity, and alleged psychological disabilities and neuroses attributed to women, have all been scorned by the following three generations.

The inhibitions and taboos of a society are important. Paraphrasing the ideas of biologist Harold Hayes, we must consider the "carrying capacity of a culture." Some things come naturally to a society, other things may be quite impossible. A given society cannot tolerate, or bear some things.

As Betty Friedan explains in *The Second Stage*[6] the movement for women's rights cannot support itself in our current society, unless it accepts the importance of the family. Our society will simply reject women's rights, as a cause, if the women's movement rejects the family.

This is important in regard to deadly force, as our analysis has run. For we are in an era when the family has been radically restructured for much of our population. Working mothers take an ever larger role in our economy, and in our concepts of what women can do, and who they are. Relevant to our own discussion is the effect on children, traditionally the responsibility of mothers in the home.

Is our present system of child-care able to carry the burden of children without a mother in the home, ready with nurture, care and concern to mold the child into a nonviolent image? Can our culture develop new norms that will take the place of those mandated by fathers who worked all day, and come home at night as exemplars of ultimate discipline and authority in the home?

To those who plead for a return of the traditional family pattern, the question must be asked, "Are you ready to give up our modern conception of a free woman, with unlimited potential?" We must ask ourselves, are we ready to put her in the kitchen and laundry room for up to twelve hours a day, bind her body in corsets and layers of underclothes, insist on her physical maladroitness, enforcing it all with the threat of otherwise being considered scandalously unladylike, and unfit to be mother, wife, or citizen? The answers are in the process of being resolved by life situations all over the United States. It is not possible at this time to be certain what the final image will be.

Advanced Technology.

The broadest question we have is: "How much deadly force will our society accept — how much can it carry, before it breaks down into chaos, and internecine warfare?"

The advent of advanced technology now permits deadly force to be applied in subtle, covert ways, with minute infernal devices and techniques. To kill with less than a milligram of poisons, such as ricin, used by Bulgarian-sponsored assassins in London is now possible. In theory entire municipal water supplies can be poisoned in less than one half-hour. The demoralizing effect on millions of people of this deadly hazard is slowly penetrating the public mind. Current reports of pesticides, lead residues, and traces of carcinogenic substances in our drinking water have made the manufacture and sale of water filters one of the fastest growing industries in the country. The possibility of terrorist poisoning of drinking supplies is felt to be a very real possibility, especially with modern devices to instill and disseminate new poisonous substances.

Advanced technology can be used, on the otherhand, to detect, suppress, and oppose those devices and techniques. Granted, that is, the desire to implement that desire with economic support, and political will.

Pre-World War II police officers carried a small revolver which fired a light, weakly powered bullet known as the short .38. The revolver, itself was handy enough to be kept in the officer's off-duty civilian trouser pocket without difficulty. On duty, it was effective only at short range against unprotected criminals, without heavy overcoats; certainly not against those sheltered in a steel-bodied car. Now police and criminals carry armor-piercing bullets powered with heavy loads that enable them to blast a long bullet that has the penetration and power to pass through a car from stern to stem, killing any people it encounters in its passage.[7]

Even criminals wear body armor, carry hand machine-guns, and ride about in armored vehicles.[8] Naturally, the pressure is on for police departments to equip their officers with equally effective tools. Rifles and shotguns are now commonly part of the equipment of radio cars. Many departments recommend 9 mm. automatic pistols, body-armor, stun-guns, and armored cars to their budget commissions.

It becomes an exciting technological race for superiority in firepower and defensive armor, for police gun fans and their aficionados. Unfortunately, the public still remains in the main unarmed, unarmored, and unprotected.

Guns for the people, however, is a continuing program, and many jurisdictions have extended the right of the ordinary citizen to bear weapons in their homes, and on their person. What this bodes for the future is presaged for us by the frequent reports of shootings by motorists, frustrated in traffic congestion. The reports are not limited to southern California, and cannot be ignored.

The issue of deadly force by and against the public, remains in doubt. That doubt will exist for a long time, it seems to most observers. Our culture is not yet in a position to deal with the problem. In fact, it is doubtful if the general public sees it as an urgent problem they can handle.

Adapting By Avoiding the Issue.

There are a number of theoretical approaches to adapting to deadly force, each locked into its own set of ideological apothegms which have been bruited about, with little observable effect on the rate of use of force. These differing points of view, may serve to dilute focused efforts at more direct amelioration.

Perhaps a case in point is the recent report of graduate medical students in Moscow who have vowed to block any cure for AIDS, calling the deadly disease, "this noble epidemic."[9]

No doubt this is a sentiment that is widespread in many countries, including ours, though usually unvoiced in public in the United States. Even silent opinion, however, must have its effect in weakening public efforts to discover means to prevent, treat, and cure this most dangerous threat to life.

"They deserve what they get!" has often been a bar to bringing common community effort to resolve a problem. By excluding themselves from the acts and the consequences, such disclaimers of interest and responsibility may be at the base of our present dilemma in deadly force in general. If we feel those who meet violent ends deserve the violence they received, we insulate ourselves from the entire matter. It is no longer our problem, we are not the keeper of our brother.

Avoiding the issue in this way not only takes ourselves out of the fray, but also tends to vitiate the activity of bystanders who might otherwise be active in the drive to control deadly force. The intentional or negligent refusal to admit possibility of contagion from this disease of deadly force prolongs our agony. Closing our eyes to the source and implications of this violence does not make it go away.

Apocalyptic Adaptation.

Is the real truth about humans simply this: Deadly force is as valid and as necessary as life-force. The urge, the force, divine or otherwise, that has created life has, and probably must, create death.

Whether this is part of some larger plan, or not, it is easy to trace the historical truth that every war brings on a higher birth rate. Every glut of food and luxury brings in train a lowered birth rate.

Is it not true that if the birth rate were to decline to zero, it would be absolutely necessary for us to arrange to reduce the birth rate to nullity, too? The alternative would be the geometric progression of squirming humanity into a mountainous, moiling pile of protoplasm, without the real characteristics we recognize as human.

The question is easily answered. No. Death, in this view, is as necessary to man as is life. "Let us," say the apocalyptians, "learn to accept the inevitable, deadly force is here to stay. For solace, we must remember that there is a better world to come!"

An Econometric Adaptation.

In one sense, we need not ponder the question of deadly force. It will, inexorably, resolve itself in response to presently existing economic pressures. As long as force is profitable it will continue, the more profitable the more force. When force becomes non-profitable, or a source of economic loss, it will be reduced by the "invisible hand" of economic law.

The basic reason for the problem is, to the econometricians, incredibly simple: There is, at the present time, more profit and less loss, in the use of deadly force, than its containment. There is insufficient economic incentive to reduce it. The model provided by economics demands removal of all profit that goes to those who apply force; and increase the losses.

The similarity to Bentham's proposals is evident except the punishment involved is economically based, even if not purely financial.

Up to now, for solutions we have proceeded in the opposite direction. Not only do the users of force and threat benefit economically in our culture, as a rule, but the broadest view of government policy reveals an interesting pattern when examined under the lens of economics.

Our efforts to control deadly force have, in the main had recourse to government bureaucratic procedures. However, the goal of every good bureaucrat is to get an exclusive franchise on what he is doing.

If nobody else is doing it, no one else can measure how well, or poorly, it is being done. Unmeasured, and uncriticized, the bureaucrat, then, need only stay busy, generating paper. As long as he does not make any obvious, or scandalous mistakes he is safe for his entire career, whether or not his position truly contributes to the public benefit.

True, the bureaucracies that are concerned with deadly force are split up into many jurisdictions throughout the country. We have thousands of police departments and other investigative agencies, in this country. Each one, however, is victim to this bureaucratic axiom: Power accrues to the bureaucracy without reference to successful accomplishment of its job. In fact, if they did the job in a completely successful manner, they would work themselves out of a position. Even the casual observer knows how rare this is.

For this, and other reasons, bureaucracy cannot reduce deadly force. In the long run, it can only compound it. The fiscal dynamics of bureaucracy call for production of symbols of performance, without real performance, lest next year's appropriation be reduced.

The social dynamics of bureaucracy call for larger and larger injections of personnel and funds to refurbish an ever more powerful administration. The more personnel an administrator supervises, the greater his salary. The greater the jurisdiction of an agency, either geographically, functionally, or organizationally, the more important that agency is in the government network.

And the less accountable it is.

A Revolutionary Adaptation.

If we accept the ethos of the revolutionary, the most acceptable route to radicalizing the issue of deadly force is to let it run its expected course. If we can endure sufficient bureaucratic bumbling and suffer the consequent epidemic levels of deadly force on the part of criminals, and law enforcement officers, we shall become completely disgusted, and reach for other more effective routes.

Danger exists along this route, however, of overreaching in the direction of either manic suppression, or passive acceptance, of crime and violence.

With either eventuality, we shall have seen the end of our concern with deadly force. Perhaps it will be the end of our time, too.

The Disciplinary Adaptation.

This method of adaptation has been called "the Cracker Barrel Philosopher's Approach." It calls for a return to "practical truths." It is simply expressed in many of the clichés of the English language. "Spare the rod and spoil the child," is one of our oldest. Why has it endured? Because, is the answer, it is the basic truth of child-training.

No doubt one can entice more bees with honey than with vinegar, but as one oldster phrased it from his rocker on the porch of a general store in New Hampshire, "We're not trying to get bees. We're trying to suppress those little sons of B's out there, who are murdering and robbing and beating on the young, the old, and the helpless."

The exhortation drew applause from elders, in the Summer of 1967, during the student demonstrations. It could draw applause in many a civic auditorium today.

In neighborhoods of our older generation, from South Miami Beach to the suburbs of Phoenix we hear the same phrases repeated. They are tried out, from time to time. The litany is invariably the same, "Spare the rod . . . and you get trouble! If corporal punishment were administered on the street, by the first person who caught a child using force, they would never learn to use deadly force, is their insistent imperative.

There are other popular comments:[10]

"When cops used their nightsticks on all tours, to suppress violence on the few occasions it appeared—well, we had a lot less violence."

"Psycholgists have proved it in their laboratories. It is the speed with which punishment is administered that corrects behavior."

"If a juvenile acts violently: Punish him immediately! He won't do it again, under those circumstances. Of course he won't like it, and he will possibly fear, or even hate the punisher. But on the other hand, the good effects are: He won't be so likely to commit the fault again—at least not where he will be punished."

"And, there's another good result: Everyone who acts properly—without violence—will be assured that there is some justice in the world. Instant retribution for violent criminals binds the good citizens together, and notifies them that we are a real community of loving citizens who have only one hate: violence."

"If history has any lessons to teach, it teaches that the juvenile, if punished for violence when young, will, when he is older, join with the nonviolent community. That's the way it was in the old days!"

Another commentator interjects, "Please note too that all punishment meted out, and all decisions made about him, by this method, will be with his full knowledge and understanding, on the basis of universal concurrence of community, friends, and even family. He would have no social choice but to agree and to voluntarily submit."

Harmony and Stability.

The harmony and stability of ancient Chinese communities was the subject of admiring comment by Marco Polo, and later American travelers and missionaries. It implied internal calm in the community, and mandated peaceful relations between all members. It removed the necessity for adapting to deadly force, by eliminating it. Peace was enforced by public meetings or trials which commanded the basic rule that individual sense of wrong was unimportant, compared with the absolute necessity for harmony at all times, and in every case.[11]

Thus to exhibit any kind of anger, to claim unfairness, or even to treat, or be treated, with discourtesy, was to "lose face," a great personal dishonor.

The people lived closely together, in cities, and in rural villages. When combined with ancestor worship, households naturally consisted of three or more generations under the same roof.

Family members were valuable to each other for their labor, thus a son did not leave his father's home, even when he married. He brought his bride to live with his parents, where the young bride labored under the supervision of her mother-in-law.

Under such a close familial situation community enforcement of peace and harmony was a necessary development, if the community, and the family, were to survive intact.

It is recorded that this tradition lasted for millenia in China. Today there are clear traces to be found of this family pattern, even among the "Overseas Chinese," in America and elsewhere.

The trade-offs are obvious. To an American man or woman, especially concerned with crime and violence, there are many attractive details. We cannot, unfortunately, successfully extract the details of one social system and transport them into another, unchanged by other elements of the new situation. Each social system must be studied whole, each part interacts and depends on other parts. Rarely can it be picked apart and one element moved into another system, to operate as it did. Social relations do not travel well, it seems.

The Power of the . . . Ism!

Honest, open-minded review of recorded history reveals one consistent model that has worked to eliminate deadly force, with great success. That is, Faith.

Faith in the efficacy of the rules set forth, and faith that all will obey them, and that—if we may be forgiven the unfashionable phrase—a state of grace comes with obedience to the rules. This has been the way humanity has ever attained a nondeadly community.

If all have faith, then all will obey. If the rules forbid deadly force, and all obey that prohibition, deadly force is wiped out.

The many rules of religious orders, aside from any divine sanction, are handed down almost invariably for the proper administration of the people. Freedom from deadly force, then, can come with obedience. In that sense, obedience to the rules makes men free. Free, that is, of deadly force. Cults and other disciplines know this well.

"Free of fear, free of crime, free of deadly force. It is all possible, if ye all believe, and obey." The exhortive tone is familiar to our ear.

But how is this faith to be attained? Here are the social tools, used by cults for many past millenia:[12]

1 Belief in a superhuman, spiritual authority that enforces the . . . Ism.
2 Rituals of devoted, exhausting practices and mysteries.
3 Rigid orthodoxy enforcing all dogma and practice.
4 Supression of intellectualism for intellectualism breeds dissent. This must be prevented.
5 Rewriting history, to conform with dogma and doctrine. Indoctrination of all members with this historical background and justification.
6 Syllogistic proof of every tenet in the doctrine.
7 Erecting tribal walls: In-groups vs. Out-groups.
8 Subjection and terror applied to all Out-groups. As a tactical

maneuver, concentrating usually on one Out-group, as the particular Beast, Devil, Heretic, Heathen, Satan.

9 Parasitism, that is, the coöpting of every cultured thought, act or artifact to the Faith.

Particularly in past centuries, but also even today, uncounted millions in many different communities have been happy with their lives under a community-wide dogmatic set of beliefs. Many of these, research indicates, were happy, nondeadly communities, at peace with their life and their common ideals.

The pros and cons of this model, for the modern American probably would be quite a personal, individualized list. We need not speculate as to the details, here.

Extreme examples of this model are well known, and have been publicly discussed, but are undoubtedly too strong for modern America to even consider for our use.

One example exhibited[13] on public service television was that of the Dervish sect of Islam. Many members now live in Kurdistan, a part of the political entity known as Iran.

These people perpetuate, in their society, a pervading desire to feel at one with God. Among them, all fellow faithful members, violation of law is unheard of, almost unthinkable. Guided by Holy Men, who have rigidly disciplined themselves and their bodies for years, they undergo hours-long sessions of rhythmic, monodic chanting and swaying to aid their entrance into a religious state of mind and mood. Thus they please God by showing their spirituality. In modern American terms, they "get high on God."

In this state, for the glory of God, they can withstand extreme physical trauma, without pain or suffering. On the contrary, enduring for religion, what would be pain and suffering to the unbeliever, the piously devout sense the greatest satisfaction, physical, spiritual, and emotional, as well as morally, that is possible to the human organism. Thousands of outsiders have seen this.

A true zealot attains great prestige among the tribesmen and religious leaders. They know the Holy Men would not call on them to harm themselves, nor to do any wrong. The demands of the Holy Men are only to please God, and obey Him: To help all brothers and sisters of the Faith, to look on no man's wife, to use only kind words to children.

In pursuit of God's Will, or to demonstrate faith, the Holy Man might ask him to skewer his flesh, or to press it against redhot iron. But the penitent devout will feel no pain because he knows God protects the faithful from pain, here and in the Hereafter. To obey the Holy Man is the way a member can show his own faith, and love of God.

"The Holy Man has disciplined himself for the sake of God. Thus God protects him, and God protects us, when we obey the Holy Man. It is God's Will," said one of the participants recorded for public service television.[14]

"Pain is good for the body. It is discipline, and helps me reach the point where I am completely in God's care, living only for Him. A sword can pass through my body, it doesn't matter. A rod can pass from the top of my head through it to below my chin. It doesn't matter. It is God's Will. To love God is to love the Prophet. To love the Prophet is to love God. One who loves neither God nor Prophet is no Muslim! We purify and wash ourselves five times a day, and pray to God five times a day, to discipline ourselves to think only of God."

Force to Suppress Force.

The methods used circle around a number of points. The literature is filled with materials about the suppression of violence by physical force. The force is supplied by agents outside the subject individual. The kind of force applied varies, pain, deprivation, incarceration, the threat of death, or actual death. Any, or several in combination have been used to deter others from deadly force for fear of that example.

If the subject complies with the demands that accompany that force, by abandoning the use of force himself, the method is successful.

Military forces who overcome an enemy, or who physically occupy "pacified" lands, are typical instances of the use of superior physical force to reduce or eliminate deadly force by others. Nonmilitary groups, governmental, or otherwise, that use force tend to adopt the tactics and weapons of the military. This country and many others, use the term police *force*, and these units often use military rank designations, such as sergeant, lieutenant, captain, and so on. This has been of telling consequence.

Military type discipline and drill is quite usual. Modern military forces are, as social-systems, the end-product of thousands of years of development, with a vast arcane lore of practical, workable ideologies, policies, and procedures. There has accummulated a huge literature documenting military theory and practice.[15]

On the other hand, no military-type despotism without recourse to other resources, has prevailed for any extended period of time. One suspects, that if the military were the best organization for society, it would have been more universally successful in maintaining regimes indefinitely.

Education: Against Deadly Force.

Another source of influence might be termed "education." That is, an effort to teach less use of force by training, or schooling. An extreme example is the military discipline used by the military itself for its personnel. Much the same type of discipline is often used for police forces. Of course, in the background of this discipline is actual raw physical force itself, in the event of mutiny.

Education, training, and discipline, of course, can be used to teach many subjects other than to suppress deadly force. What is implied in use of the term 'education' is that the teaching will tolerate or even encourage critical thinking about items of knowledge.

It must be noted that this type of influence, the most common type of education, tends to depend on a certain kind of order. In fact, almost any type of disorder tends to frustrate the educational process. Although in the early stages of child education the necessary order is buttressed by a latent power of force available should it be necessary, experienced teachers report that the pupils can usually be cajoled into becoming so interested in the subject matter that disorder and force no longer become factors in the teaching-learning situation.

As interest intensifies, it is claimed that order becomes the norm that is not only expected, but preferred by the students. There are a few communities of adults who are so immersed in learning, gathering new knowledge, that other constraints of behavior become irrelevant. Usually, however, even in those few communities, other influencing factors have played significant parts in guiding behavior. We can discuss some of them.

Early Indoctrination: Against Force.

Indoctrination implies teaching a system of thought uncritically. In that sense it might be considered a type of education. The significant difference, as stated, is that education customarily encourages critical thinking about the topic of discourse.

Indoctrination in its purest form declines to engage in critical thinking. It discourages its students from questioning the matters it proclaims to be truths in many ways, although it may present a facade of critical discourse to promote credibility.

When indoctrination commences in a child's earliest years the effects have been noted to be extremely persistent. As noted above, Abbe Dimnet,[16] an educator of the first part of this century commented, "Give me a child up to the age of seven, and he will be mine for all his life." But by now, most people are beginning to understand that.

Analysis.

Of course, there are hundreds more ways that violence in humans has been dealt with, that have not been discussed. Can ways of adapting to deadly force be summarized? There are probably almost as many routes to analysis as there is to deal with violence. What questions should be asked? What questions can be answered? Let us try to respond.

We are interested in deadly force, its causes and consequences. That is a social matter, involving many people. Nevertheless, ultimately, deadly force involves a social entity, of some kind. We could consider a single individual surrounded by others, or a group, or an institution in society that wants to reduce whatever may be the tendency impelling an individual to use deadly force against other human beings. Since, however, force as we have discussed it always involves more than one person, we must infer that social forces must be used to oppose the deadly force we fear.

Summary.

The above several approaches were presented for whatever they are worth. Perhaps they are of most relevance to our study of deadly force because of the energy they draw away from direct action programs, soundly based on behavioral science principles. Their existence provide sufficient distraction to have made a concerted antiviolence program politically impossible up to this time.

Whether this disability can be overcome remains to be seen.

PART THREE
WHO ARE THE ASSAULTERS?

Chapter 11

KILLERS IN THE STREETS

*"My intention was to – do
anything I could do to hurt them."*

Bernard Goetz[1]

Fighting Back: Violence Against Violence:

The fan mail, admiration and support received by Bernard Goetz for shooting four would-be muggers in a New York subway is an index of the hate and fear that stalks our streets. Not only the actual muggers and robbers, but all those who fear that they are potential victims have accepted violence as a solution. All of us have become symbolic killers in our own minds.

Whoever walks down many of the streets of our decaying cities, lives that fantasy. Can we kill before we are killed? Why should we not? For we believe our lives are in danger.

This belief overrides all other considerations, and in Bernie Goetz we sympathize with that same fearful belief. He was found not guilty because the jury felt Goetz was truly in fear of his life and limb. This, even though he admitted all of the following: He armed himself, knowing he was going out to look for muggers; he then shot the four youths before they had harmed him; shot after they started to run away; shot repeatedly after they clearly wanted to leave the scene; and he shot one of them in the back. On the face of it, any prosecutor in the world would have thought it a clear-cut case of premeditated, deliberate attempted murder. The jury understood all that, but they appreciated Bernard Goetz state of mind: fear, unremitting fear, of violent youth in public places. Understanding and themselves feeling his paranoia, they approved of his action. They, too, had found no way to cling to a nonviolent urban life-style. It has become our ideology to believe that violence is omnipresent, and is properly met with prior and greater violence. It spills

101

over into our international relations, it affects our decision to fly to Europe for vacation or for business. We all know how it is, who is left to dream of how it might be: Without constant fear of violence?

Is it merely paranoid illusions that startle people into fear in public places? No. It appears to be a perfectly natural and logical worry. They fear they will be attacked without mercy.... That they will have no able defense.... That there will be no other citizen to help them.... Finally, that the institutions of government will not be there to provide protection. They fear the police will not respond—or if they do, will arrive too late. They fear that they will be intimidated, injured, killed. If, in the unlikely chance there is an arrest, it will be long after the fact of their personal catastrophe, and the perpetrators will escape punishment and be released to do it all over again.

These fears are not imaginary. Sadly, their fears are all too true.[2] Repeated studies including those conducted by the research group known as The Rand Corporation,[3] indicate that most violent criminals are released quickly, to repeat their violence. The crimes for which they were charged: homicide, rape, kidnap, assault, robbery, or burglary—crimes that have the potential for immediate physical or psychological harm to victims.

Inconsistent Alternatives.

What policy options are available to deal with high recidivism rates? Even the most learned investigators respond with inconsistent and impractical recommendations:[4]

> ... while crime could be reduced substantially by incarcerating more offenders or incarcerating them longer ... this is a difficult option to implement because of existing and worsening prison crowding.

To reduce crime and prison crowding simultaneously, we will have to generate support for increasing the resources devoted to correctional institutions, develop considerably less expensive ways of incarcerating offenders, or find other methods (and funds) for closely supervising and monitoring released inmates.

Thus we see practitioners and policymakers are advised to do the impossible, the impractical and the ineffectual. It does not seem either possible or desirable to turn our country into a camp for criminals confirmed in violence. Whether in prison or out, we must constantly be "closely supervising and monitoring them. The army of the violent is too great to be so guarded. As jailers, we would be jailing ourselves.

Thus it goes far past mere matters of budget and resources. Do we want to spend so much of our national time or attention in this essentially self-defeating process? For, in so doing we would polarize our nation into two opposing adversaries: the jailed and the jailors? A point to ponder: It has been calculated that some 20,000,000 persons are serving, or have served some time in jail. When we add relatives and sympathizers, we have quite a significant self-interest group. All of whom can and do, vote, demonstrate, vote and demonstrate . . . for which they have a constitutional right, but at great cost in treasure and confrontation.

Back to Square One.

We are back to the problem: The fears of victims and potential victims are valid, because we have permitted our system of freedom to be distorted so that tens of thousands of children are being brought up with the firm conviction that they have been marked for life with a stigma that bars them from fair participation in a country that promises full participation in all the best that a society can offer. They believe, with all the firm conviction of ideology, that they are justified in their resentment, and in striking out against the system in general, and against innocent individuals in particular. Those are the individuals whom they maim, mutilate, and murder.

One notes the similarity this situation has to the jihad—the holy war—that thousands of Palestinians and other Moslems believe in, and cling to as an ideology to live by, and kill for.

One can always rationalize seemingly logical reasons to justify a faith. Once firmly implanted, no amount of contrary argument has any significant influence on that system of opinions. These obstinate bigoted presumptions can become so strong that they deafen one to other pleas. They are past listening or caring about another side of the story. To intolerant outsiders it may sound inane, or even insane, but if the self-conviction is strong, it will inexorably guide the unshaken faithful to their preordained actions.

One finds much the same situation in North Ireland. Americans often deplore the Irish strife, remarking that "the troubles," have become a tradition in Ireland. So it appears to many Americans who are sympathetic to the Irish, but convinced that the entire situation is pointless and irrational. But Americans are outside the belief. It is not a mad ideology to the participants, and that is what counts. They have powerful beliefs. They act on them. There is killing on both sides.[5]

There is no alternative, no cure. To extract, by some traumatic psychological surgery, the creed that motivates most of each day's labor, would be to destroy their personality, as they recognize themselves. They would not, they could not, tolerate that.

We Study the Wrong Subject.

We do not study in any profound way how these beliefs overcome entire peoples.[6] There has been more study of how individuals come to have obsessions, hallucinations, visions, and delusions. We seem to be more fascinated by this, than the far more harmful and deadly ideologies and group beliefs which sustain mass hate and killing.

Individual mental and emotional problems are always tragic, and deserve the most compassionate consideration. Their significance to humanity, however, is infinitesimal, compared with mass delusions and indoctrinations. These are the great embarrassments of our time. These are the overwhelming sources of deadly force in our century. Modern scholarship is now commencing to address this subject.

We Study Individuals.

There have been countless news and feature stories about "Sam" the New York killer who received ghostly messages to kill lovers in parked cars. Charles Manson is thrillingly billed in a recent book as "The Most Dangerous Man Alive." Countless books, articles, and television shows have been built around such psychotic individuals. We even have prime time shows consisting of mass interviews of people who have been "confidants" of deadly killers.[7] They and others have written books about such notoriously deadly killers. Joseph Kallinger, with the aid of one son, killed another son, and numerous other innocent people, committing the most scandalous sexual mutilations in the course of a criminal career which ended in a Pennsylvania state hospital for the insane was interviewed on a national network television show for the doubtful edification of millions, who thus received additional support for their own ideologies of violence, and its proper response.

Very often these psychotic killers acquire fan clubs, marry while in jail, and carry on an extensive correspondence with sympathizers. There is much help proffered to rehabilitate these prisoners, but of course, very little can be done really to change these people. In that sense the sympathy and help are wasted. Their well-intentioned donors, are left with only a spiritual feeling of wellbeing at having tried to do good.

The Real Problem.

The bulk of the problem, however, lies in the ideologies, the basic beliefs of large groups who feel they have a common ground to hate. This feeling, this deep-rooted ideology, which is so pervasive, damaging, and so dangerous to us all, is hardly ever examined in ways that would possibly reveal how to reverse this persuasion.

On the contrary, we see more people acquiring a cultish viewpoint on life, and a dependence on the value systems thrust upon them.

How we got into this bind is treated in the next chapter.

Chapter 12

IS AMERICAN JUSTICE A CRIME?

"I have never been more struck by the good sense and practical judgment of the Americans than in the manner in which they elude the numberless difficulties resulting from their Constitution."

Alexis de Tocqueville

Inconsistent Policy Principles.

"The May 13, 1985 police-initiated fire bombing of a Philadelphia neighborhood in an effort to force the members of the radical group MOVE from their hiding places was charged with being an unmitigated disaster against all the people of that city."[1] That is the way the reported story goes. Other analysts claim examination of the facts of that case reveal quite a different story.

Although the media made much of the errors such as the use of .50 caliber machine guns and military-type explosives to knock down walls, and the eventual firebombing which caused the fire that spread until 61 houses burned down, the complaint of most of the people of Philadelphia was even more directed at the long period during which the hyperorthodox organization known as MOVE was permitted to terrorize that neighborhood. MOVE members continually threatened violence against other residents, intermittently assaulted them, threw trash and excreta at will in front gardens and backyards and prevented the regular trash pickup from remedying the matter.[2]

Where were the police and other government agencies of justice? The answer was: They were there, but they were unable to mobilize the political backup to take effective action to enforce simple laws of public health and public nuisance.[3]

MOVE as a hyperorthodox group, had been able to screen itself from complying with the basic sanitary norms the rest of Philadelphia felt to

106

be necessary for urban living. If the government has any function other than tax collecting, one would think that protection of peaceful citizens from violent ones would be at the head of the list. The many assaults involving MOVE that occurred were viewed by the justice system on an individual basis, and easily dismissed by the city justice system as inconsequential, transitory, left to private resolution or dismissed out of hand. No one considered that here was an organization indoctrinated to hate, which had repeatedly expressed hate in many unlawful organized ways. Justice policy was inconsistent in that other individuals were not permitted to escape police prosecution for the same type of petty crimes. The police had lost their most precious possession: Their reputation for impartiality.

Small violations uncorrected resulted in rising community awareness of bias, increasing polarization, and ultimately the necessity for extreme force.

After the debacle of the massive fire-fight and helicopter bombing the police and the city were charged with "overreaction." On the contrary, the true charge should have been a long-time policy of *"under-reaction."*

It is in point to remember James Q. Wilson's edifying parable.[4] Assuredly ignoring boarded-up homes and schools leads to youthful stone-throwing and window breaking. If there is no police action of apprehension, no guarding and repair, this leads inevitably to invasion of the buildings, stealing plumbing and fixtures, muggings, and assaults. Shortly thereafter, occupancy by vagrants and drug addicts, finally arson and complete destruction. And it all started with a child breaking a window!

Another source of inconsistent policies lies in the charge that the rich, the powerful, the influential, and those that control voting blocks, all encounter a different kind of justice from the rest of us. Large organizations have the clout that protects them from legal action. Thus they need only nominally to comply with local laws. This is a charge that cannot remain unanswered. If not laid to rest, it becomes a social reality, with all the evil consequences of the evil itself. Justice in a democracy cannot endure the most trivial hint of impartiality. The slightest accusation is intolerable, and must be answered.

The Public Media Fulfill Jefferson's Hope.[5]

The public media community has become cynically aware of the flaws in the justice system and undertakes to investigate many tips that at one time would have been ignored. Newspaper editorialists and executives have in print and at public meetings called for change.

"For those who live in poverty in the slums of America, the 'Blessings of Liberty' are a dicey proposition at best," said a leading speaker at the 100th annual convention of the American Newspaper Publishers Association.[6]

Positive approaches seem to have failed. It was pointed out that financial aid, in the form of loans to minority groups, have not improved conditions in the ghettoes of America. Nor has any lasting benefit come from sympathy for the ghetto, expressed in touching speeches, community meetings, and editorials.

Nor have negative approaches, such as harsh enforcement policies resulted in either law compliance or reduced violence in our ghettoes.

It is claimed we need new institutions. However, such institutions, whatever form they will take, cannot be developed, until there is acceptance that a new ideology must be created out of new values. For a repetition of adversarial moralizing, log-rolling and pork-barrel politics offers no credible hope for improvement.

Deadly force is frequently decried in the campaign rhetoric of those seeking public office. This gives the illusion that politicians have a continuing interest in the subject, but the truth of the matter is that as soon as the topic has lost political value for the current campaign it is dropped for the next newer and more attractive issue.

Federal funding dumped into projects in devasted slum areas typically disappears into the pockets of evanescent local figures, or provides short-term make-work jobs for nonemployables.[7]

Our Judge-Ruled System.

In our judicial system there are a number of strange quirks and inconsistencies which stubbornly resist amelioration.[8] Judges are expected to be impartial arbiters of difficult questions involving adversary, partisan issues. Our law demands it and does its best to enforce it. This ideal has echoed through the halls of man's dreams, of a good society, for at least two millenia. Plato[9] provided an early model in his *The Republic.*

In this work, Plato argued that executive leadership in the ideal state should be the responsibility of dedicated Philosopher-Judges, who were to guide Plato's ideal city-state, without concern for any private interest, least of all their own.

However, most judges in our various states are elected. To be elected they must solicit votes. Today the solicitation takes the form of television, radio, and newspaper advertisements. This calls for a sum of money invariably much more than an entire year's salary for the coveted position. Where are those millions to come from? Most of the funds must come from "contributions."

Then the following even more pertinent question: What will the person who puts up the money for the judge's campaign be given in compensation for advancing large sums? The only lawful answer is: Nothing. Does that make the judge an ingrate, disloyal and not worthy of trust?

Or, must the judge keep in mind his own future, consider that he will want to run again—and again—and necessarily must keep old friends and backers satisfied. The existence of "matching funds," from government coffers merely doubles the influence of individual backers. A contributor of $100,000, with matching funds, is worth $200,000 to the candidate, doubling his pleasure!

How do other countries handle this dilemma? In France judges are the product of a long specialized education, simulating the Platonic ideal. They are judges for life, their allegiance is to the national government.[10]

In England, judges are appointed by the Crown, after a long, distinguished career. Their tenure, too, is for life.[11] Their loyalty does not belong to the lawyers and the contestants who come before them, it belongs to the mystical concept of the Crown, which encompasses all the British people, the Parliament, and their equally pervasive Constitution.

Thankfully, the Federal system[12] consists only of judges that are appointed for life. Perhaps this is the reason that Federal judges have established an exemplary record of honesty and dedication. The entire Watergate inquiry has been said to have been opened by the judicial indignation of Judge John Sirica at the revelation that perjury was being committed in his court.

With that example at the start of the investigation, and the pressure of honest adjudication hanging over the conspirators, further revelations and exposure of the entire affair was inevitable. Until that climactic point had been reached, there was nothing but rumors and suspicions with no hard evidence to go on. A strong judge, without obligations to anyone or anything but his own conscience and his oath of office, seems to have been the key to justice in this case.

That is not so among the various state judicial systems. Their record does not compare favorably with the federal. Compounding the flaw, they are many times their number, handling on the whole, thousands of times the number of cases in the Federal courts.

Many state judges are elected, and the obligations of campaigning bring in many potential abuses. Often the names and careers of the running judges are unknown to the public. There has been no practical way discovered to make the facts and the personalities involved known to the electorate so that the people can make the informed decisions that are held to be necessary to a good judiciary.

Unfortunately it often ends with citizens running their finger over the list of names in the voting booth, as they search for names they recognize. That should sound incredible to anyone interested in a sound judicial system. The truth of the statement is, however, undeniable, proved countless times in formal and informal polls. The "popular" names vary from county to county. But pollsters have identified them, and some of the variables involved in voters' selection motives. It has been found that a familiar name has great drawing power in any free election. Candidates will spend inordinately on television advertising to make their name known, expenses often run into hundreds of thousands of dollars to win name recognition in a single election.

A name that is easily recognized because of prior familiarity can be far more valuable to a judicial candidate than learning in the law. A familiar name has great drawing power in an election. This phenomenon is exaggerated when it is announced that a large number of judgeships must be filled at one election. Democracy reaches a nadir then, opening up, as it does to every mindless influence over voters' favor. As many as forty or more judgeships have been opened to candidates from the various political parties in a single election, in a single county with often a candidate from each of the two major parties, plus a few from splinter organizations.[13] With eighty or more candidates in the field, a voter's choices for forty positions is bound to be constrained by as many uninformed choices as a traveler equipped with a map to Blunderland.

To be named Du Pont in Delaware, or Jackson in Georgia, is a leg-up on the ladder to political success. We can only speculate the effect on politics of the name of a successful candidate for Chicago's Mayor: Washington. No doubt, however, it was considerable.

Recidivism.

Seventy percent of released prisoners return to prison, either for new crimes committed or for gross violation of the conditions of their parole. We cannot rehabilitate because we don't know how. We cannot keep convicts in prison, because we can't afford to. We cannot release them, because they commit more crimes. That would cost the public more than even their exorbitant keep, not to mention the loss of lives and injuries that are inevitable concomitants of their deadly tresspasses.

People resent the criminal justice system. Who can blame them? They know the horrendous work-products. The system released from prison a convict who had been imprisoned seven years.[14] His crime was raping an eleven-year-old child. That not being sufficient, he chopped off both her arms, blood spurted, slowed, and stopped. Left for dead, miraculously the little girl survived.

After serving seven years in prison, the prisoner was released on parole, to live in town. The community to which he was released rioted, and the public was treated to video interviews of outraged demonstrators, dismayed community speakers and random representatives expressing the sympathy of the nation.

The authorities, hastily found another community to settle the ex-convict. That community rioted, too.

Here we had a real Catch-22 situation. The parole authorities felt that under the existing law they had to release the prisoner on parole. Release necessarily implies the former inmate going into a community and finding means to support himself and try to carry on as a responsible, stable citizen. They had no other alternative.

It is easy to take either side, community or parole authority. Our justice system, as presently constituted can find no reasonable way out. The doubtful resolution was: Administrative secrecy. The ex-convict was removed to an undisclosed location.

Keeping the matter secret violates the obligation to make parole actions public lest they become abusive and self-serving. Making the matter public invites intractable resistance, justified because, among other things, the known recidivist rate looms as a promise of repetition for at least 7 out of 10 former criminals. *Quo vadis?*

Uneconomical Justice.

Ex-Chief Justice Burger has commented that the United States is known as the most litigious country in the world, but that we have less judges and more lawyers than most of the other advanced countries.[15]

The consequences are that fewer cases are dealt with by court-controlled methods of fairness and justice, court calendars are swollen to ridiculous dimensions, and the wait for resolution of a case is so long that almost any other means becomes more attractive. The judges are so pressed by their pending calendar there is no way they can convey the majesty, dignity, and essential fairness court administered justice requires.

The fact that we have such a surfeit of lawyers has, it is held, encouraged litigation, controversy, and confusion in the insurance industry as well as affecting the very quality of life we experience, and encouraging confrontation and adversary positions instead of peace and harmony.

To accommodate the suing-society we have become, tort law has been expanded to permit money awards for every imaginable consequence, even the unforseeable.

Racketeering Influence Corrupt Organization (RICO) statutes in states, as well in the Federal government, have been held to be a golden goose ready to lay golden eggs of money damages to reward everyone who feels insulted or hustled by a police officer.

One might think that this is a good measure to enforce better performance on the part of our police officers. That possibility is negated by the fact that the police officer is invariably defended by a government attorney, so he need pay no attorney fees, and the award, if any—and some of them amount to hundreds of thousands of dollars—come, not from the police officer, but from the taxpayers. There has not been observed any visible improvement in performance, but municipal treasuries have been depleted, and in a few cases, the towns have been rendered bankrupt.

An interesting sidelight, on the economic scene is that many urban counties not only hire hundreds of lawyers to prosecute criminals, but they also hire hundreds of lawyers to defend them. Taxpayers pay the gladiators on both sides of the criminal trial show piece.

With up to 90 percent of cases being plea-bargained, both prosecutors and public defenders retire from the arena with honors for good performance, the guilty get off lightly, and the taxpayer. . . . pays the bill again.

It costs over $8,000 per jury trial, and often a case may come up on the docket ten or more times before it is actually reached for trial. Lawyers on both sides, sometimes witnesses, police officers ... everyone is very busy, but the assembly-line justice that is provided is quite unproductive of acceptable results.

Confidential evaluations of judges, by hundreds of lawyers, reveal their opinion that many judges are utterly incompetent, and worse. Yet, the same lawyers publicly endorse the same judges, because they fear disciplinary repercussions from the sitting judges, and their friends. These "evaluations" are a substantial part of the documentation for campaigning judges who have the power of supervision, and discipline over those who subscribe to these evaluations and polls.

In 1982 US taxpayers paid $4 billion for the management and administration of criminal courts. Additionally, litigants spent unknown billions of their own funds. Former Chief Justice Warren Burger has repeatedly urged the country to find alternatives to litigation, that are faster, cheaper, and as equitable as going to trial.

The vested interests, however, are so strong, not to mention the natural inertia of bureaucracy, that few attempts are made that can be seen as offering even a partial solution the the problems. At most, we "muddle through."

One promising approach has been tried in Allegheny County, Pennsylvania, where court-supervised arbitration has cut public costs of the average case to $65. Amazing, that! Especially when one compares it with the enormous unit expense budgets of urban courts, where one would think that principles of mass production would enable greater economies.

More than one-half of the pending cases in urban areas in the northeast, southeast, and west are drug related. They usually have multiple defendants and therefor tend to be inordinately complex and time-consuming. Thus the cost of running the criminal courts in these areas must, in largest part, be laid to drug-related law enforcement. Probably the costs attributable to drugs can be estimated as much higher when we add the many burglaries, assaults, and murders which are drug-related. Is it worth it? some academics ask. The answers are made by those whose beliefs demand that they answer: "Yes! Any amount of money is worth one life that is saved from the vicious maw of crack."[16]

That decision, however, has not been tested in a public forum. It remains in the arena of conflicting beliefs, reduced to moralizing on both sides.

Inmates Run the Asylum.

America's prisons are run by vicious inmates who terrorize not only other inmates, but control the system itself.[17] It is standard operating practice for a prison administration to enlist the assistance of the meanest characters the administration can co-opt into doing management's bidding.

These bullies are given the rank of "trusties" with a hierarchal organization paralleling that of the regular guards, but with less compunction about using violence, up to and including deadly force to maintain the kind of order that is to their liking.

On the occasion of a riot they are in their best fettle. Most of them violent since childhood, now they have the patina of official right to exercise unremitting ferocity. Customarily they arm themselves, without official permission, but with the knowledge and implicit consent of the administration with "trashcan lids, pipes, clubs, weight-lifting bars." One of the trusties remembers they also had knives, chains, bats, clubs.[18] The adrenaline flows and the rampaging berserkers carry the fight to the rioters.

The most brutal and overcrowded prisons, those most susceptible to riots, sometimes become the subject of action in federal court, which then usurps the state executive function. Directed reform, under court order arrives under penalty of having the administration of prisons taken away entirely from the state administration and placed under independent commissions directed and controlled by the federal court. Sometimes, in the alternative, the prison administration is directed to release the entire prison population over a certain arbitrary figure set by the court. The confusion and added expense, and most of all, the injustice and harm to the innocent public has been incalculable.

Even under reform, the killings do not stop. Directed to reform by a federal court, the 27-unit Texas prison system, in twenty-one months from January 1984 to September 1985, saw fifty-two prisoners fatally shivved and mangled by other prisoners.

Every week we need space for 1,000 more inmates. The total now is 450,000. Even if we spent $10 billion on new prisons in the next decade, the number of prisoners will still be more than 20% over capacity in year 2000. And with overcrowding, the already disgraceful situation reaches the point where our justice system adds, within its own prisons, rather than reduces, the total crime and deadly force exerted in the land.

Often we get sidetracked by collateral issues of doubtful relevance to deadly force, and the effort to reduce it. One of these bypaths is the "charge" of racial disparity in prisoners. This is not really a charge, it is simple fact. What is back of it is that disparity is erroneously interpreted as racial discrimination.[19]

The factors that are the criteria in sentencing guidelines are simply more prevalent among blacks than among whites.[20] That is where our true attack should be: to eliminate, or at least reduce the factors which experience has shown leads to bringing up violent children who become violent unrehabilitatable adults.

Chapter 13

SCHOOL FOR VANDALS

"To go to school and fenisch my
Schooling whithout getting prenant."

A 15-year-old Detroit girl's definition
of the American Dream.

Children Learn Evil As Quickly As Good.

Children, we fondly assume, tend to see the world with greater clarity than adults whose eyes are blurred by myth and prejudice. If there is any truth at all in this assumption, we should refurbish the world we present to their view.

No one would charge children with responsibility for the culture into which they are born. As the child lives, and grows, however, he does affect in some degree many people, his family and others, as well as his general environment. There appears no purpose embedded in a child's psyche, ineluctably teleological, that will make his effect on his environment, beneficial and nurturing. All the evidence indicates that if it is true the growing child can accept and learn the good, it is also true he can accept and learn evil just as handily, if not more so.[1]

What Children Really Learn—and Do Not Learn.

A recent issue of the *American Bar Association Journal*[2] wondered about the lucidity of youth. Its cover story considered major cases of alleged ritualistic child abuse and asks, "Are the Children Lying?"

Nationwide we have been scandalized by allegations of child abuse cases in many widely separated parts of the country.

"In each case adults (usually teachers or parents) were accused of sadistic acts running from sexual abuse of infants, to animal mutilation, satanic rituals, crucifixions, and stabbing of babies."

Charges were dropped against five of seven indicted teachers in one

116

case. Many of the other cases were dismissed, for lack of evidence sufficient to support prosecution.

It appears, most claims were fictions fed by adult hysteria. All of this is the part of a world we have created for children on which to feed their fantasies. These are not their inventions. As adults, we have taught all these deadly fears, fantasies, and forces to the children.

Newspapers publish in their local news section, the addresses where illegal drugs can be purchased.[3] A typical comment accompanying such information is, "Our estimate is that in this city, 75 to 80 percent of crime is drug related." And schools are centers for drug distribution.

After providing children with this kind of environment, it is no surprise to find that 40 percent who enter the ninth grade will not stay to graduate.

One grand jury reported finding that in one county alone, 8,000 youths drop out each year.

Ominously inner city Black youths disproportionately leave school. Dropout is "followed by unemployment, and self-perpetuating alienation and failure."[4]

On analysis of the statistics, it appears the reasons for leaving school can be attributed to "faults" in (a) the school, (b) the neighborhood, (c) the Home.

That just about covers the entire social environment we have provided for school-age children. A grand jury, in at least one report, soberly comments that youths, "Need all three!" So much for sober analysis.

Certainly then, is the recommendation, we should concentrate on the dropout problem, establish committees in each community to provide oversight for the public institutions concerned with youth. This would include schools, welfare centers, juvenile courts, and other institutions.

This oversight should encompass plans for revitalization of inner city schools, and many other efforts.

Jon Miller of Northern Illinois University has stated,[5] "In the United States only about 10 percent of adults could be considered scientifically literate. That's too low. It doesn't meet, in my view, the basic test of democracy, because we really have a lot of important science policy issues that at some point are going to have to be decided."

Some of the important lacunae in the mental armentarium of our children have been listed:

1. Basics of specific scientific disciplines, such as chemistry, physics,

physiology, mathematics. Perhaps astronomy, geography, meteorology, and others.

2. Understanding the way science, technology, and society interface.

3. Knowing the nature, goals, and history of science.

4. Knowing how to interpret numerical information. Applying numerical information to life-situations, from keeping track of their money, to evaluation of public policy based on numerical data.

With all due respect to the well-intentioned analysts, exactly the same lacks are evident in the education of our adults, as well as our children and youths. As a people, if we are candid, we just do not know too much about those listed subjects. Is that bad? Well, that's a judgment call. Our educators say it is, and they compare the level of information learned by European and Japanese students with an equal number of years of education behind them. And of course, they are correct, as to those facts.

The most recent plaint from educators is, "Have Our Kids Lost Their Past?"[6] They have discovered that

"Johnny—that infamous American schoolboy—is about to get another bad report card. Back in the '70's he flunked reading and writing. By the time the 80's arrived he'd picked up F's in math and science. Just last year he failed geography when he couldn't tell Brazil from the United States on a map."

The National Endowment for the Humanities studied the matter for six months and issued a report of its findings that 68 percent did not know when the Civil War happened, and one out of three thought Columbus arrived after 1750.[7]

Literature scores alarmed the NEH, too. Eighty-four percent did not know who wrote, "Crime and Punishment." Sixty-four percent did not know who wrote "The Canterbury Tales," and 60 percent could not identify Walt Whitman as the author of "Leaves of Grass." This report is something to laugh at.

To anyone who has been in a classroom the report comes as a shock. It is so naive! For the kids not only have lost the past, they have no concept of the present, or their own future.

The fact of the case is that children are not given enough demanding school work to learn much at all. The NEH report finds fault with the schools for giving too much "practical education," and "vocational training." Well, they are not learning that either. They do not come out of school trained, either practically or vocationally.

Actually our children are not being educated. They do not have nearly enough, and long enough exposure to the huge amount of valuable information that they must learn while young, because once they are grown up it is too late. Is it time to reconsider the discontinuance of Project Headstart for preschool children? Can we reinvent early intervention programs? There is a host of other well-known recommendations calling for inquiry.

Where Youth Interest Lies At Present

There is one area where youths seem to be in possession of abundant information: Guns.

You can't expect adults to be armed to the teeth without expecting teenagers to be armed, too. We have innumerable cases such as the one where a 16-year-old youth had a gun he found a month before, took it to high school football game, and in the school bus killed another youth of only 14 years.[8]

Sports events cause irrational reactions among fans. What happened in the bus was similar to what happened in Detroit after the Tigers won the World Series, and that was adult behavior. Such observations cast some light on youthful death dealing. They are accepting the environment we have provided for them. We indulge our children. Doesn't this help to explain why informed adults are no longer shocked?

Reducing Violence in Youth: Pabulum Prescribed.

There are many suggestions for ways to cut down on such violence, and everyone reads about them. "Stronger family ties, along with better schools, higher standards and greater expectations would work against continued rationalization of aberrant behavior. More decent job opportunities would give youngsters something to look forward to and give them and their parents enough of a stake in society so they would take better care of life and property. Fewer guns would make it less likely that 16 year olds would "find" and use them." This is merely a wish list.

Though child psychologists disagree about the extent to which personality in general is shaped by early childhood experiences, there is not much dispute over the fact that *male aggressiveness tends to be stable in a given individual from his early years on.*[9]

We have at least that to go on. There is more on which we can rely. Contemporary "research by Paterson and by scores of others, has placed the family at the center of any effort to explain and reduce unruly or violent behavior."[10]

But we already knew that. In fact, it's been known for centuries, certainly long before Roman times. Now, at a scholarly level also, we are coming to realize that, "The role of the family in producing such behavior seems to be a greater mystery to social scientists than to parents."[11]

Almost half a century ago, the Gluecks studied the family as a factor in juvenile delinquency. But then crime scientists turned their attention to the youth gang as a prime force in initiating and perpetuating violence in children and adults.

When that concept seemed to have all the research juice squeezed out of it, social scientists reached for a new culprit: the Social System. This took blame away from delinquent youths, and exculpated worried parents. But of course, blame is not really in point, except to those who want to preach, and hope by this simple method to save souls and lives. By tempering accountability and removing responsibility from parents and the individuals involved, behavioral scientists fostered the very flaws we complain about today.

For neither youth-gang associates, nor a vague "social system," have the power, to instill values during earliest family years.

Today, clearer-eyed research sees that in many cases, lower-class boys, convinced from childhood by their families that money cannot be saved for a better future, and that work is punishment, "may come to disparage the conventional ethic of success and embrace instead the values of toughness and immediate gratification."[12]

The ambition that once was cited as inspiring the hardwork and saving ways of fictional Horatio Alger, and real-life Andrew Carnegie, can reach for other goals. Paraphrasing Robert K. Merton's words, "A cardinal American virtue, 'ambition,' has come to promote a cardinal American vice, 'deviant behavior.' "[13]

When Does Violence Start?

We now know that early manifestations of hostility and aggression are a strong indicator of later criminality. The aggressive five or six year old becomes the aggressive youth and adult. Our grandparents knew that, but that was too pessimistic an idea for us to accept.

Every child should have a chance, was our hopeful thought, while we extended the idea of "child" through the teens into the early twenties.

The entire idea of youthful offender statutes and programs was based on that hope.

To come to grips with the error of our way, we have had to turn research viewpoints upside down. As Travi Hirschi argues " . . . the first question is not why men break the law, but why they obey it."[14]

To rephrase the idea: Conformity, not deviance, is what is most in need of explanation.

Hirschi's answer is that people obey rules to the extent that they form bonds to society. That bond is composed of four elements:

attachment, chiefly to the family;

commitment, by which Hirschi meant a prudent regard for the costs of wrong actions and the benefits of right ones;

involvement in conventional activities, such as schools; and

belief in the moral validity of society's rules.

Herschi did his empirical research in and around Richmond, California. His findings supported what he calls a "social control" theory.[15]

We can note well, that one of Herschi's findings is phrased, " . . . after one takes into account the bond with the parents and doing well in school, the contribution of . . . (social) class nearly vanishes, and that of delinquent friends sharply drops."

As a corollary a very large body of data has demonstrated beyond much doubt the powerful effect on aggressiveness and delinquency of being raised in a family that is discordant, lacking in affection, or given to inappropriate disciplinary practices.

Children Are Acculturated Before They Arrive At School.

Some things about schools, schooling, and youths are indisputable. For the young child, schools become the setting for playing out roles already learned at home. The preschool child's mind is not a primary blank, the *tabula rasa,* presumed by worshipers of the free public school. The school does not, nor can it, by itself impose middle-class values, or any other set of values, on passive minds and bodies. At best there arises an interactive classroom subculture. In many ghetto areas the subculture of the children overcomes that of the teacher, if, in fact, there is a difference. The particular influence any school setting will have on a child will be the resultant of a complex of situational variables, quite dependent on priorly established personality variables.

The concept of the Headstart Program of the 1960's in retrospect, appears to have been correct in concept, though faulty in performance. We must seize little minds and hearts long before school age.

At the present time we are presented with dilemmas such as was laid in the lap of Black Hawk County Attorney James Metcalf of Iowa when police arrested three children, 3, 4, and 7 years of age.

The charge was: breaking into a day-care home and stealing three bicycles with which they went to another building to commit another burglary. Mr. Metcalf refused to prosecute any of these children, and ordered the police to stop arresting any young children. Mr. Metcalf stated for the record:[16] "Law enforcement has more important things to do than arrest toddlers."

Well said, Mr. Metcalf. There is no job there for lawyers or police. There is nothing they can do to remedy the situation. But certainly sending kids back to the home and street where they learned the tricks, somehow, does not go down too well, either. Such blind optimism is something we can no longer afford.

The Long-Term Effect of Early Child-Experiences.

Long-term studies in the London area lasting from before 1937 to 1955, concluded that the impact of early child-rearing practices, is quite permanent in limning the outlines of a child's future personality. This was well-documented, particularly with regard to child-rearing practices the researchers denoted as "adverse." Generally, this term was used as a catchall for what can otherwise be described as harsh, uncaring or inconsistent treatment of the child in his earliest years.

Another long-term study, by West and Farrington, tracked 411 boys in London starting at age eight. The study continued for 17 years. This research concluded as follows:

1. Delinquent boys conspicuously exhibited a lower intelligence quotient, as measured by standard tests. (N.B.: Other studies have found that I.Q., as so measured, correlates well with school accomplishment as measured by school grading systems.)

2. These children had parents who were "perceived" as cruel, neglectful, or passive.

3. Aggressive boys were revealed to have the same background as the youths adjudged delinquent.

The researchers rephrased their findings, to conclude that five factors they deemed important to predict delinquency and violence in children were:

1. Low intelligence
2. Large family
3. Parental criminality
4. Low family income and
5. Poor child-rearing practices.

Refining the concepts of the last item, poor child-rearing practices were analyzed to consist of: parents who were less concerned about their children's doings, whereabouts, fixed rules, punctuality, manners, bedtime, television, tidying up.

Have We Learned How School Can Affect Behavior?

Many recommendations were given by the above cited principals of long-term research in juvenile delinquency and most, if not all, appear to have been confirmed by even more recent research:

Punishment, when used, must be contingent on what has been previously clearly defined as bad behavior. Further, such punishment should be relatively mild, and consistently applied.

Reward for good behavior was recommended, although not necessarily on an itemed *quid pro quo* basis. Rewards or benefits received without apparent reason may be less influential on subsequent behavior.

It was recommended by these researchers, too, that violence *not* be a normal and acceptable mode of expressing one's feelings. This radically differs from the past half century of advice, perhaps initiated by Sigmund Freud's psychoanalytic studies which were interpreted as encouraging "release" of feelings, even of aggression.

Shortly afterwards, John Dewey,[17] an eminent and influential writer on educational philosphy, inspired two generations of teachers with the conviction that encouragement of a child's "self-expression," was the best educational tactic. Some teachers were charged, probably unfairly, with misinterpreting Dewey's teachings, to adopt a laissez-faire approach to classroom ambience.

Beginning in the 1960's, behavioral scientists and school psychologists acquired more influence than ever before. With B.F. Skinner,[18] and other social psychologists as leaders, these scientists looked on child behavior for the most part, as learned in interactive experiences, especially on the basis of reinforcing stimuli.

As used in schools, foster homes, juvenile institutions and adult prisons this type of discipline, training, or influence on behavior came to be called "behavior modification."

Certain programs, those that used punishment, as negative reinforcers such as electrical shocks, or nauseating drugs, fell into disrepute. Not, however, necessarily because they didn't work, but rather on grounds of humaneness, or constitutionality.

Those that used reward, or satisfaction, as the stimulus toward desirable behavior, received friendlier welcome. The programs that exploited rewards in "token economies," have received quite favorable publicity.

The basic rationale for the use of reinforcing stimuli, both reward and punishment, can be summarized: To change behavior by changing its consequences.

Persistence of Learned Behavior.

Changes in behavior do occur under either style of program. However, the changed behavior tends to disappear on leaving the institutional setting in which it was learned.

The problem was to go from theory and temporary laboratory situations to permanent real-life school and family living.

By 1982 a "teaching-family model" had been developed with 170 such groups in operation, in six regional centers. Considerable improvement in peaceful and supportive behavior was remarked. Also, there was much less aggression and violence among the children placed in these model homes.

Unfortunately within only one year after leaving the model teaching family, the children returned to their old, violent, aggressive behavior.

There have been many other attempts at developing models complying with the precepts of the scientists. As a war correspondent might say, "The issue is still in doubt." Again, however, we do not know how to transfer the new ways of parenting to real life families in ghetto areas.

Current Beliefs.

Thus the key belief today is: "We must learn how to improve child-rearing practices in the delinquents's natural home."

Now that the problem is clearly stated, why are we not making more progress with this new idea? The reasons are many. Here are some of them all dealing with affirmative aspects of behavioral change:

First, many parents do not know how to raise children. Further, we do not know how to go about teaching the parents how to do better.

Second, usually, by the time a child is labeled as delinquent, it often is too late. The child is too confirmed in delinquent-type traits to be able to reverse the habituated behavior patterns.

Third, whatever benefit can be obtained in the short term, the calls of peers, neighbors, and even potential victims prove to be too seductive an inducement to return to violence.

The belief of the majority of current investigators, however, remains strong. The basic rules remain the same: monitored behavior; rewards contingent on good behavior; punishments contingent on bad behavior.

Reward has been variously tried as: responding in pleasant and supportive ways, or with "points" as token money, exchangeable for small privileges, such as ice cream for dessert. Other rewards have been tried, with invariable, measured standards.

There have also been experiments using reinforcing stimuli that are random in kind or amount. There is some difference in opinion as to which schedules are likely to be most effective, but the general outline of how to proceed seems reasonably clear. On this basis, training centers for parents and prospective parents have been instituted on the model developed in 1980, and various modifications developed since.

A hugely popular writer, James Q. Wilson, sees continuing difficulties in the following terms:[19]

> "Today children are a burden, children have more ways to avoid parents, traditional social and moral supports for family life are more precarious, opportunities for distraction and entertainment outside the family are greater.... And, Given the deepseated and poorly understood causes of discord and incompetence, it is hard to imagine mounting any national program to deal with the problem directly. One shudders at the thought of developing.... a national family policy. But at the same time, one also wonders whether, ... we might not do more to prevent the frenzied or apathetic incompetence of so many families from producing monsters ... "

Turning Concepts Into Programs.

A large number of programs have been devised to implement the current ideology of how to nurture less violent children who will grow up into peace-loving adults. Thus far no particular program has attracted widespread approval. We are backing and filling, ready for the next move. Perhaps, in this present state of disarray we might consider the following sequence in which the schools can participate usefully:

Families resist help, therefore we must, in the first place, avoid the formation of incompetent families. This can be done by using the existing schools to teach young people, long before they become parents, the proper techniques of parenting.

Videotapes of actual families in trouble can be shown in school. The students would score each family sequence, as to "good" and "bad" items. Then their scores would be compared with scores made by trained family behavioral scientists.

Of course, the usual indoctrinal techniques of showing anticipated "good" results of acceptable parenting techniques with film strips can be another item on the menu.

Granted cooperative schools and parents, many existing families can be reeducated to some degree, for whatever community benefits there may be in such a program.

Possible Objections.

We must stop to consider. Would this merely add another unjustified burden to an overburdened school curriculum? Possibly. As we have shortened the school day and year, we have added program after program. We have reached the fringes of marginal return. Look at what we do today. We try to train our children in responsible sex, and we have more than one million teenage pregnancies each year. Sex education as presently administered has not been the answer to unwanted pregnancies.[20] Teenage pregnancies are at an all-time high.

Would training in parenting be more successful? We won't know until we try it more, it appears.

We try to teach good nutrition, with little success. Of course, the effort to teach children to avoid drugs has reached enormous costs in money and school time. Thus far, there is no credible progress to report on this score either.

We overload the too-small school day: Little children are given lessons in cooperative behavior, which somehow produce exploitive little people. In the higher grades, we have gone even further: auto driving, social studies and hygiene, physical education, sports psychology, band, study hall, ethnic studies. How useful has it been?

The question is especially relevant when we admit that we graduate people who can hardly read or write.[21] Mathematics has become a lost art, as far as the average school child is concerned. With these fundamental lacks, it is hard to see that the time spent on some of other subjects is worth the dubious results obtained.

We try to do too much in the schools, and we accomplish too little. This has been a recurring failure in bureaucratic management of human problems. Police departments that have reached out to deal with general community problems, such as health issues, drunkenness, licensing of cabarets and taxicabs have had the same failure in performance as our schools. They tried to do too much. In despair at the failure implicit in overreaching, today, police departments tend to refocus on police work, and leave other tasks to other agencies.

Admittedly only schools can teach English, arithmetic, history, and geography. There is plenty of work for them in teaching those subjects, if the administrators want that to be done. At present schools do a very poor job of it. We have cut down on the hours of school, while trying to add new subjects. Attendance in school is for less hours than the time children have available for rock video. We give our children plenty of time for exposure to violence at home and on the street. Indeed, yes. As a Georgia school administrator said,[22] "Students have a right to their own personal time." The American schoolboy, unwillingly in school in the first place, will be glad to hear it.

Thus our concern with school time and curriculum. With everything else that schools try to do there is no time to do their proper job on the subjects they do best. School administrators, teachers unions, and under-educated parents all have agendas that argue against what the facts seem to say: Twenty-four hours of every day is still not enough time for everything that's worthy. Perforce, a child's time must concentrate on learning what is *necessary, and do a good job of it.*

Basics and Beyond.

What only schools can do is: Educate our children in specific skills and knowledge that will improve their lives.

We must establish priorities. What must be at the top of the list? Each of us will have a preferred sequence. I place at the top of the list: How to make a living, and live in peace.

Next down the line are: Where the world is, and where it has been. Finally, the skills by which they can participate in managing the world on the basis of knowledge, rather than uninformed opinion and emotion.

How does this translate into school procedures and practices? Here is one way to analyze the problem:

1. Every hour of the day a child will learn something. It is not reasonable to expect that without guidance the child will stumble into learning useful skills and knowledge.

2. The hours of guidance in school, in this country, are far fewer than in countries which have a more notable success in educating children than we do, such as Switzerland, Japan, the USSR, and other developed countries.

3. Thus we must extend the school day, and perhaps the school week.

4. If it is acceptable that the two prime educational objectives, applicable to all children are: (a) How to make a living, and (b) How to live in peace, then we must seek the advice of professional educators as to which skills and learning serve as a proper foundation for the two prime objectives.

5. These experts, when consulted, suggest that without overly deforming present curricula and subject-content, we can offer at the earliest school ages: Reading, Writing, Arithmetic in contexts which encourage cooperative interaction in small group settings of two to four children.

6. Since high level skills in these subjects, as well as the other complex subjects necessary for competing in an increasingly technological workforce call for many years of training, at equally high intensities, it is suggested that longer school days be extended to higher grades as well.

7. All this, because high level skills in the above subjects as well as the systematic fields based on them, engineering and bookkeeping, tax analysis, preparing reports and summaries, taking and giving orders, management, are all necessary for living and competing in an increasingly technological workforce.

Alternative Approaches.

"The Devil finds work for idle hands," is an old cliche that like many others, may have truth at its core. Perhaps with that inspiration, one approach that has been suggested, is to motivate youngsters to earn money, working at real jobs, and so to avoid the cycle of idle time, hanging-out, petty crime, and violence. The thesis is: If kids have jobs they will be good, and nonviolent.

We have a living laboratory available to study this hypothesis. Youth has relatively easy access to jobs with fast food emporias. Fans of the work ethic and chain restaurant personnel managers enthusiastically claimed confirmation of this favorite dogma.

Behavioral researchers, however, have examined the facts, seeking verification of the benefits of this simple application of the work ethic.

Excellent as one would expect the results to be, the returns, as they have come in, have been ambiguous, if not negative. The results do not directly deny the work ethic. Nor do they disprove the thesis that work and jobs will reduce youth violence. Rather they highlight an interaction between work and its objectives. That is, what may be an important, and critical variable is the *purpose* of the work. Here is what one study at the University of Michigan found: Kids working to buy things make the shopping-mall the center of their lives, instead of the school.

Researcher Jerald Bachman[23] calls it "premature affluence." Instead of "learning the value of a dollar," as the old saying goes, many teenagers are simply learning how to spend, and spend again . . . and their school-work suffers. Immediate gratification becomes the grail.

Of course, implicit in old ideas about the work ethic was the idea of innuring one to delayed gratification, until the completion of the labor necessary to attain a *worthy goal.* Apparently the value system of the University of Michigan researcher did not include satisfaction of the desire for fashionable clothing, VCR's, and other modern consumer merchandise as a worthy goal.

No doubt that is oversimplification. Dr. Bachman's research confirms what the most casual inquiry reveals: that many youngsters save their money for large ticket items, help out at home, or even open savings accounts for education or marriage. The question of how having a job impacted on youth violence was not directly addressed. However, it seemed to be reduced.

The question of how much does youth employment damage school learning has not really been given as much attention it deserves. It may be that the effect on school education varies depending on whether the youth's purpose is to avoid school, and uses the job to switch his attention and ambition from the chores of school, to immediate financial independence. Or there may be other factors. We really have to inquire more fully.

Fearing loss of school time, and overfatigue, most states limit the number of hours a child under seventeen years may work at a job out of school. Typical statutes put a cap on an entire week's work at 18 hours, though some states, permit as much as 30 hours per week.

This is particularly important because it is now claimed that liberal arts training is becoming increasingly valuable as background education for success in corporate employment.[24]

This is a reflection of the often observed fact that the trend for the past few decades is for much better employment opportunities for better educated job applicants. In our society, with its continued emphasis on technology, there is less of a need for unskilled labor than in prior years. Thus the time taken by a youngster on relatively unskilled tasks in low level restaurant, or similar service jobs, may not be productive of the skills they will require to join the rest of their upwardly mobile generation. Especially so, if they are not learning to become frugal, provident hard workers, with large ambitions.

This is not to say that learning to work cooperatively in almost any work situation does not have its values. Learning to endure fatigue, boring tasks, harsh supervisors, and waiting for a paycheck may be part of what we should all learn. The important point may be, perhaps these personal qualities are best learned in a context and for a purpose that is desirable in the long view.

While most people would not see any harm in a youth working to buy a new pair of jeans, some would like to see effort devoted to more socially advantageous uses. Thus we find active recruitment going on for community service in slums, for churches and other such services. The response to this call has been prompt and impressive in numbers.

All of these kids—the workers for money, volunteers for good works, the college-bound who concentrate on academic studies—are for the most part, nonviolent. Study of them, their values, and their actions has utility for us only in providing alternative nonviolent life-styles, if we could only persuade the potentially violent to accept them.

Still another approach has been to study the remarkable success of Asian-American children in school from the earliest years through doctoral programs. Coming to this country without a firm knowledge of the language, most of them in straightened financial circumstances, the children of these new Americans move rapidly through the grades and many go to college where they are taking an ever larger share of top honors.

The question immediately presented is, "How do they do it?" The answer that has been provided by reporters and others seems to be capsuled as, family support and self-discipline, directed to education ... all of which, incidentally, would reduce violence in youth.

Whether this is true, or merely the values of the reporters being projected onto the subjects probably requires more inquiry. Even if true, however, we are again faced with the problem of "How do we promote family support and self-discipline for education?"

The inquiry becomes even more interesting, and perhaps important, when statistical studies show that in this country Asians, though discriminated against quite thoroughly in the job market, overcome that handicap and earn a substantially higher net annual income than the average American.[25]

There have been a number of scholarly studies of this phenomenon worldwide. The findings are monotonous in the repetition: In innumerable instances, in a wide variety of geographical contexts, even persecuted minorities, granted the correct balance of family support and self-discipline directed toweard social goals, such as education or material success, have prevailed despite severe political and economic intolerance. Also, their youngsters rarely get involved in violent situations.

Most of the cases cited involve groups that are easily identified as foreign to the majority of the population, such as the Overseas Chinese, Indians from that subcontinent, and Southeast Asian refugees.

This makes the inquiry both simpler and more complicated. That is: Can it be that being a member of an easily identified minority adds to group solidarity, and so facilitates their mutual support, leading to success? Or, is it that being so identified, the individuals and their families, accept the demanded role and work persistently at it? Or, does feeling estranged from the majority energize and motivate toward accomplishment? Or ... ?

Aside from the many new research issues that may be raised, there remains the brooding possibility: Does this presage the obverse side of *Brown v. Board of Education of Topeka, Kansas?* Will the Asian-American success, for instance, in schools result in a wide-spread movement to establish quotas against them?

One would hope not. A better move would be to try to emulate their methods, and their success. But what is working there? Could it be that being persecuted, scorned, and driven down to take menial jobs. . . .all work to create material success for a group? It sounds insane—but is it really?

Certainly any change at all would promise more success than does the present teenage pregnancies, school drop-out rates, graffiti, vandalism, and violence.

Chapter 14

AIMLESS IS NOT HARMLESS

*"Human history becomes more and more
a race between education and catastrophe"*

H.G. Wells

Solutions Become Problems

When issues of society come up for discussion, many people will rise and claim to know the causes of ills, and how to cure them. Almost invariably these people turn out to be false prophets, for their solutions turn out to be problems, even more insidious than the ills they sought to cure.

Why do we listen to these false prophets? Is it part of our nature to do so? It would seem so. We seek charismatic persons to rely on. We want cure-alls. And each new medicine show brings new performers on the stage, clowns and charlatans, with new palliatives. Distracted by the patter of Mr. Bones and his cohorts, we lose our sense of direction. We lose our clear aim at attaining personal and national purposes.

Without an honest standard to follow, it is not surprising that we take words for fact, and self-serving statements as words of wisdom.

In the end, however, we realize we have been harmed by their false words, and our own lack of wit. Aimless is indeed not harmless.

Then Prophets of Doom.

Despairingly, there arises, when we realize that we have been mislead, a great urge to surrender, to submit to what seems inevitable. As the old prayer goes, "Do not ask why. We do not know. Just pray for strength to endure." That ancient refuge has suppressed creative thought long enough, one would think. Even behavioral scientists succumb to this, from time to time. Thankfully, they come back, eventually, to deal with the facts.

"What works?" was the anguished cry of Professor Robert Martinson[1] as he sought for solutions to prison and parole corrective practices. He never found them, and, as an honest man, he reported this. In retrospect, it seems eminently logical that had to be the case.

As we move aimlessly from one program to the next, hoping against hope that we will stumble upon a solution, our frenetic efforts ensure failure. Trial and error, as we use the method, can demonstrate "success" only after a failure has occurred.

But if the failure has happened, it is substantially too late, for we shall have already suffered the consequences of the failure, and the new method, stanching the old damage, provides its own sequences of failure. Thus our trial is a burden, and error inevitable. We seek success aimlessley, but in doing so, we truly direct our efforts first to failure.

Goal-Seeking Behavior.

All experience tells us we must keep our eye on the ultimate, distant value, the end we seek. Interim "solutions" if not constrained within narrow channels leading to the distant goal, develop dynamics of their own. In doing so, they become ends in themselves, and develop other objectives unrelated to what we seek.

Joint human effort is usually costly in time, lost individual initiatives, and personal gratification. It involves submitting to compromises of values and ideologies, and is worthwhile only when directed to productive ends. Considering the sacrifices incurred, it should not be mere makework, or busyness, with no more point than to fill out idle time.

Nor is it helpful to tarry in byways, or to invent unrelated problems. If there is no truly clear, though distant, objective, joint human effort can have only ceremonial impact, with no more permanent value than gossip or empty ritual.

True, we cannot always march directly to our goal. Nor do we want productivity at all costs. We will not tolerate productivity at the destruction of human dignity or lives. For we have many ends in view, in addition to productivity.

One is fairness to every individual, within the limits of reasonable practicality. Another is freedom from interference in private affairs; another is the right to contract, to make binding agreements with other people. We want to be able to promote our ideas; to believe, or not to believe. Some of these goals in any given instance, may conflict with others. If we are to keep our aim true to our mosts important goals, we must find ways to accommodate all these and others, lesser objectives.

Conflicting Goals.

We have a number of movements within our nation which run counter to our ultimate shared values, or goals, as expressed in our Constitution. This is not to say that the Constitution is the complete and unchanging dogma some organizations seem to think it is. As interpreted, it has changed in two hundred years. It has grown in breadth of its concept of liberty; it has explored nuances and bypaths. It is, nevertheless, a fairly clear statement with which we can start.

At its very beginning, in its first amendment, we were provided with a goal of freedom of expression. This was limited to four specifcs: religion, speech, assembly, and petition. As we have implemented those freedoms we have found, over the years, that there should be reasonable limitations even on those basic freedoms.

For instance, in the United States, we boast that we have complete freedom of religion. We can worship as we see fit, and preach that worship to others, and promote it in almost any way. Even to promote the supremacy of our own religion over all others is lawful. From that point limitations start on the freedom of religion.

Crime is Harmful, and Never Our Aim.

To commit an action that is denominated a crime in either rational or irrational promotion of that freedom, is nevertheless a crime, and punishable as such. The Constitutional protection of freedom of expression does not carry over to all action in furtherance of that freedom. That restriction has been applied to peace-loving religionists who want to stop war; or priests who want save San Salvadorans, and in their zeal break criminal immigration laws.[2]

Crime is a definition of what has been deemed harmful to society. If an act is defined as crime, it has been so defined as presumptively harmful. There may be good reason to exculpate the individual, but the presumption is all the other way.

In the same way, we have in this country developed a unique and valuable right to privacy. This precious right, for the most part, has been constructed like Galatea, by the United States Supreme Court, using as molding clay, the simpler basic rights of the Constitution. Thus essential, fundamental fairness rules have been applied Gemara-like to the written words of the Constitution to reveal the intrinsic need in a good society for respect for the dignity of the individual, which demands a right of privacy.[3]

It is therefore a police-crime to unnecessarily invade a home. It is not the aim of this society to encourage the harm of unrestricted police surveillance and intrusion into privacy. Thus in the privacy of our home, we are free to do as we like. We can even plot as Aryan Nazis, Black Panthers, Islamic Jihad, or to have a world congress of similarly-minded individuals.

Such scheming will tend, perhaps inevitably, to evolve into action forwarding programs which easily could become crimes. Not until, however, an actual crime is committed, may government lawfully take action to suppress those criminal acts.[4]

There is, of course, the complaint that such arrests would be no more than a reaction taken after the fact of crime and damage has already been done to society, and to all victims concerned. This may be considered unwise policy and practice, by certain zealous lawyers and enforcers. It may be "inefficient" police work.

So be it, we seek a conflicting, and in this case, a higher goal: Privacy for the many. We exclude police interference until there is clear probable cause to believe a crime has already been committed.

Under our present system there is no other possible lawful police action. Government agents who infiltrate peaceful organizations before they contemplate or commit crime are subject to severe criticism. Their action probably would be construed as being illegal, under present statutes and decisions.[5]

A New View of Liberty.

That is one side of liberty as we have developed it over the past two centuries. We are now facing problems which offer us the opportunity for a new view of liberty. Perhaps, even an extension of freedom. Let us put it this way although there are countless other examples from which to choose:

A headline in a Georgia newspaper in the Fall of 1986 read as follows: "Executed Killer Blames Society," The story went on to describe, " . . . a 5th grade dropout who beat and kicked three elderly people to death in a drug-induced rampage died in the electric chair Wednesday, blaming his plight on "being born black in America.' "

One reaction to this all-too frequent type of news item is to scorn the murderer as either demented, or cowardly. He tries to exculpate himself by blaming someone else for his own misdeeds. There is both good sense, and good morals, to such a conclusion. But there are other ways of looking at it. Here are only a few alternative views.

First, such headlines, and accusations are given credence in many quarters. Second, such lingering doubts about our system weaken our social fabric, and encourage crime and violence. Third, a society which permits kids to dropout in this fashion is a participant in the design of the problem he becomes. Fourth, a society which, in effect relegates utterly helpless babes, and small children to social environments which mandate the development of violent attitudes and criminality, is charge-able with reckless neglect of their persons and personalities. That society must stand charged with cruelly harming that child by invading the dignity and privacy to which he is entitled. It would not be overstretching our current law to find civil, and perhaps criminal, liability against state and municipal authorities.

No Defense.

It is no defense to claim that the child is with his parents, and the responsibility is on the parents, not society. At one time that may have been a sufficient excuse. It no longer is, today. For we readily take children from their parents when the parents are abusive, incompetent, or dangerous to the child. That is the law, and it is followed by every court in the land—sometimes with an excess of zeal.

Does not the same rule follow? If the child, for whatever reason, is exposed to danger to his character, to his life, to his ability to earn a living and to have a reasonably hopeful future, society must assume the obligation to correct the condition.

This not really so startling. We have already, in company with numerous other countries, taken on that burden. The only thing in error is the way we do it: We provide, "Aid to Dependent Children." But we do so by giving money to a parent who may not use the funds to correct the child's environment. On the contrary, the money is often used to support generation after generation of violent families, continuing them in their abusive condition of life. Perpetuating a bad condition in no way can be conceived as remedying it. As has been said many times before, we perpetuate a cycle of failure.

A good society does not let the safety of its members depend solely on the self-control or judgment of those with either bad motives, or weak conscience. No human community allows the individual to exercise his passions or vices without restraint. It is the community's responsibility to minimize the harm individuals might do to others through ill will, error or bad judgment.[6]

How the Cycle of Failure Can Be Interrupted.

This country is founded on a First Amendment which forbids government to make laws respecting the establishment of religion, or prohibiting the free exercise thereof. Without a doubt, religions provide aims to guide the thoughts and actions of a people. The exclusion of the government from establishing a religion, or from prohibiting its free exercise, did not prohibit early Americans from having quite complete consensual ideological systems and aims which did not concur in the formal dogma and tenets of any one of the various religions practiced at that time. Generally speaking, however, they did consent to quite a full system of values, which served our country well in its formative years of the early 19th century. Different scholars and historians have differently phrased this "American Dream," but we all know the broad outlines of what it was, and much of it remains as a firmly held ideology to this day.

Such ideologies are not formal religions. Religion demands belief in, and reverence for, a superhuman being. Bare ideology does not.

We have persevered and succeeded as a nation with this profoundly sensed ideology which has been variously described from before colonial times. Hector DeCrevecoeur caused a sensation in 1768 when he published his *Letters From An American Farmer.*[7] In French, and in then in English, he thrillingly told of his experiences in America where all traces of European royal lineage and national prejudices had been erased, Where all Europeans had become equal. But this was only part of the American Doctrine. Other parts dealt with self-government, and protection from government tyranny. These ideas grew and were formalized with years and experience, developing in part out of resistance to British administration, expressed in local laws and constitutions, reaching a peak in the Declaration of Independence. Until finally, we had the fashioning of the Constitution as our national totem.

Not finally, after all, for we have since blazed and scratched new icons of liberty, in all the decisions and discussions numbering in the thousands which have reached to complete and clarify the American Dream, in doctrinal form. What has been the effect on our people, imbued as they have been with this exceptional doctrine? One may say that the effect has been similar to every indoctrinated group.

It is indoctrination which sets the broad outline of subsequent performance. A group without a purpose, without common goals, accomplishes little. True, overly rigorous constraint can be stultifying, inhibiting dreams and schemes, as well as performance. But that has not been the quality of our dogma.

Our national beliefs have revolved about vigor as well as virtue. It may be instructive to examine other groups and organizations which have exhibited high performance in the face of difficulty. Such groups invariably have been imbued with an ideology of ever improving themselves and their people, as an aim, have mandated useful purpose to every act, with no harm intended to any worthwhile cause or person.

If our aim is true, we have a chance at avoiding harm to children, to adults, to our entire society. If we have no accuracy to our vision, not only is time and treasure lost, but the harm to our people continues, and is compounded.

Grandiose plans often fail. Long-term plans often crash before they mature. This is not a call for detailed five-year or twenty-year structured methods and ends. If the phrase, "Aimless is not harmless," has any useful meaning, it is: "Know where you want to go, accept the responsibility for getting there." Otherwise we must all accept the moral blame for tragedy.

Chapter 15

WORKERS AND SHIRKERS

*"Man, unlike any other thing . . .
grows beyond his work . . . "*

John Steinbeck

"Work is love made visible."

Kahlil Gibran

Work is Joy or Pain . . . It All Depends.

If there is any benefit to an individual from joining a social group it must be, among other things, to gain satisfaction, to be better off than he was alone. Among the satisfactions that philosophers and others have noted are safety from enemies and natural hazards, more and better food, clothing and shelter and happiness in social intercourse. Wherever societies have been found on earth, or left their traces in books, records, pyramids, or stellae, we find people have worked together for their common benefit.

Over time, individuals can come to find satisfaction in the existence of the community itself, and even in working for the common benefit of all. Of course, that is an ideal, and like all ideals, it has an obverse side. Balancing the aphorism "Work is Joy," is its opposite, *"Trabajo es castigo,"* "Work is Punishment."

The last adage undoubtedly arose when people found themselves forced against their will to work for the benefit of others who held power over them, with a variety of unpleasant alternatives, should they refuse to work. When work is punishment, the avoidance of work becomes a happy goal. Even Thomas Jefferson, convinced his slaves were shirking, indulged them in what he stated was laziness, but in view of the very personal interest he had in them, he recognized as simply a natural reluctance to become fatigued for no gain.[1]

140

When a belief-system that does not demand work as a valued and necessary part of life becomes paramount in a people, it becomes difficult to maintain a high level of employment or production. That is our situation, today. Many people have become convinced that hard work is not rewarding in internal satisfaction, nor in substantial material gains. Is that a loss for us all? It appears it all depends on what you want out of life, and what you want out of other people. At least, in this country, with its "dollar-democracy," work-wages make possible the acquisition of money, provides some ease and liberty of action, and even some political and social power. When work-income is supplemented with frugality, money can be accumulated in large quantitites sufficient to serve as capital for investment and further wealth production. Here is the way incomes are distributed in the United States.

Who Gets the Money?

Analysis of the 1980 census data[2] reveals that although we are all living within the same economic and political system, there is a differential return of benefits to each ethnic group. For full-time American workers' median average annual income is distributed as follows:

Black:	$ 11,327.
Vietnamese:	11,641.
Hispanic:	11,650.
Filipino:	13,690.
Korean:	14,224.
White:	15,572.
Chinese:	15,753.
Japanese:	16,829.
Asian-Indian:	18,707.

There has been little recent similar econo-ethnic analysis of such oldline hyphenated American immigrants as Irish-; Jewish-; Gerrman-; Polish-; French-; Italian-.

One possible reason this area of research has been neglected is that for the most part, these Americans no longer are considered, or consider themselves "hyphenated." In this sense, the assimilation process may be more extensive than Glaser and Moynihan wrote about.[3]

There has been even less research seeking distinctions inside those groups, to differentiate between North and South Irish; between Sephardic and Ashkenazi Jews; Catholic and Protestant Germans; North and South Italians, and so on. Certainly there has been no political positions taken on these subgroups, as there has been on that of the economic positions of blacks, women, hispanics, and asiatics in general.

One would wish that the repetitious assaults on the public ear of arguments for or against the economic interest of one group or another would cease. Perhaps, in a proper society that would be so. In the real world we have made for ourselves, however, delineation of groups who claim special privileges for possible past transgressions is a fact of political and economic life. It is simply explained: Groups that can swing votes will find political figures willing to "lead" them. If this be a problem, so be it; so it was for the Founding Fathers, and for every generation of Americans since.

"The First Principle of Law."

It is estimated that about one in four businesses have a gun on the premises for defensive use.[4] There is considerable evidence and widespread common belief that self-defensive use of a weapon against robbers is an effective deterrent. We can expect continuation of this business policy, and even more extended use of weapons by business people in protection of their premises.[5]

Our business people feel a basic need for the availability of deadly force in their hands, to protect their lives as well as their premises. They feel that government does precious little for them, thus they feel justified in such violent reaction. A frequent response to objections made at a business person's possession of a firearm is, "The first principle of the law is self-defense." It is an intimidating reaction to objectors, and is usually supported by other business people in a dangerous neighborhood. That it is not an idle claim is the fact that "mantraps" placed in business establishments, despite the clear phrasing of the law, rarely result in indictments against the business people who placed these clearly illegal machines.

Of course, mantraps have been against the law since the Middle Ages in England, and in America as long as the country has existed. However, when a malefactor is caught or killed in one, set in a business establishment it is difficult to support a law that would punish the defender of property, and justify the thief. Recently a storekeeper in a Miami ghetto electrified a bed spring, placed it near the ceiling opening that had been burglarized before, and . . . a burglar was electrocuted.[6]

There was complete neighborhood support for the storekeeper, but when the national news picked up the story, few scholars or law deans were willing to espouse his cause.

Prentice Rasheed, the storekeeper, need not have worried. The prosecution was unable to prove to a jury that he "had intended to kill." On that basis, according to the newspaper reports, the storekeeper was found not guilty by a jury of his peers.

The law on the books is unchanged, however, and it is doubtful if this case has established any precedent. Most lawyers are convinced it is a case "unique to its particular facts."

For the argument against the use of mantraps is overwhelming, as a matter of law and fact. A first consideration is: deadly mantraps can, and do, mete out much greater punishment than would be enforced by the criminal justice system, for the crime of burglary. In the second place, the use of mantraps is crushingly placed in the area of public nuisances, if not contraband, because of the fact that public safety employees, from police and firemen, to health inspectors could easily fall victim to a mantrap. No, the law is not changed . . . but juries do look at who the criminal victim was, and how evil was his purpose.

The rebuttal to these arguments is finely reasoned by retail-business people: The crime and the punishment spelled out in the penal law, do not establish a contractual equality. There is no validity to the criminal's objection: "Let me do the crime and *if you catch me, . . . I will pay the price of incarceration, for a minimal time period!*"

The purpose of the criminal justice system, and all its works, is to prevent crime, not merely to endure it.

There is no proper sense for society to set up a plan, in which it will occasionally capture some of its criminals, and, after all the civil rights of those few are defended, releasing some criminals because of errors of apprehension, all at enormous public expense, finally incarcerate the residue, again at public expense. The plan is grotesquely crimogenic, and an infringement of the obligation government owes to the noncriminal public.

As one businessman interviewed said, "I did not go into business to became a participant in a duel. Even if I would be willing to accept that role, let me be equally armed. I am not a vigilante. I keep my gun to defend myself."

When phrased in that fashion, the logic is bemusing, if not irrefutable.

The anger, of course, is justifiable. Local communities and even some states are recognizing this community rationale, and are broadening the right to possess and bear arms.[7]

Ultimate consequences of more ready access to small arms in densely populated urban areas are still unknown. It seems reasonable, however, to anticipate an increase in deadly confrontations.

Violence Against Workers.

The violence-for-cash that is visited upon storekeepers to force them to open up the money box is developing in irrational form against employees and agents, even when there is no possible value-return to the violator because the employee has no key to the vault. It is violence for the sake of sheer violence, without possibility of monetary gain.

For instance, there has been a great increase in the number of assaults on traffic ticket agents in New York City.[8] Geoffrey Perrin, spokesman for the New York City Department of Transportation describes how ticket-agents have been smashed in the face with bricks and other blunt instruments. From time to time this punishment is augmented with a vicious stomping.

Meter maids calmly ticketing parked cars have interludes that are not so calm. A motorist double-parks his car, walks over to the meter maid, and punches her to the ground. Satisfied at a good job done, the irate motorist drives off. The cause unknown.

In one such case, the assaulter was apprehended only due to the lucky chance that a witness wrote down his license plate number, and gave it to an investigating police officer. On being queried why he committed such a senseless battery, he complained about a particularly noxious money-based scandal in the Parking Violations Bureau which "bothered me!"

People are certain that the coins they place in the parking meters are stolen by the collecters, or by the cashiers in the central office. Unfortunately, each investigation reported reveals much evidence to sustain their suspicions. The report is widely publicized. The peculations do not stop, nevertheless. Exposure becomes just another cost of doing business, in petty crime, to the new employees who obtain the job of handling the cash from the parking meters.

In the public resentments build on resentments, finally a random representative of the public, venting spleen, blows up in mindless personal violence.

Few of us believe our workers can be relied on to do good day's work, or do it honestly. No one in a position to know can assure us to the contrary. We are coming to hate and be suspicious of our work force.

Repeated stories about entire auto assembly lines being forced to close down because of failure of employees to either have reasonable attendance on the job, or do a reasonably good job, have become common.[9] In some instances, routinized sabotage has been discovered.[10]

Would it be too ironic to comment that today, should there be a revolution, no one would follow the workers traditional cry: "To the barriers." They fill us with distrust, as do their managers and employers.

Workers in the Vineyard of the Lord.

In the past those who were called to serve God in a ministry did so at great cost to their time and effort.[11] Gospel workers were expected to, and usually did, lead lives of piety and poverty. They were exemplars of morality and good works. A nation of admirers, we were then, we tried hard to follow their models of deportment and demeanor.

We were known, from our inception as a nation until this century, as a nation of church-goers who carefully guarded the morals of our families and our neighbors. Most of this was inspired by charismatic spiritual leaders.

Today! The example of the electronic evangelists on television is of a rags-to-riches life-style. "Pursued properly, studying for the ministry can be the first step toward achieving one's monetary goals."[12]

It can also be a first step on the path to a television career, especially if the lust for immorality and peculation is avoided.

Once again, the old idols are left in shards, with no one to pick them up, and put them together again.

PART FOUR
RIGHTS OF A FREE PEOPLE

Chapter 16

FREEDOM FROM ASSAULT

*"The best laid plans o
mice and men Gang aft a-gley."*

Robert Burns

The Search For Safety.

Philosophers and anthropologists have mused that in early times
people planned to find protection by grouping together in cities. On
data and inference based thereon, it appears now to our learned scholars
that ancient peoples who wanted peace and safety joined to maintain
that peace against violent dangers from outside their perimeters.[1]

That plan has gone astray. Today the danger is inside the city. People
desiring to avoid assault move away from city, to the country, or to
distant suburbs. But that is an old story, now. This emigration from the
central city has been going on for decades, closely paralleling the rising
crime rates of the cities.

The Urban Jungle.

How did it happen that the city changed from being a refuge, into
what some writers have called a "jungle?"[2] As a people, how did we learn
to criminalize our cities? Further, how have we come to view the
crimogenic, violent city as a natural fact of life?

There are any number of ways this question can be answered. One way
is through examining how and why we learn. When cities were first
formed people lived in submission to a society and environment that
quickly gave pain for error, and reluctantly gave pleasure and benefit for
correct behavior. Angry blow was instantly returned with blow, and
universal community disapproval of a transgressor. Forbearance from
returning righteous punishment was a rare and notable characteristic.

149

People who demonstrated it were set apart either to be revered as holy, or exploited as fools. They did not become what today we call role models. People, young men particularly, strove to survive within constraints of their physical and social world, set by strictly enforced codes of behavior and attitude.

How Do We Learn?

Much of our education today is symbolic, with no constraints of penalty or pain or harsh reality. Much of it is presented as visual entertainment. Even in school, there is no anxiety to learn. The only negative is boredom.

The large and small screens are our teachers. From them we have learned that cars can happily career through crowded urban streets crashing car after car, ultimately smashing into a hydrant, sending a spout of water skyward as the hurtling auto slides up the rear of another car to fly through the air, landing upside down to go skittering along the sidewalk, with pedestrians leaping out of the way. The auto comes to a shuddering stop. Of course, the occupants squeeze out of the bent and battered sedan to continue to run after the bad guys. Good guys (with whom we identify) rarely encounter serious injury.

Would it were so in real life. From film stars, and a playboy Prince of Wales, decades ago, we learned to smoke too much, and do without undershirts. No great harm there, but we went on to see images of people, and so believe it to be true, that after being knocked unconscious a man can get up and go routinely about his business of being a movie leading man. Physical blows are not so much. Gunshot wounds are half-humorously shrugged off, "It's only a flesh-wound, Colonel!"

The ancients said, "He laughs at scars who never felt a wound." Quite a different point of view, there. Different, too, from the shuddering nightmares of veterans of real fire-fights. For the most part, those realistic-minded elders do not talk much. They weep.

On the contrary, in brilliant technicolor, even battles in Viet Nam are glamorized and bloody death is offered as a thrilling alternative to a boring lifetime of passive entertainment. The attraction of an active life of crime, under these circumstances, is undeniable: Profit, pleasure, little work, no pain. Urban crime is *good* for you!

Where We Are.

The statistics show a different story. Urban crime is reaching the point where we cannot even warehouse the convicted. In 1986, our prison population reached 546,659, though that is only about 10 percent of all the criminals being "treated" by the system. Probation, parole, community-based treatment programs, pretrial intervention, and other dispositions absorb the other 90 percent. That is an increase from 1980 of about 66 percent in the 6-year period. Every state, and the federal government, are building more prison capacity in expectation of ever higher prison populations. The female prisoner population grows at an even faster pace than the male. This, despite the notorious reluctance of our courts and juries to find women guilty, to convict and to incarcerate them. Should women attain equality in this, we would need even more prison capacity.

Our justice system, as presently constituted sees no alternative to building more prisons to confine the huge number of convicts we will have in the near future

Where We Will Be.

We need the new prisons, it is claimed, because the recidivism of young parolees reaches 69 percent within 6 years of their release. They were arrested for thousands of new felonies and violent crimes.[3] An estimated 37 percent of the parolees were rearrested while still on parole. Apparently the only thing that assures the public's safety from young-sters convicted of violent crime is actual, physical incarceration contin-ued for long periods. Probation and parole, despite the claimed economies, are a sham, they find from the evidence, that while cost of their food and keep is thereby saved, young parolees and probationers continue the depredations that first brought them society's condemnation.

Significantly the longer the parolee's prior arrest record, the higher the rate of recidivism—over 90 percent of the parolees with six or more previous arrests were rearrested, compared to 59 percent of the first-time offenders.[4]

None of this implies that violent youth are less assaultive while in prison. While in prison they assault each other at ever higher rates. Our prison's are the scene of more assaults each year. All the system can do is to protect the general public by separating those prone to violence from the community. Criminologists know the violent are easily identified, because they come to the attention of the authorities early in life, and repeat their pattern inexorably. Thus our prospect is for us to boast of a "Land of the Free and the Imprisoned."

Incapacitation as a Solution.

What can be called an ad hoc attempt at a solution to the problem: statisticians have noted, that while out of custody, our violent minority are without inhibition to exert their violent personalities. Their conclusion: Keep them in prison. For, on the streets, our ability to control the assaulters, is almost nonexistent. Confidence has waned as to the ability of correctional programs to rehabilitate offenders. Public attitudes toward crime and criminals have become more punitive. Prisons throughout the United States are crowded, having reached an all-time high. Recent research efforts suggest that it may be possible to identify and incarcerate high-rate offenders, thereby promising an eventual ability to reduce crime without crowding the prisons. Our bests minds, funded by our best research organizations have taken on the problem. Here is the way some of it has proceeded:

Public policy advocates distinguish between collective and selective incapacitation. "Collective" strategies involve identical sentencing for conviction of a designated offense. For instance, conviction of robbery would mandate a five-year sentence. Research shows that such a policy reduces crime only a small degree. Rigorously following such a policy results in dramatic increases in prison populations.[5]

"Selective" strategies involve individualized sentences based on predictions that particular offenders would commit many crimes if not incarcerated. The thought is that the crime rate could be significantly lowered, without seriously increasing the prison population. This strategy, when proposed in a notable research report in 1982[6] received much favorable comment, and considerable active response from enforcement agencies. Teams were formed to concentrate on 'high-risk,' criminals. Many were apprehended, prosecuted, and imprisoned.

The problem, as one would anticipate, was that whatever predictive scale was chosen it was based on retrospective factors, with unknown accuracy as to prospective crimes. Further such a scale lacks internal and external validation. Also, there are serious ethical and constitutional questions related to so harrassing a particular offender.

Career Criminal Patterns.

Offering a more hopeful approach is one based on analysis of criminal career patterns. This method relies on recent empirical research on criminal careers.[7] The key variables are: Empirical estimates of average individual arrest and crime rates and the average length of criminal careers. The goal is to identify classes of offenders who, on average, would remain active at high rates. Extensive data was collected, analyzed, and organized in graphic predictive models.

In these studies it appeared that convicted robbers and burglars had high crime rates and relatively short careers. It also appeared to predict that minimum two-year terms imposed on all adult offenders convicted of robbery would result in an 8 percent reduction in robberies by adults, while increasing the total prison population by 7 percent. This seemed promising in 1983, and enthusiasm was high.[8]

But now it is half a decade later, and we have a higher crime rate than ever.

After the fact evaluation is rarely helpful. Often it has merely led to more speculative repairs to a system that is intrinsically self-defeating in policy and style. Very probably the criminal justice system is simply overloaded with attempting to control, and service too many people who commit violence. Improving the efficiency of the system to handle larger and larger numbers is at bottom a no-win approach.

Reasoning By Analogy.

Theories on an *ad hoc* basis having failed to gain much success or support, perhaps we can be forgiven the hope that there is benefit from reasoning by analogy. One remembers: When the problem was too many cars on a given road, the solution proposed of adding an extra lane did not reduce the congestion. It merely resulted in more autos taking that route.

When the problem in India, after World War II, was too many infants being ill-fed, the solution proposed of providing special supplementary payments to the mothers of such children did not reduce the number of ill-fed children. It merely resulted in more poor mothers having more ill-fed children.

When the problem was too many North Viet Nam soldiers infiltrating into the South, the solution tried, reinforcing the South Viet defenses, did not reduce the fighting. It merely resulted in more and deadlier fighting, and the ultimate defeat of those defending South Viet Nam.

If this remembrance of things past is to provide any benefit we must find a way to apply the lesson to the present issue: Violence.

Doing so, one is impelled to suggest that perhaps what we need is *not* more and better response to violence. On the contrary, the solution may be simply: *Reduce the incidence of violence.*

Is that suggestion too simple, . . . or too complex?

Since violence is initiated by people who have that tendency structured in their personality, the only reasonable approach must be: Avoid structuring violent personalities.

Can this be done? There is much reason to believe it can. We can start in the home.

Chapter 17

SAFE HOMES

"Charity begins at home,
is the voice of the world;
yet every man is his greatest enemy,
as it were, his own executioner"

Sir Thomas Browne

Most murderers kill relatives and acquaintances.[1] Where do these murders occur? Simply, it is where a murderer first learns violence, in the home. Why in the home? That is where he learned it and where it is most comfortably exercised.

The Unsafe Home.

Almost invariably, the murderer and others guilty of using deadly force, experienced and learned violence as a child. Early in life they showed many signs of a violent tendency.[2]

But early childhood is spent almost entirely under control of a family. We have no adequate institutional approach to controlling, or even understanding what goes on inside a particular home. However, we do often have information coming out about what went on there, after the fact.

Figure 17-1 graphically demonstrates the percentage of households touched by selected crimes of violence and theft, 1975–1985.

The decline in the percentage of households touched by any crime between 1984 and 1985 was caused by a decrease in the reporting of personal theft. Have people just given up on reporting minor thefts to police? There was no decrease for crimes of violence reported. In absolute numbers, 4,235,000 violent crimes are listed in one year (see Figure 17-2).

Despite the decrease in reporting minor crimes, most really unpleasant life events occurring in the household are still crimes. It is astonishing that crime is more common than any other negative life event in the home (see Figure 17-3).

155

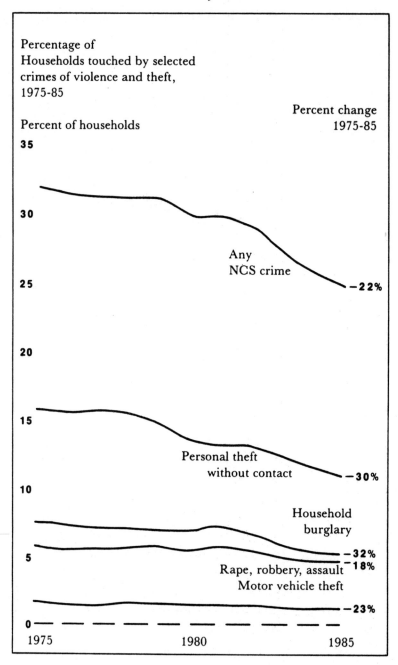

Figure 17-1.

Safe Homes 157

Households touched by crime, 1985
and relative percent change since 1984

Households	1985		1984		Relative percent change 1984-85
	Number of households	Percent	Number of households	Percent	
Total	88,852,000	100.0%	87,791,000	100.0%	
Touched by					
Any NCS crime	22,191,000	25.0	22,806,000	26.0	−4%*
Violent crime	4,235,000	4.8	4,392,000	5.0	−5
Rape	125,000	.1	161,000	.2	−22
Robbery	842,000	.9	914,000	1.0	−9
Assault	3,488,000	3.9	3,566,000	4.1	−3
Aggravated	1,246,000	1.4	1,308,000	1.5	−6
Simple	2,459,000	2.8	2,542,000	2.9	−5
Total theft	15,699,000	17.7	16,330,000	13.6	−5*
Personal	10,233,000	11.5	10,776,000	12.3	−6*
with contact	439,000	.5	520,000	.6	−17**
without contact	9,910,000	11.2	10,353,000	11.8	−5*
Household	7,240,000	8.1	7,467,000	8.5	−4
Burglary	4,713,000	5.3	4,792,000	5.5	−3
Motor vehicle theft	1,201,000	1.4	1,202,000	1.4	−1
Crimes of high concern (a rape, robbery, or assault by a stranger, or a burglary)	6,876,000	7.7	7,063,000	8.0	−4

Note: Detail does not add to total because of overlap in households touched by various crimes. Relative percent change is based on unrounded figures. Estimates for 1984 differ slightly from those published in *Households Touched by Crime, 1984* to correct an error in rounding of weights.

* Difference is statistically significant at the 95% level.
** Difference is statistically significant at the 90% level.

Figure 17-2.

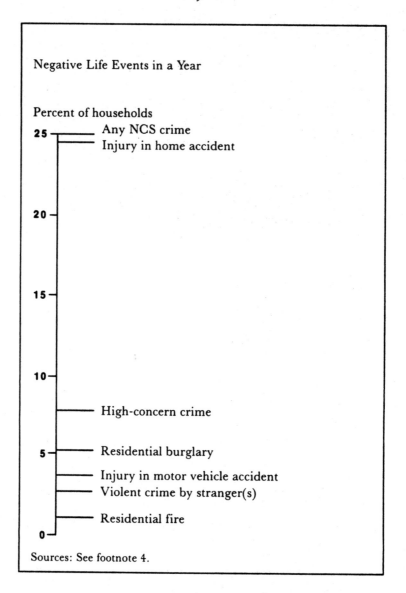

Figure 17-3.

Family violence has been receiving increasing attention from citizens, policymakers and the criminal justice system. The National Crime Survey[3] does not specifically try to measure all criminal violence, but in its various surveys, many interviewers provide data about family violence in response to questions not truly designed to explore this subject.

Thus the statistical base is weak. One basic difficulty is in defining what is to be measured. There is little disagreement about extreme cases when a family member is killed or seriously injured by another family member. There is dispute, however, about the kinds of behavior that should be regarded as acceptable for disciplining children, and resolving conflicts among family members. When does spanking become child abuse? When does a big brother's abusive behavior to siblings cross the line between undesirable action and criminal assault?

Family Violence As a Pragmatic Issue.

Family violence is often a legal issue, that is to say, a crime. It is also a social, moral, and psychological issue. Certainly the class of people who have suffered psychological and physical abuse is larger than those who have been brought to the attention of the authorities as victims of crime. But we have no adequate method to measure this larger figure.

One thing seems quite certain, however. Family violence is an issue of pragmatic consequence to the nation. What goes on in the family home is no longer a private matter. The consequences have reached out from the home, to affect us all. Unfortunately, we do not yet realize the true dimension of the problem.

Methodological Puzzles.

Even criminal assaults cannot be numbered accurately, for neither the Federal Bureau of Investiation's Uniform Crime Reports nor the Bureau of Justice Statistics National Crime Survey can provide reliable estimates on the overall incidence of family violence. The total figure, however, is undoubtedly enormous.

Research findings, drawn from data collected by such organizations as the American Humane Society, and others, using spot surveys,[4] estimate that as many as five or more million couples may experience violence ranging from any at all to severe violence.

When that violence spreads out of the home to the rest of society, can—or should—it be ignored?

We are in constant receipt of subtle messages encouraging us to use violence, even murder, to remedy family problems. The popular approval of many such films as *The Burning Bed* have received is an indication of the pervading resentment and violence within families. We are treated in great detail to the newsy items of abusive parents who are not restrained until murdered by their children.[5] It is no wonder that we learn to condone, and subconsciously, even approve violence. In confirmation, the usually reliable statistics on homicide reveal astonishing numbers of relatives kill relatives in this country (see Figure 17-4).

Percent of homicides reported to UCR, by victim's relationship to offender, 1982	
Victim's relationship to offender	Percent
Husband	3.4%
Wife	4.8
Mother	0.6
Father	0.7
Daughter	1.0
Son	1.7
Brother	1.1
Sister	0.2
Other family	3.3
Acquaintances	29.7
Friend	3.4
Boyfriend	1.4
Girlfriend	1.9
Neighbor	1.6
Stranger	16.9
Unknown relationship	28.1
Total	100.0

Note: Because of rounding, percentages may not add to total.

Source: Federal Bureau of Investigation, *Uniform Crime Reports, 1982.*

Figure 17-4.

The National Crime Survey interviews about 60,000 households throughout the United States. Each person in the household (a total of about 132,000 individuals) is asked a series of screening questions about whether he or she has been a victim within the past 6 months of any of the specified crimes. If a person answers affirmatively to any of the screening questions, a detailed incident questionnaire is administered for each incident. Households in the sample are interviewed every 6 months for a period of 3 years, allowing the survey to track serial victimization.

These survey findings indicate that family violence is significantly under-reported, both for methodological reasons and because of the sensitive nature of the subject. Among the many possible reasons for the apparent under-reporting are the following:

1. Many victims of family violence do not perceive their experience as crimes.
2. Although interviewers are encouraged to view each respondent privately if possible, there may be other family members present during the interview. If the offender is present, the chances diminish that the victim would feel free to describe the event.
3. Many victims of family violence are reluctant to speak of their experiences because of the shame and revulsion they feel about the matter.

The National Crime Survey asks a series of screening questions that are phrased in nontechnical language to determine whether the person has been a victim of rape, robbery, or assault. The survey respondent is expected to report all events, regardless of whether the offender is a stranger, acquaintance, friend, or relative. Since the survey included crimes not reported to the police, it permits measurement of family crimes in which police are not involved.

The most difficult information to obtain from such a survey methodology is information on child abuse. When the National Crime Survey methodology was being developed, research was conducted to determine whether accurate statistical data could be obtained from children using self-report techniques.

A proxy method of questioning the parent or other adult for children aged 12 and 13 was developed: information was not obtained at all from children under age 12; thus we have no data on abuse of very young children from the National Crime Survey. Additional research is being performed to discover newer methodologies for surveys, especially those involving interviewing younger children.

There are a number of specialized problems encountered in interviewing young children about their experiences as victims of any type of crime.

Professionals working with abused children have found that a high level of trust is necessary for the child to feel free to describe what has happened to him or her.

A survey interviewer who spends only a few minutes, or even an hour in the home, or on the telephone, asking general screening questions is unlikely to be able to establish the required trust in that brief time.

These problems are compounded when the offender is a parent or other close relative. The offender may be present, or within hearing during the interview, making it even more unlikely that the child would describe abusive experiences.

Still another possible source of error has occurred in the experience of prosecutors in California and other states, who relied upon detailed descriptions of abuse of child-interviewees, and of other children and commenced prosecution which failed to stand up under further investigation. Whether the errors were the result of imaginations overheated by the attention and inducements conscious and unconscious of the interviewers could not be determined.

In court cases, in times past, child witnesses' statements were often excluded because of the presumed oversusceptibility of children to suggestion. The power of suggestion works in reverse, too. When we are overly sympathetic to children's tales of abuse and violence, as adults, we overreact, and encourage exaggeration. Even wilder accusations become credible, and perhaps are reinforced.

Since the National Crime Survey screening questions are designed to measure behavior that people regard as crimes, estimates of family violence from their surveys reflect only those forms of abuse that victims are willing to label as criminal and report to interviewers. Thus there are many limitations to the information collected by these surveys. The data is to be viewed within these constraints (see Figure 17-5).

Of the crimes committed by relatives measured by the National Crime Survey, 88 percent were assaults, 10 percent were robberies and 2 percent were rapes. Of the assaults, about a third were aggravated, indicating use of a weapon and/or serious injury. The remaining two-thirds were simple assault, indicating either a minor injury or a threat of harm. Serial victimization within 6 months occurs in up to 25 percent of family cases.

This is notwithstanding the fact that many victims of family violence do not report their victimization to any authority at all. The most common reason for not reporting the crime to the police was the belief that the crime was "a private or personal matter." This, it certainly is.

Family Violence Reported to NCS By Relationship of Offender to Victim		
Relationship	1973-81 total	Yearly average
Total by all relatives	4,108,000	456,000
Spouses or ex-spouses	2,333,000	259,000
Parents	263,000	29,000
Children	173,000	19,000
Brothers or sisters	351,000	39,000
Other relatives	988,000	110,000
All estimates rounded to nearest thousand.		

Figure 17-5.

When ultimate consequences affect the individuals outside the family, however, it acquires public interest.

Conclusions To Be Drawn.

It becomes clear that violence starts in the home, is learned at home, and moves out from the home to the rest of society, as a confirmed practice that the youngster has learned, of how he should deal with frustrating problems of all kinds.

One must comment about Senator Daniel Patrick Moynihan's iconoclastic approaches to social programs[6] which, among other items, support a "national family policy" to promote the preservation of two-parent households, with parents encouraged to be responsible for each other, and for their children. It may be impossible to provide two-parent homes for all children. In fact, the two-parent model may not necessarily be the best, especially with the high possibility of having two violent parents. The true goal is: Nonviolent parenting, to bring up nonviolent children.[7]

Nevertheless, with all the errors and sins of urban life being so assiduously promoted in our unsafe homes, one is tempted to say "Aye," to Senator Moynihan's cry, against violence in the home: "Enough! We can't let this happen to our children"!

Chapter 18

LAW ABIDING POLICE

"When constabulary duty's to be done
The policeman's lot is not a happy one."

W. S. Gilbert

"You must obey the policeman,
his authority comes from God."

"Whoever opposes the existing authority
opposes what God has ordered."

Romans 13

The world has been treated, recently, to the spectacle of a few people in the National Security Agency, sure of the justice of their cause, assuming power over the might of the entire United States government.[1] The Iran-Contra Affair will recede into history, but the dynamics involved in that situation, are everpresent, when people are charged with a mission, but do not have the legal authority to do the things they consider necessary to accomplish the task.

Missions, Tasks, and Nonperformance.

Police officers are by definition charged with the task of controlling crime, maintaining order, and preserving peace in the community. Their powers, however, are quite limited, and in many ways become more limited each day.

Sometimes the result has been that police have overreached. On occasion they have mistakenly used more force on a scene of suspected crime, than a court with more time, and the benefit of hindsight, judged to be warranted. On such occasions the police action is called "illegal," and offenders are chastised, sued, fined, or sometimes jailed.

"Why can't police obey the laws?" is an often asked question.

For many of the police, and for many law-abiding citizens, too, the answer is: "They can't do the job we want done, without cutting corners." Thus they succumb to the lure of violence, if it seems to them at the time that it aids mission-performance.

Technical Violations of Law.

In many cases, investigation reveals that the charge of police illegality is of a quite technical nature. That is to say, without intention to break the law, but merely a failure to completely follow complex procedural rules.

Centuries ago, when police had difficult cases, the traditional interrogation method was to use punishment as the prime method to extract the truth from the suspect.[2] He would be terrorized, beaten, hung, or other excruciating tortures would be applied until he confessed. Machines for this purpose were invented, given colorful names as the Iron Widow, the Wheel or the Rack, that were held to be efficient at extracting the truth.

Of course, given enough punishment most people would confess to anything.[3] The risk of thus receiving incorrect information and confessions had to be reduced by the skill of the torturer: Enough punishment to get the full story, not so much as to so demoralize the sufferer so that his confession or statement was without truth.

These interrogative techniques were an intrinsic part of the art and even science of investigations from before written history. In the cuniform markings made in the 18th century B.C., during the kingship of Hammurabi in Babylonia, is found a statement that the King's agents went out to investigate a crime and commenced the investigation by a giving a thorough bastinado to a witness.[4]

As late as the 1920's, in the United States, pain and torture in police interrogations was picturesquely called the Third Degree.[5] The lure of force in police interrogation was strong, because for the most part, it worked wonderfully well. From, that is, the point of view of the inquisitors.

But in 1966, the Supreme Court of the United States laid down new requirements in the *Miranda v. Arizona* case[6] which mandated that no longer could police interrogators have a free hand with anyone in custody. Henceforth very great care was to be taken that any admissions or confessions would be made intelligently, voluntarily, and knowingly. Under no circumstances could punishment be used to facilitate police investigation. Even mental pain, or suasion was not be permitted, at risk of having the entire case thrown out of court, as violative of the Fifth

Amendment of the Constitution privilege against self-incrimination, as well as other amendments and laws.

When that case became law, and Mr. Miranda was released from jail, there was an uproar in the law enforcement community. Police had always felt that their main task, as investigators, was to find the person who knew the facts of the case, and then get him to talk.

For a criminal to be released even though he had confessed to the crime seemed eminently unfair to the police, the public, and to justice itself. A number of alternative solutions were suggested, from legislation by Congress or States, civil or criminal action against officers' violating the law, or other methods that time and study could devise which would maintain the conviction of criminals, and not send them out to prey upon the public anew. Nevertheless, the decision stood, and became the law of the land. The technical details of how a confession could hereafter be admitted became part of the literature, known as "Miranda."

Further, Chief Justice Warren's opinion had suggested that a person in custody should be given four specific warnings before any police interrogation to assure the complete constitutionality of any custodial interrogation.

Such was the prestige, and influence of the Supreme Court, every police officer in the land was issued a card with the four "Miranda Warnings" printed on it, to be read to every prisoner in custody who was to be interrogated.

To some police, lawyers, and courts, the new law seemed quite clear. But the protection of the Fifth Amendment, as procedurally explicated by the necessity for voluntariness, and the Miranda Warnings, still held technical procedural details secret from the world. We are still exploring them. One interesting, and quite technical item became apparent in 1977. In this case, *Brewer v. Williams*,[7] two Des Moines detectives tried to tread a narrow line between the lure of violence and ineffective police work at two extremes, and compliance with "Miranda," somewhere in between.

In the *Brewer v. Williams* case a 10-year-old girl, Pamela Powers, had disappeared from an athletic event at a YMCA in Des Moines, Iowa, the day before Christmas, 1968. A young boy had seen Mr. Williams, a resident at the YMCA, carrying a large bundle wrapped in a blanket with two thin legs hanging from it. He had put the bundle into his car and driven away.

Mr. Williams' car was found the following day 160 miles away in the town of Davenport, Iowa. A warrant was issued for the arrest of the suspect. The Des Moines police received a phone call from a lawyer stating that he represented Mr. Williams, and he had advised him to turn himself in to the Davenport police. The lawyer then went to the police station, and while there the Davenport police notified Des Moines authorities that Mr. Williams had surrendered himself.

The lawyer requested that he speak on the phone to Mr. Williams, and in the presence of the Des Moines police chief and a detective, the lawyer advised Mr. Williams it had been agreed that he would be picked up by two detectives and brought back to Des Moines, and that the detectives would not question him during the trip.

Here was a dilemma for the police: A horrible crime had been committed against a young child. Certainly the suspect could not be expected to confess on his own volition. No one knew if she was alive or dead, or where she was. Certainly there was not enough evidence then available to convict Mr. Williams of any crime.

The two detectives were directed to pick up the suspect from the town of Davenport, where defendant Robert Williams had been arraigned on the warrant, and drive him back to Des Moines where 10-year-old Pamela Powers had been last seen, and probably where she had been killed, for booking and arraignment.

Further investigation was absolutely necessary to obtain more evidence, otherwise the killer would eventually have to be released. The only lead they had was in the mind of Mr. Williams. Being experienced detectives they were aware of the powers of brutal interrogation. But they had discarded the lure of violence as an alternative. They also knew that in Davenport the Miranda warnings had been read to Mr. Williams. They felt they had to do some*thing....* but what?

On the long drive to Davenport, they reviewed what they knew: Williams was a former mental patient, and he was deeply religious. He probably was the only person who knew what had happened to Pamela Powers, but violent interrogation was completely out of the question. In fact, they decided to comply with every letter of the law as they understood it at the time: They would not interrogate him.

On arrival in Davenport, and meeting Mr. Williams, in custody of the police and conferring with another lawyer there who represented him, the detectives read Mr. Williams the Miranda Warnings:

> You have the right to remain silent.
> Anything you say can be used against you in a court of law.
> You have the right to the presence of an attorney,

If you cannot afford an attorney one will be appointed for you prior to any questioning, if you so desire.

Charged as they were with the heavy obligation of finding a child, possibly her murdered body, identifying the perpetrator, and obtaining evidence sufficient to convict, they believed they could tread a fine line between illegal police work and an unsuccessful investigation. Hanging over them was the knowledge that going too far in either direction would result in the release of the defendant from custody.

The detectives put the defendant in their car and started the 160 mile drive back to Des Moines. The solution they grasped at was to avoid formal interrogation. In their judgment, however, it would not be a violation of law to tell him what they were thinking.

I want to give you something to think about while we're traveling down the road...Number one, I want you to observe the weather conditions, it's raining, it's sleeting, it's freezing, driving is very treacherous, visibility is poor, it's going to be dark early this evening. They are predicting several inches of snow for tonight, and I feel that you yourself are the only person that knows where this little girl's body is, that you yourself have only been there once, and if you get a snow on top of it you yourself may be unable to find it. And, since we will be going right past the area on the way into Des Moines, I feel that we could stop and locate the body, that the parents of this little girl should be entitled to a Christian burial...

The appeal struck a chord. The suspect led them to the body where he had hidden it in the woods. On trial, with testimony as to the above, his attorneys objected to the admission of the evidence. The objection was overruled, it was admitted, and the jury found Williams guilty of murder.

Many commentators, analyzing the case at the time, felt the practices used by the detectives were acceptable to the law. They were wrong.

It was not until years later, in 1977, after appeals in which the question of possible waiver was raised that the Supreme Court held that "there is no need to review in this case the doctrine of Miranda v. Arizona.... to secure the constitutional privilege against compulsory self-incrimination." Mr. Williams was held to have asserted his right to have counsel present, under the Sixth and Fourteenth Amendments, and not to have waived that right. His voluntary statements and actions were not admissible.

Police and prosecutors and many in the community were appalled. Many older police officers, were particularly dismayed to see a case, "go down the drain, when a good, hard slap in the face, would have gotten all the evidence needed."

To this day, the quick resolution that violence can bring remains seductively just out of legal reach to police officers in the United States. However, we are becoming more resistant to the lure of violence for this purpose. Communities no longer will support an abusive resolution to crime problems. Our police have had to bear up under what used to be called "technicalities," as further case law explores the nuances of private rights and public needs.[8]

Borderline Violations of Law.

The Rochin Case[9] can be cited as, "borderline." Here the evidence, illegally possessed narcotics in capsules, was swallowed by the suspect, when he was approached by the police. The police, in hot pursuit as it were, called for the services of a stomach-pump, forced the suspect to swallow the tube, found the evidence in the effluvia and charged the suspect with the crime of illegal possession of a controlled substance.

Here the decision of the court was that it would be unconscionable to permit police to follow their hunting instincts so closely as to invade the body of the defendant, however sure they were that evidence of crime could be found. It smacked too much of the tortuous indignities visited upon human bodies and spirit, by inquisitors in the Middle Ages. As Justice Felix Frankfurter in his opinion stated, this "breaking into the privacy" of the accused was "conduct that shocked the conscience."

Should the police have had the sensitivity, the squeamishness, or known how the U.S. Supreme Court would decide, to avoid pursuing the contraband even into the body of the suspect? Well, they know now! Some, including the majority of the Court, insist that the police action was intolerable and insufferable. Others, placed emphasis on the fact that the packet of drugs was swallowed in defiance of the officers and the law. Further, the evidence was recovered, with no substantial pain or discomfort incurred that had not been instigated by the suspect himself.

An old-time police officer informed of this case commented, "A quick punch in the belly while apprehending the subject would have made him throw up the evidence with less trouble, and less law suits."[10]

The modern police resisted this lure to violence, but found themselves "in trouble," nevertheless. The case was reversed on appeal.

Could this borderline area be further refined? Probably so. As one instance, the contraband is inserted by the suspect into one of his body cavities, mouth, throat, rectum, or bladder and cannot be removed by the police without instruments and force. How much force will be considered, "shocking to the conscience" and therefore denied to police?

Or, if the police do not have certain knowledge that evidence has been secreted in the body, nevertheless use instruments and force to "explore" body cavities and tissues. Can X-rays be used by the police, to discover body secrets, despite the known damage to tissue caused by X-rays? We do not know the legal answers to these questions at the present time. Force is invariably involved, but, how much force is too much?

We do know, however, that the human body can lawfully be invaded by the police to the extent of taking a very small blood sample for blood-typing purposes. How do we know this? A United States Supreme Court decision so held.[11]

Clear Violations of Law.

It is much easier to identify and decry clear violations of law by police, particularly when unnecessary use of violence is a part of the events.

Police, to balance the special privileges we grant agents who are paid to guard our lives and property, are charged with special obligations of honesty, and self-control. They are exposed to many opportunities for illicit gain. We expect them to deny themselves the luxury of being as susceptible to greed as an ordinary mortal. Often the officer will receive much more severe penalties than the citizen involved in the same crime.[12]

No one in the United States tries to make a brief for clearly unlawful actions by police, except for apologists who use arguments: "They're only human. They overreacted." "We must support our local police." "They are the only bulwark we have against the vicious criminals out there."

The response to such excuses is as undeniable as it is unavoidable. We must, in all cases:

1. Train police to act only in compliance with the law.
2. Enforce all laws against police as is done equally against others.
3. Use supervisory bodies to monitor performance of police.

The roles of independent prosecuting attorneys, grand juries, citizen-volunteers in such programs as Courtwatch, and investigative reporters are all-important here.

Experience has shown that when officials, police included, are permitted to evade the full enforcement of the criminal law against themselves, the hole in the web of community protection is gradually widened until it is entirely in shreds. The light of day, full information to an informed public, is the greatest deterrent to crime. The more the public knows about its police department, the more it participates in its affairs, the better the results, in terms of law-abiding police.

Entrapment.

Entrapment is another example of how difficult it is to draw the fine line between lawful and unlawful police work. In fact the psychodynamics of the situations that arise in alleged entrapment cases almost always involve the police in situations where a citizen reveals to the police his full criminality. Officers tend to view that as almost daring the police to arrest and to convict. The temptation to use whatever force may be necessary to accomplish that objective, is sometimes irresistible.

The dictionary meaning of he word "entrapment" is to lure into a compromised act such as a crime. But police have always been permitted to use trickery, deceit, promises, and lies as part of their routine techniques to obtain evidence of crime. The investigation of crime and the detection of criminals is not a game to be governed by Marquess of Queensbury rules.[13]

There is, as always, another point of view: Professor White of the University of Pennsylvania Law School[14] holds that effective protection of constitutional rights demands that whenever there is an "unacceptable" risk of infringement, the trickery should be absolutely prohibited.

One would think that from the defendant's viewpoint, all such risks are unacceptable, and therefore should be prohibited.

Current law, however, does not go so far. Generally, the "totality of the circumstances" is examined. Thus an exhortation to tell the truth has been held to be proper.[15] But suggestions that things will go easier if the truth is told, can have a different result. Is that over the line into unacceptable false police promises? The decided cases on the question are not to be reconciled.[16] Some states will permit police to make such deceitful promises, but deny them to district attorneys.

Self-Defense.

It is indeed a rare police academy that counsels restraint when the police officer himself is under direct attack. Implicit in such a situation is a diffused community feeling that such a reckless, violent assaulter deserves the worst of the encounter, if only to reestablish a proper respect for the law. This is an attitude in which a police officer can join heartily.

Unhappily, in the nature of physical confrontation, sometimes the force used goes over the line permissible and the officer stands subject to investigation on a charge of unlawful use of force, or assault, or even homicide. Of course, a claim of self-defense could put the officer in a kinder light.

Aware of this, sometimes officers may shade their report of the facts of the confrontation to prove, or at least suggest that their deadly response was elicited by necessity, a clear case of self-defense.[17] However, internal affairs divisions, and supervisors of police are well aware of this and generally look with a jaundiced eye on such a claim, when unjustified by other evidence.

Cops and Politics.

Some police strive to avoid politics, others have politics thrust upon them.

Eighteen police officers sued Mayor Harold Washington of Chicago for being demoted after supporting an opponent.[18] Twenty-nine officers had been demoted, with substantial loss of pay although they were informed that they had done a good job, and fifty-nine others were laterally transferred. The pay loss varied from $5,010 to $20,000 a year, for each officer.

Politics is almost an invariable complication of criminal justice administration in this country. Despite the assumptions of President Woodrow Wilson, at the time president of Princeton University, in the late 1880's, that politics and administration could be separated once and for all, later more sophisticated reviews have revealed that politics and police are inevitably intertwined.[19] We have not yet determined a way to separate the two.

Chapter 19

PROTECTION FROM CRIME

"During the time men live without a
common power to keep them in awe,
they are in that condition which is called war;
and such a war as is of
every man against every man."

Thomas Hobbes

Old Problems.

Criminal justice problems of two or three decades ago were:[1]
1. Competent legal representation for accused
2. Police discretion
3. Police encounters with juveniles
4. Supreme Court insistence on adherence to strict rules to protect the "rights of the accused."
5. Doubt that correctional punishment is necessary.

Have these problems of a generation ago been resolved? It will be noted that all five of them can be summarized as "Protection from the justice system" itself. Each of the topics was the subject of intense debate at the time, and in case form, struggled through the system to be substantially resolved.

As to "1": Most of the states now provide adequate legal representation for accused, either in the form of state-paid legal defender systems, charitably financed legal aid systems, or well staffed *pro bono* representation provided as a service by the working bar.[2]

As to "2": Police discretion today is narrowly channeled by federal decisions,[3] state-mandated restrictions on the use of deadly force, internal affairs divisions within the police departments, with fearsome reputations as disciplinarians, extensive manuals of procedure for each police department, and a public educated in its civil rights, including the powers of 42 U.S. Sec. 1983, a federal law designed to provide criminal

173

and civil remedies against improper use of discretion by individual police officers, or improper training by department or municipality.

As to "3": Juveniles now charged with crime are as a matter of law, carefully segregated from adults. The In re Gault decision[4] mandates the provision of competent legal representation for juveniles charged with offenses serious enough as to put them at risk of commitment to incarceration. This is universally enforced in the land, with extremely rare violations.

As to "4": Not only does every patrol officer now have on his person a card with the "Miranda Warnings," but all police, and the public as well, have been well rehearsed in their lines: "You have the right to remain silent . . ."

Video cameras maintain a vigil over many formal police interrogations, and there are very few shocking instances of police brutality in station houses, such as was common a generation or so ago.

As to "5": Regarding punishment, we have developed a very non-punishing justice system. In fact, society itself, and the public media, in some respects have shown great unhappiness with that fact. Repeatedly, public surveys have supported a more punitive approach to crime and criminals, even to capital punishment.[5]

A New Problem.

The list clearly shows that the major problems that were with the operations of justice system as it was a generation ago, if not completely resolved, no longer pinch the public nerve as poignantly as a new and pressing concern: The increased need and demand for better protection from crime.

It is not that there are no complaints about the justice system now. But in a relatively short span of time we ameliorated in large part the routine workings of the criminal justice system. We still have instances of the old type, but they are exceptions, and properly receive the condemnation of the entire country, on the relatively few occasions that they do occur, at least in comparison with the past.

Was This An Exchange of One Set of Problems for Another?

The question remains, in doing so have we merely changed one problem for another. . . . or for a complete set of other problems? A subsidiary question comes up, too: Is there a *relation between the way we solved the old problems and our new problem with crime?* Were the old problems not so bad as the new? Did those old ways of doing things, in some way, prevent crime?

Our problems today have to do with the need for public protection from crime, committed by youths alienated from all submission to public weal or zeal.

Legal representation for the accused is guaranteed today by an institutionalized defense counsel system that in the dangerous urban areas is often judged to surpass the competence of the prosecution. Customarily they receive a higher salary than the prosecution, and turnover is less, thus the more experienced attorneys defend the accused in a system that has increasingly become too complex for a young lawyer just out of law school. It takes experience, talent, and time, before a youngster newly admitted to the bar can reach his full potential as a trial lawyer. The prosecutor's office is often the first job of a new lawyer. Many feel it necessary to gain trial experience before looking for another, better paying position, with a large private firm, or going out on their own.

Legal representation for poor defendants, a generation ago, was pitifully lacking in skill and dedication, compared with the present day. Public legal defenders, as a group, exhibit more more competetence, and more availability than ever before. No longer do judges throw cases to worn-out hacks, lounging about the court room, waiting for a quick cash fee, easily earned by pleading a beaten, cowed client, "guilty, as charged, your Honor, with a plea for mitigation of punishment."

Now, the defense lawyers we see are energetic and courageous in defense of the most obdurate and confirmed offenders, as well sympathetic and supportive to clients who are crime novices, caught up for the first time in the web of the law.

In fact, some have accused the new justice system of going overboard in fiercely defending the undeserving, and being excessive in providing aid they do not merit.[6]

Discovery proceedings are available without charge to the client of a Public Defender. Paid for by the taxpayers, they are extremely expensive, at an average cost of more than five dollars per page of deposition. The average taxpayer could not afford as extensive a discovery process as he makes available for every indigent criminal, however vicious and degenerate he may be.

Additionally, public defenders have much the same power to investigate as do prosecutors. The person of average income, if arrested and charged with crime, would find that the services of the public defender are not available to him. He would have to pay exorbitant fees for private investigators to gather the evidence necessary for his case. The fees are calculated at a substantial per diem rate, plus generous expenses. It is unlikely that the lawyer the average taxpayer could afford would be as familiar with the courts and criminal procedure as the public defender counsel assigned to guard the interests of the indigent accused. Nor is it likely that he would have the backup office and clerical staff available to the Public Defender.

It's All Part of a Game.

Thieves and muggers know well the many resources and benefits available to them. They are aided in locating them, and they use them to the hilt. It has been charged[7] that we have permitted the greatest machinery in defense of liberty ever devised, the adversary system, to become a game that empties the public coffers, and provides macabre sport to the direct participants:[8]

> If you do get busted, don't panic. You will be out in several hours. The juvenile justice system is such that you will not be held for very long.

The above is from an instruction manual issued by social workers to a gang of 75 Brooklyn teenagers who take buses to shoplift at suburban malls.[9]

Perhaps the most significant thing about this item is that it was prominently republished on a page of cartoons with other peccadilloes, in a national news weekly magazine.[10] Everyone knows that this goes on. Criminals, defense lawyers, and many prosecutors laugh embarrassedly, coconspirators, all. Nobody does anything about it.

The New Oppressors.

Why do we do nothing about it? Is it because we feel that *anything* done to sustain the morale of kids charged with crime is acceptable as a humanitarian gesture? But these kids are acknowledged criminals, some of them the subject of other news and feature stories detailing their *modus operandi*, their tricks with burglar tools, and disguises.[11]

One effective device they use is to shoplift, or purchase with loot, two-colored reversible windbreakers. They wear the garment while on a caper. Immediately afterwards they slip off the garment, turn it inside out, and put it on again. Dressed in another color, harder to identify, they skip happily away, their escape made good. On their sorties, they chortle enthusiastically as they patrol for targets of opportunity, like Robin Hood's merry highwaymen, but they do not give to the poor, nor do they spare damsels in distress. They do not fight against an oppressive king or sheriff. They are the oppressors themselves. They mug oldsters, terrorize storekeepers, and rape girls, with music, sometimes from their "ghetto-blasters," but without the color and romance of *West Side Story*.

Conspirators Against Youth.

Is it proper "social work" to assist them in their depredations? Is it humanitarianism to sustain the morale of such children? Most behavioral scientists would agree it is a disservice to them, in the long run. But our consent to this careless waste of youth-potential is proof we all are truly coconspirators in our own mutual destruction. For these youngsters do grow up to be killers.

The case of Robert Excell White, called "Excell the Executioner," by law officers who had evidence that he murdered four men just to know what it felt like to kill, is instructive in the same vein.

After a long career as a juvenile delinquent, Excell the Executioner was convicted of a killing. After all procedural delays and rights to the accused were provided, he was sent to death row for the last mile before delayed justice was to prevail.

There were, however, more delays. After twelve long years on death row, the court ordered retrial. There seems to be no question that Excell did commit murder. Do the procedural delays comfort idealogues or the convicted criminals, or does it make victims of the convicts? Do we really want to torture convicts and public with such dissembling. It titillates the media, and the fringe group of scandal sheet readers who enjoy the struggles of the system.[12]

Is there a parallel with our three-year political campaigns for president, compared with England's legal limit of four weeks for a campaign? "Why not have do and be done with it!" say some authorities.[13] Certainly whatever deterrent effect the apprehension and conviction of Excell the

Executioner had was dissipated long before the tenth year, ... or the fifth year, for that matter.

There is no need to stretch out the agony for defendants and for public the way we do.

Artistic License ... and "Heightened Reality."

Artistic license to heighten reality is an accepted technique in all communication. Mr. Steve Horn, the brilliant director who made the "Reach Out and Touch Someone," commercials for AT&T, explained his art.[14]

"In any medium, including newspapers," he says, "the truth is altered. "Everything is a lie. You can't give the truth ... I can't give the truth ... So what I do, I do what I do best, so I make it look good. I try to make it look dramatic and heroic ... "[15]

Continuing, Mr. Horn said, "Heightening reality makes things come across a little better. I think it helps to make it more *real* more emotional."

Horn is not embarrassed by his use of artisic license. That's just the point, for this approach, attitude and method is not unique with Mr. Horn. It's just that he phrases it so well. It reveals the tenuousness of the link from fact to message, in modern communication.

Facts are too simple, the boring reality used merely as a take-off point. From there we mold a new creation: the artistic reality of the fact.

Now, though the phrase uses the word "fact," it has no real relation to those cold, sober details of life itself. This is poetry we speak. That is to say, it reaches for a "higher" truth. Perhaps, more honestly said, for an emotional impression or impact.

Admirable as it is in ingenuity, and powerful in influence on its human subjects, it is revealed as often completely confused with the foundation stones of its starting point.

Less charitably stated, "The information we receive is predicated on the calculated fraud of 'heightened reality.' "

Grant us the artistic license to "heighten reality" and we can go a long distance away from the objective truth of the fact-message. To instigate emotion becomes the prime purpose. With emotion comes "interest," for without emotion there is little interest. If we are interested we can be influenced.

There remains the key query: Influenced to what end? Certainly not to appreciate the truth of the original message. For that was stained, and washed away long before, when the "heightening process" began.

Often we do not know of this process at the time we receive the message or see the presentation. If we do know of it, we forget it, for the only the heightened image is before us. It commands our attention. Clothed in its emotional ambience, of course, we accept the image as the reality. One of the heightened-realities we have come to accept is: That this is a violent crime-ridden society. A further heightened reality which immediately follows is: That because this is a violent crime-ridden society, we must accept it. To refuse to so accept, would be merely deceiving ourselves.

With image-realities all around us, in every medium of communication, our perceptions are overloaded. We succumb, to the image as reality, we no longer perceive that it is all really what behavioral scientists call a "construct." Finally, we accept the "heightened reality" as truth itself. We also accept the construct, that there is nothing we can do about it.

"There Is Nothing We Can Do About Crime."

Among the heightened-realities that we accept almost without question is: "There is nothing we can do about crime, in the long run." This is the doctrinal belief that there is no real protection from crime. We have all come to believe this utterly preposterous credo.

It is all a part of the "artistic license," with which the entire process commenced. Originating in a desire to convey information in an interesting way, to dramatize it, crime stories have come to be accepted as current wisdom. We have gone from artistic license to images, from metaphor to melodrama. Admittedly, the images are often of compelling interest. However, when they masquerade as facts, conclusions, or acceptable doctrines of faith, they are frauds.

Simply stated: *Images are not reality!*

Gatekeepers of Information.

The emotional images and symbolism that have persuaded us that there is no protection from crime come from somewhere. They arrive as communications, and their sources are easily identified. Some researchers in communication have called these sources, "gatekeepers," of information. Who are they?

For television, one of the important gatekeepers is the Ad Council—"it tells America what is right and wrong."[16]

"The Ad Council is a collective of executives from the big business branch of advertising agencies, the networks, and large corporate advertisers. Naturally they are concerned with profits. There is nothing wrong with that, but it certainly has an influence on the tenor of their activities. Thus the censorship and control of the symbolic heightened realities we see are motivated by emotions and beliefs that underwrite that purpose."

Advertising codes are prepared and used as standards to measure advertising, commercials, and, inevitably to a large degree, constrain the artisitic creations which attract clients, readers, and viewers.

Implementation is performed by copy and script writers, producers, directors, and newscasters. Rarely do any of these individuals have purposes other than those of the Ad Council or its executives. They are product of the same beliefs and attitudes. They, as we, are all trying to make a living. That is simple economic reality—the real kind.

Images and Realities.

In this view of heightened reality, our American system is not discriminatory, racist, or inept in dealing with crime and violence, except in minor instances, which are thoroughly scorned. The heightened reality perceived, and transmitted, is that the system simply asks that everyone play by the rules: acquire an education, get a job, buy lots of nice things, and enjoy being an American.

As to racism, the image-reality messages say racism is bad, but only bad people think it, or do it. Almost invariably in the narrative-messages, and shows, racists get their come-uppance. Upon the defeat of the rogue racist, our world appears whole again.

As to dealing with crime and violence. The heightened-reality stories show us that crime is done by individuals, and those individuals are quite unpleasant people, who usually practice great violence, and are punished by circumstance or an appropriate hero before the final fadeout. In the odd chance that the story admits of failure in this, we all feel a vague uneasiness. The story doesn't end right!

Nevertheless, all the above is a charade, isn't it? What is left out might be summarized as follows:

As to discrimination against poor children: The system does not arrange things so that children are taught to be frugal and prudent with money they earn. Children do not absorb into their personality an acceptance of monotonous tasks, and delayed gratification as an acceptable and natural part of life.

Just those two sentences describe what would be a route to escape from the ghetto and its violence.

As to racism, the truth of the matter is that we are, as individuals, not only racist, but quite manic in our stereotyping of every aspect which distinguishes ourselves, and "our people" from others. As groups form, the same phenomenon is merely magnified.

As to dealing with crime and violence: The symbols presented by our communication channels, through the Ad Council and other gatekeepers simply do not send the message that:

1. Crime is almost completely suppressible by force applied quickly and firmly to the criminal violent.

2. Crime is almost completely suppressible by early indoctrination by well-known, loving techniques that operate from the second year onward to age fifteen.

There you have the challenge. Protection from crime is available, but at a price. It is a price we should be willing to pay gladly.

The power that is needed to "keep them in awe," in a Hobbesian sense is constitutional, and completely in keeping with the American Dream, without legal or practical bar. In fact, the method would assist quicker, earlier, and easier accomplishment of the American Dream.

Chapter 20

TO BE A MINORITY

*"It is the minority that have stood in the van
of every moral conflict and achieved
all that is noble in the history of the world."*

John Bartholomew Gough

At one time to be a minority in this country meant that you were expected to be meek, humble, and a couple of other words meaning you were not very important. That is no longer true.

The Majority.

The majority now are thought to be not very important. As such they are not newsworthy. In times past, the heroes of this country almost always were representatives of the majority. In those days that was an impressive position, with prestige and what is now called panache. The panache is all possessed by the minorities now. And there are so many of them!

Old Heroes Fade Away.

We have been the recipients of a great deal of revisionist history, and investigative reporting. Every day sees another hero cut down to less than human dimension. Unfortunately, we don't feel any the better for it. We miss our heroes. They were the respository of our conscience; they gave us peace of mind.

It affects our feeling of stability when the spot newsbreaks on television crash another contemporary hero for us. Presidents and presidential contenders bite the dust. It's open season on Senators and Congressmen. We are used to media stars being put in the pokey for drug possession, assault, and worse. But we are not happy about it.

Regularly, even the old-time heroes are having their reputations shattered, and the shards cut us painfully. Fawn Brodie's revelation[1] that the great hero of political liberals, President Thomas Jefferson, kept a black girl closely confined to his personal service was shocking. The revelation that she was literally what another generation called a love-slave, did not soften the blow. It certainly put a cloud on the great repute that surrounded the sage of Monticello. His magnificent work on behalf of the Revolution of 1776, and for the nascent United States, has lost its pristine aura. Feet of clay, indeed! Jefferson's previously widely reported graciousness for freeing his slaves, has lost whatever credit it gave to the luster of his name. Today, it is emphasized that this was after his death, as a near bankrupt, despite the free labor they had given him for all their lives. In a word, he exploited them as long as he could — while he was alive.

It made many suspicious of George Washington's similar largesse in freeing his slaves, by will, after death. Most scholars have stayed away from that one, for sentiment's sake, one presumes. Washington, never-theless, has had his detractors.[2]

We are treated to a long list of Washington's peccadilloes, an assorted variety of scandalous revelations.[3] One that unwillingly comes to mind is a revisionist report asserting that Washington had an exceptionally heavy hand on his expense account, to the dismay of the Continental Congress. And to the dismay of all of us who learned at our father's knee to worship his name, his life and meaning as the Father of His Country. One hopes that the cherry tree story will not be taken from us. At least we can cherish his boyish honesty.

There are many old and new heroes that have bit the dust of revisionist history, but there is no need to dwell on that at this time. We turn, now, to the revisionist allegation that minorities are members of a prestigious and privileged class.

Privileged Minorities.

It hasn't reached the stage of, a breathless, awed, "Oh, he's a minority! Oh, my!"

It's more of a case of subvocal thinking, "Aw, he's a minority. I better be careful of what I say."

"If he pushes past you at the ticket window of the ball park, better let him get to the seat first."

"In schools, at all levels, if a minority-child's answer to a school question is almost, but not quite correct, give him the benefit of the doubt."

"On the job, if we don't have an employee of that minority, we better hire the guy."

Thus runs the plaint of the unregenerate. The "heightened reality" of the complaints. The unadorned, "unheightened" fact is quite different. For intolerance still lives, along with race hate, in localized places, on both sides.

There are white bridge clubs, and black bridge clubs . . . but it is almost impossible to find an integrated black and white bridge club. A white family's friends are almost invariably white. A black family has only blacks to call friends. Not even churches show much of the integration for which a generation has fought. Hallelujah, there is progress, but not much of it.

The facts reveal continued envy and resentment as affirmative action assistance is given to specified, politically designated groups. The representatives of those who desire such aid, call this resentment "racist," and exhibit their own racism. Rebuttal by the majority is a new response of racism, with some allegedly factual research claimed as foundation for the charge that affirmative action does not perform the function for which it was designed.[4]

Alleged Dysfunctions of Unearned Aid.

This is not something that's talked about frequently. It is there, nevertheless, lambently suspicious, as it were. There is no sustaining laboratory-type research, just some judgments by authorities who command an audience.

One of these conclusions is that money rewards buy neither loyalty nor submission; neither relief from riots, or from citizen disaffection.

When one thinks about it, we should not expect money to buy those things from free Americans.

Another finding is that after a minority has been given the opportunity to perform — such as affirmative action opening of a job opportunity — further aid after that may be dysfunctional.[5]

Some commentators charge unearned assistance appears to suppress efforts to maintain high-level performance. Perhaps even more significantly, the desire to improve performance, it is alleged, may virtually disappear.

There are more judgments made by investigators and practitioners:[6] Teacher time and effort is not the critical variable politicians and community leaders believe, in improving pupil performance. The more time teachers lavish on their pupils, the more the teachers tends to do their work, — and the students let them do it. It was observed that students became experts at cutting corners. That becomes the game to play. In one study, it was found that the students would provide only the minimum, "half-assed job" of study and schoolwork.

The Super-Ethnics.[7]

Some minorities demonstrate amazing diligence in school studies.[8] These Asian and Southeast Asian ethnic and cultural groups show strong family support of education, and business, as a route toward upward mobility. Once again we find present the triple-play toward upward mobility in America: Strong families, self-discipline, and desire for self-improvement by education and savings.[9]

It is important to note, that these super-performers are not born into privilege. Their families have not brought either wealth or education from their country of origin. On the contrary, most arrived in the United States without any financial resources whatever. Many had minimal formal education before becoming refugees.

In school they earn outstanding grades and scholarships. After entering the job market, the super ethnics earn incomes significantly higher than the average American, and grossly higher than other ethnic minorities, all of whom are below average in annual income.

Crime and Income.

All low-income people, majority or minority, are the core group of those who resolve issues with force and violence in the United States. This statistical correlation has incited the often stated fraudulent wisdom, "Poverty causes crime."[10]

The statistical correlation is more correctly interpreted: Poverty and crime appear together in the same individuals to a high degree. To claim one causes the other is an unjustified inference.

In fact, the mathematics involved would equally sustain the reverse comment: "Crime causes poverty."

If there is any real "causation" involved, long-time observers of the crime scene are tempted to say the latter is closer to the truth. Their position is: A youth who spends some of his time waiting for a score, wasting any proceeds on drugs and consumer goods, and spending all the rest of the years of his life sitting in a prison, is necessarily poor. The super ethnics spend all that time working, saving, and investing. That program necessarily ends in riches.

If there is any insight in this comment, it would appear that low income is not to be corrected by any of the traditional approaches. They just have not worked. We can list the failed programs: crime prevention, classes in work-skills, make-work jobs, open college enrollment, food stamps, aid to dependent children. None of them dilute the despair and ennui of the ghetto teenager.

The missing ingredient is the lack of the kind of inner motivation, home-built by the families of the super ethnics.

Low School Performance.

When low performers in school are given projects that come close to issues already of concern to them, they do demonstrate concentrated effort, give time to these projects, and demand less of the teacher.

That has been the basic principle, following John Dewey's philosophy, of structuring school projects around the child. The teacher's task becomes: "Find something to interest the children on the basis of their existing interest structure."

No doubt it is better to have the child interested in school work, rather than to become an early dropout. But we must remember that school must reach past keeping them interested to keep them busy. Mere "makework" without real-life value is soon discovered to lack any real point.

Could not the time spent be used to learn a wealth-producing skill that would provide present earning power, and also lay a foundation for even higher capacity?

Constructing an individual personal family tree has been typical of the kind of project that captured a sense of personal responsibility in many pupils in at least one research instructor's class. Another way of putting it is that the work demanded had to be made a high personal priority. Otherwise, in the words of some of the teachers, they "feared the project would crash."

That comment, however, is circular in reasoning and conclusion. The teachers' research simply came to the same conclusion Benjamin Franklin did, "Tell me and I forget. Teach me and I remember. Involve me and I learn." True, but trite.

It is easy to appreciate the researchers' good intentions. But that is a trap to clear thinking. To praise a result for the "good intentions," of the effort, is to beg off the hard reality that the only thing that matters is: results.

These well-intentioned teachers, instead of controlling the children, were controlled by them. Instead of creating motivation for *useful* work, the children created motivation for the teacher to follow the child.

The "experiment" was productive of no worthy end other than to encourage submission to childrens' goals.

There's really not much use for such skills as may be learned in writing out the names and relationships of one's ancestors. Uncharitable, but true.

The objection immediately arises: How, indeed, can a teacher involve a recalcitrant pupil, if not to start with what the child wants?.... And, then, ever so gradually, to bend that interest toward more useful skills.

Perhaps there is at least one answer in Samuel Johnson's off-hand comment: "When a man is to hang in the morning, it wonderfully concentrates his mind."

Basing Theories on Empirical Findings.

Some psychologists confronted by youthful violent criminals have reached for dramatic, even fanciful theories. They treat us to hypotheses of a primal instinct for aggression, a genetic flaw, a crashing traumatic event, or a "lurking Oedipal complex."

Gerald R. Patterson and colleagues at the Oregon Social Learning Center have delved elsewhere.[11] Their observations summarized in specific findings indicate that what is crucial is *the way parents define, monitor and control the behavior of their children in routine settings.* Simply put: "Coercive family processes," come to define the future behavior of children.

Avoiding cliches such as recommending love instead of punishment, Patterson and a growing following find violent adults are merely violent children grown up. Further, that violent children are the product of a socialization process which is carried out by reflex displays by family members, particularly the parents, of irritation, interest, disinterest, attention, approval or disapproval of the child's activities.

After the study, a program of reeducation, in the nature of treatment at the Oregon Social Learning Center followed. Objectives were clearly set forth: They proposed to try to teach troubled parents how to establish clear rules, monitor behavior, and make rewards of supportive and pleasant approval, contingent on good behavior.

The parents were taught to respond to a child's bad behavior with prompt and consistent application of minor punishments, such as "time-out" of five minutes of seclusion, without scolding or long lectures.

A difficult problem was, as one would expect, encountered when the parents themselves were violent or recalcitrant or otherwise unmotivated. Often they put their own convictions about how to raise children far above the innovations to which they were introduced.

A pervading ethic of, "Sparing the rod will spoil the child," was one of the more easily identified obstacles to learning the new techniques of child-raising. There were many other reasons why parent-training proved to be almost a difficult as child-training.[12]

Among those reasons, one of the few of which the researchers came to be quite convinced was simple parental hostility. Often this was the same reason for the child's lack of performance. Hostility to the teaching situation, the school, the neighborhood community, the city, and things and people in general, may be the critically relevant variable, was the thought of this group of investigators and teachers.

If so, that may be the most difficult of the problems in teaching children nonviolence and success in school and later life. Hostility has been noted as a continuing characteristic with the lowest performing minorities.

At this point, no solution has been discovered. Although there has been great material progress made by educated blacks, and Chicanos, as they have moved up the income-scale, their urge toward education has not inspired most of the other poor whites, blacks, and Chicanos to do the same.

Have we created a system wherein to be a member of a poor minority is almost to mandate hostility to "the system." That would be much to be deplored. For despite the grand political promises of the past, present, and undoubtedly the future, in our type of economy there will always be a spread of incomes along a continuum. Some will have higher incomes than others, and that's the "good" side, but the obverse is statistically, and practically just as true: some will have lower incomes than others. Those people will always be called, "poor." In a system such as ours, is it possible to have a social class that is "poor" but remains happy, or at least satisfied? It appears unlikely.

We have discovered no credible solution or program that addresses the basic dynamics involved. The approach that is being tried with most promise is to organize to form bases of political power. What happens when organizations are based on poverty? What happens when organizations are based on race? What happens when a member of a minority refuses to organize? We consider these questions in the next chapter.

Chapter 21

NOT TO BE COUNTED

I count myself in nothing . . . "

Shakespeare

Bureaucracy Replaces Democracy.

The bureaucratic ways we have gone about dealing with violence and crime have restricted our choices. Everyone, in every developed country, has adapted his way of thinking to the bureaucratic system in almost every field of life, from administration to politics, from justice to war. Since we are primarily interested in deadly force, let us consider the way we fall into military conflict, in the hope that it will reveal how we bureaucratically fall into deadly policies.

We have lately been presented with a plethora of films, books, and articles on the fine points of killing and being killed in the jungles of Viet Nam. They all take that war as a given fact, and display the tactics, techniques, and consequences. Rarely are we prompted to look back to the times *before* the killing in Southeast Asia started. Let us do so now. How did we get into that war?

However we view the propriety of our actions before or during the war, it must be remembered that it occurred because this great nation slowly slid into that bloody unwanted conflict through reams of memoranda prepared by anonymous government and military bureaucrats. The alleged monopoly of crucial and secret information in the bureaucracy was touted as justification for insistence that only the bureaucrats knew the truth of the data, therefore only they could draw valid conclusions.[2] We discovered, later, that they had no essential truth and no validity,[3] except for body counts.

Some things, however, are not to be counted. Counting, a distinctly bureaucratic function, distracted from what was really important.

We have recently been treated to the spectacle of the bureaucracy of

190

the National Security Agency coöpting our foreign policy regarding both the Middle-East and Central America by means of the secrecy to which bureaucracy is prone, as well as the compartmentalization and isolation of decision-making facilitated by bureaucracy, all leading to "absurd" conclusions, programs, and consequences.

Bureaucratization not only clogs up the movement of truthful unbiased information, it tends to falsify the data itself.[4] In any case, counting data does not confer relevance or validity on the data.

Bureaucracy is portentous. It counts the men under arms we have, the money and weapons we have available. The bureaucracy impresses itself. Since the bureaucrats are impressed, everyone else, they judge, should be impressed, too. They sent our Marines to "keep peace" in Lebanon, but the terrorists were not impressed, and bombed them to death.

That is history, and the history of our dealing with domestic deadly force is not much different. Not to learn that history lesson is not to learn from our mistakes.

We count criminals but do not understand them. We count crimes but don't understand the personal dynamics or psychology of those who commit crime.

Thus we have often overlooked what is relevant, with the consequence that we have failed to see what was really going on, and what could really be done, or would be impossible to do. One is impelled to speculate that if Thomas Edison had been working for a government bureaucracy he would not have invented the light bulb. He'd have made a bigger candle. Regarding issues related to deadly force perhaps the following is acceptable reasoning by analogy:

"Is He Sane Enough To Die?"

So reads a headline in a contemporary news magazine.[5]

The people who wrote the article are concerned because, if a convicted criminal is insane he cannot be executed. This is so in virtually every state with capital punishment on its books.

Originally the concern was founded on religion. The prevailing religion presumed that since a madman could not make his peace with God, executing him would be a sentence to eternal hell.

Lifting our eyes from this Christian premise: Isn't this an establishment of religion in our criminal law, in defiance of the First Amendment? Recall the phrase: " . . . shall make no law respecting an establishment of religion . . . " Every state, as well as the federal government claims to be bound by the substance of this bar against promoting religious practice.

We make here no statement against religion. We merely comment about what is in the Constitution, and how channeled our thinking can be when we do not examine our premises, and do not even perceive the conflicts between them.

The nation can refuse to execute madmen, merely by passing a law so declaring. But the reason should not, under the Constitution, be by incrementally accepting religious rationale. The Bill of Rights forbids that. The wit of man being what it is, other arguments can be, and have been brought forth to support the thesis against capital punishment. As the Common Law of England developed, Lord Chief Justice Edward Coke in the 17th century rendered his judgment:[6] "Execution of a mad man . . . is a miserable spectacle . . . of extreme inhumanity and cruelty and can be no example to others." The eminent jurist did not feel that way about the execution of sane men, women, or youths.

Most Americans, today, would hold that execution of anyone is a miserable spectacle. But whether it would be a deterrent example to others, is a different issue. According to current polls the current opinion is that capital punishment is quite exemplary to others.[7] Common sense agrees. There is considerable empirical evidence in the literature which is consistent with, and confirms, this judgment.

To return to how bureaucratic, channelling of thought prevents new ideas from being recognized, in this case, the issue of what is best for the country, what is best for the individual or the community in regard to the insanity defense was not considered. The entire issue is narrowed, by confinement to a bureaucratic determination of whether or not the inmate is insane.

The discussion is immediately further narrowed to who decides if the inmate is insane? In many states this judgment is left to the governor, aided by state psychiatrists. This method was endorsed by the United States Supreme Court in the 1950s.

During the last few years, however, death penalty opponents and at least two influential law review articles have called for more punctilious procedures; they want a hearing at which the condemned's lawyer can present evidence and cross-examine the state's experts.

In one such examination, the inmate mailed letters to lawyers and journalists stating that his family was being held hostage in the prison, and that he was getting secret messages from a radio station. Two defense psychiatrists concluded that the inmate was a "paranoid schizophrenic who could not understand why the death penalty was being imposed on him." In a criminal law without regard to established religious beliefs, why is that relevant?

For purposes of argument, let us concede that capital punishment is warranted for horrendous crime, proved after a full adversary trial. Now, if we grant that, the provision of another full adversary trial, to determine if punishment should happen, is mindless. It is equally mindless to batter Ted Bundy about the criminal appeals courts for ten years, and at that point send his case back to determine his competency at the time of trial.

It can be nothing but the start of an endless series of adversary actions without ever any clear resolution.

"Insanity at the present time" can save the convicted from punishment, anywhere along the line. With his mind "focused," and his motivation strong, insanity becomes another suit of clothes to be donned when invisibility to the justice system is desired.

The bureaucracies of the executive mansion, the prosecution and the defense counsel haggle over the socially inconsequential, while the issue of whether or not the insanity defense is useful or functional is ignored.

It Was Glorious Then to Be an American.

As is remembered by Constitution "buffs," in 1787 and 1788, James Madison wrote to support the impending vote for the Constitution in the newspapers of the time. Collected with other essays in the Federalist Papers, he warned about the danger to democracy implicit in self-interest groups which he called "factions." He pointed out the dangers involved in either suppressing them, or in submitting to them. His proposed solution for the still unformed United States was to encourage so many factions, that they would balance their interests between them, to the mutual benefit of all.

Already in existence, however, was an indigeneous movement that tended to resolve that problem, in part, although it was not seen as such as clearly as later vision perceived it. This was the New American as has been elsewhere described who lost old allegiances of the land from which he had emigrated, and formed new loyalties devoted to the problems and interests of the conditions in the new land in which he found himself. They had found a unity of purpose in resolutely facing the labor and hazards of making a living in a harsh and dangerous land.

The polarization of war during the Revolution called for these New Americans to even more actively reject the British King. Those who would not, or could not comply were scorned, in some cases tarred and feathered, and pressured to conform to the new loyalty. After the new government was formed, in 1789, many left the country to settle in Canada or return to the England, the mother country.

Those who remained, loudly and fervently proclaimed their loyalty and unity as Americans, with proud celebration of this solidarity at all reasonable, and some unreasonable, occasions. The slogans of the day attest to that: "Give me liberty of give me death!" All other communications available, in print or speech, were supportive of their common quest: Maximum personal liberties against whoever would infringe upon them.

The Fourth of July, was dedicated as a national celebration of the Day of Independence, with torrents of excited speeches, pageants, fireworks, bonfires, parades, and every conceivable type of ceremony.[8] The Glorious Fourth became a national orgy in praise and honor of the idea of America and Americans, insistently unique, they claimed, in their devotion to liberty and Americanism.

This passion continued for over a hundred years. As late as the 1920's each year there were regularly Fourth of July bonfires in the streets of New York City that commenced with weeks-long piling of wood and other combustibles in the street, in the center of a block of tenements, that would often reach above the third story. Many an old piano was tossed out the windows onto the pile, mattresses, old wagons, even telegraph poles and railroad ties added to the mass.

There were too many such bonfires prepared for the police to attempt to remove them all. The sites were prepared from the south end of Manhattan Island, at Battery Park, to Harlem Heights. Besides, how could anyone, certainly not a loyal American, object to the planned celebrations?

At 12:01 A.M. on the Fourth, to the accompaniment of rattling gunfire, and great hurrahs, the giant piles would be touched off. The flames quickly would climb up the great mound, to reach the peak. Pausing to gather force, the flames would then shoot higher than the six and seven story buildings on each side. A grand and inspiring sight indeed to young and old.

Carried away by the excitement of it all, rifles and pistols would be fired with abandon, thankfully, most were fired into the air . . . but not all, of course.

Rockets would go streaming against the sky, crackling fireworks would have the men and children jumping out of the way. The ladies decorously stayed indoors, hanging out of the windows of the tenements on either side. They would join the fun by lighting sparklers, and they would toss the scintillating hot wires toward the bonfire. Falling short, of course, they added to the thrilling hazard of being on the street during a Fourth of July night celebration.

An occasional "bombburster" would sound off like a thunderclap, making everyone jump and laugh. Oh, it was a happy time!

The next day the newspapers would carry the names of the dead and injured. Everybody would shake their heads at the carnage. But that was part of the blood-dedication to America, and its Independence Day. No one could ignore it, no one could fail to be moved. Each and everyone knew he or she was an American and that "there's a hundred million others, like me!" Oh, it was glorious, then, to be counted an American.

There was so much to be rapturous about: Sacred documents, so excellently phrased in the glowing words of our Declaration of Independence and the Bill of Rights. Adventure and fortune was to be found, "Out West." Plenty of work, if one is willing and strong. A growing country, a place to make one's dreams come true.

There was an obverse side to the coin: To refuse to be counted among the Americans was truly to be beyond the pale of society. True, Americanism was an ideology that accepted all who had faith in the promise of the country. But not to have faith . . . to be a communist, an anarchist, a "Wobbly," or "Molly McGuire," was to be scorned, discriminated against, and to be subjected to cruel suspicion and treatment.

The International Workers of the World, an early international labor union was reviled because its initials, I.W.W. were held to stand for, "I Won't Work," with ultimate unfairness descending on two of its members, Sacco and Vanzetti, who were found guilty of charges of bombing and murder in Massachusetts. Years later the charges were revealed to have been groundless.

Yes, not to be counted an American was a dangerous thing.

The Invention of Cultural Pluralism.

In 1915 in *The Nation,* there appeared two articles under the title, "Democracy versus the Melting Pot."

In these articles, Horace Kallen, a Harvard-educated philospher objected to the pressures for "Americanization," He reveled, instead, in the variety and richness of the different cultures of the different races and the hyphenated Americans as they still persisted in particular regions. He praised the tendency of each group to preserve its own language, religion, and communal attitudes.

He did not object to the reading of the bible or other school prayers, but he did object to the school assembly's, "Pledge of Allegiance, . . . and to the Republic for which it stands, one nation, indivisible . . . "

He felt that people wanted to form their own groups, like choosing like, proud of their unique, diverse heritages, whatever they may be. Irish-American, Italian-American, Jewish-American, and others were the tribes he gloried in. Nor was he restricted to these particular congregations. All hyphenated Americans, whoever and whatever they may be, were to be signalized, and honored. Naively, he was sure this activity would result in more and better cooperation between them. His rationale ran like this:

" . . . since individuals are implicated in groups, and since democracy for the individual *must by extension also mean democracy for his group* "[10] (emphasis added).

The Fraud of Cultural Pluralism.

The ineradicable flaw in Kallen's argument was not immediately detected. It implies that a given group as it may exist, is natural, and inevitable. Further, it implies that these groups form without any conscious effort and intention. As if they "just were there," and utterly harmless to others.

Of course, we now know that isn't true. Any group that identifies itself as a group can be the product of intense conscious social interaction, specialized education, and indoctrination. We also know, that each such group not only builds a pattern of integration within, but also often an even stronger pattern of hostility to other groups. That is the nature of the beast of indoctrination.[11] Invariably it is competitive with other doctrines of the same order, with compelling dynamics leaning to hostility toward all opposing doctrines.

The groups so indoctrinated are not designed to honestly and fairly cooperate with other groups — they are designed, and generally function, to compete, combat, and confront other groups (see Appendix B, and citations included).

Horace Kallen compounded his initial error, with promises of a new era of blissful, even heavenly happiness:

> The outlines of a possible great and truly democratic commonwealth become discernable. Its form would be that of the federal republic; its substance a democracy of nationalities, cooperating voluntarily and autonomously through common institutions . . . [12]

Unfortunately, the author propagandized his thesis with great success, inventing the term, "cultural pluralism," which attained great support among powerful opinion-makers, the "gatekeepers," of public information. In article after article Kallen pressed the theme of cultural pluralism at the New School for Social Research for the next forty-five years. Long before then, others had taken up the crusade as a doctrinal approach to solving most of the problems of crime and delinquency in the cities.

Particularly since World War II, cultural pluralism as a concept has worked its way into the imagery and value system of leaders in ethnic communities and specialists in intergroup relations.[13] No longer does anyone speak of assimilation or Americanization. Little analytical attention has been given to the dark meanings or brooding consequences of cultural pluralism. Nor have social scientists or practitioners of intergroup relations come to fully understand, "its nature and relevance for a modern industrialized society, and its implications for problems of prejudice and discrimination."[14]

The Melting Pot Was Democracy.

The assimilation of individuals, or, to use the more popular term today, to *integrate* individuals into a cooperative, cohesive, close-knit society can be analyzed into a number of distinguishable concepts, although there is much overlapping of patterns and ideas.

Assimilation can be seen as of at least two quite separate types: 1. Behavioral 2. Structural

Behavioral assimilation refers to the absorption of the cultural behavior patterns of the "host" society, with, at the same time, some modification of the behavioral patterns of the host as well.

Structural assimilation is the entrance of a new group into jobs, civic life, institutional activities, and formal associations of the host.

The first type frequently develops what sociologists call primary groups.

"Primary group" is the name given to the warm, intimate personal assemblies composed of people who come together for the simple pleasures of associating with each other. Examples are families; friends; neighbors, if they are frequently seen, and enjoyed. In this group, too, are social cliques and arrangements, which grow into personal friendship patterns, and home visits. This would include many whose first encounter may be joining in common recreation and worship patterns.

Structural assimilation, however, less frequently develops into a primary group relationship. Often the relationships will remain impersonal, and, in the legal phrase, "at arm's length." Often these associations are identifiable as having contractual relationships which demand communication and interaction. Such relationships may continue for many years without developing primary-type, warm, personal relations. This has been the case in the United States. Whatever unifying forces have existed up to the middle of this century, they have not overcome old barriers of ethnicity, religion, or race.

It need not have been so, if the example of the Caribbean is taken as a model. To a lesser degree in Central and South America, there has been some assimilation on both behavioral and structural levels.

In the United States, on the other hand, there exists a large body of informal and formal sanctions which permits, encourages, and often mandates members of ethnic or religious groups to remain within the confines of that ethnicity and that religion for most, if not all, of their primary relationships, and many of their secondary relationships for their entire life.

As if that weren't enough to divide society, we, as do other countries, recognize social class barriers between high, middle, and lower income levels.

Fortunately, despite the warnings of Marx, Engels, and Lenin, deadly force has not tended to be used by any of these contained groups in the United States, in any sustained way.

No specific group has found themselves so harrassed, and so imbued with common loyalty as to turn to violence against their tormentors. We cannot identify the violent in our society so easily as to ascribe them to any identifiable group. They are not to be counted. At least not so easily.

However, the violent children that are the progenitors of violent men, tend to be found among the poor and lowest classes of our society, whether white, black, Hispanic, or other. These children of poor parents, early on develop a functional personal doctrine of believing in the effectiveness of violence, and develop a personality that is easily provoked to violence. It has been seen as a conditioned, learned response of acting out violent solutions to personal problems. As troublesome as these people are, however, they constitute a relatively small percentage of our population.

In our land we have been saved the kind of massive, revolutionary class violence, one might have expected, in view of the great social distance between our richest and our poorest. In a more homogeneous population such as was Russia, or France at the time of their revolutions, it was easier to draw a distinct line between rich and poor. In America the line is indistinct, for we latch onto other differences that drain off economic class hostility, into other channels. We are obsessed with race, ethnic, and religious differences.

We have, however, institutionalized certain controls over manifestations of violence based on these hostilities: Blandness is the approved response. We are encouraged to suppress all large-group hostilities, to be released as individual "cases or controversies," dealt with administratively, or, as a last resort, the courts. The rest of us are neutralized in our homes by symbolic television violence, and give-away shows reminiscent of ancient Rome's bread and circuses.

We do not focus on economic class differences in this country, as a rule. Most of us proclaim "middle class" aspirations. Our violence is generally our individual or perhaps, local gang response to our life situation. The great number of differences of which we are aware bar us from organizing into the violent associations which rent post-World War I Germany, post-World War II Africa and Southeast Asia.

Thus organized violence has not affected the total amount of violence in our society up to this date. We have too many groups, working at cross purposes to develop massed violence, except for the relatively short period of mass protest against the Viet Nam conflict. Even the violence was not anything at all like the continuing presence in other countries. The Black Panthers disappeared, the Students for a Democratic Society petered out, all we have left are a few Aryan, Klan, or Nationalist organizations with only nominal membership, and little actual violent activity.

There is always the possibility that there are more such groups that are not being counted and identified, which thus tends to diffuse official perception of potential violence and disorganizes any concerted attempt to deal more directly with the problem.

All of that, however, is a negative way of dealing with the problem of violence. Granted, we could have had a higher level of violence, had we been victims to terrorist or militant organizations operating in the land. We are, for the most part, concerned with the level of disorganized violence that comes from known nascent criminal activity, alarms our citizenry and is not being dealt with effectively.

That can be changed, it is submitted, if we go about it with clearer eyes than heretofore. Part Five, following, is devoted to tracing the path toward real personal liberty, and freedom from deadly force.

PART FIVE
TOWARD REAL PERSONAL LIBERTY

Chapter 22

A LESS DEADLY SOCIETY

"Morality, thou deadly bane,
Thy tens o' thousands thou has slain!"

Robert Burns

We Need Mystery In Our Lives.

Leonard Bernstein commented that we are all still romantics at heart.[1] For romantics return to us the mysterious moon which science tried to take away from our dream of love, and make just another airport. We want the hypnotic, inscrutable moon to be unattainable, serving only to light up a luminous sky. The sky should symbolize something beyond any conceivable reach. We want love to be profound and transcendent, not a set of therapeutic rules for personal relationships.

We want our ideologies, our faiths, to be mysterious and not completely understandable if we are to cleave to them with all our might and yearning. If they are not, we tend to deride them.

"Honesty is the best policy," is denied by life itself, as we learn about the scams on Wall Street, and 100 million dollars fines that are paid cheerfully out of the proceeds of the loot.[2] That, to be fair, is only one out of hundreds of reported instances of profiteering, peculation and pelf. Any American who is not living in a glass bowl has lived as many private experiences of skimming and scamming as are reported.

Black Is White; Virtue Is Vice.

The movies teach us that driving carefully is wimpy, for we see that cars can career through urban streets, pedestrians will leap wildly to safety, and the car can crash repeatedly into other cars, eventually strike a wall, slide up, go flying through the air to land upside down, a mass of contorted metal and shattered glass. Not to worry. A hand reaches out of the broken window, followed by the unharmed body of a man who rises, brushes himself, and walks away.

Honesty and safety are boring. They are not mysterious. We do not know how to make them a part of an appealing ideology. We don't care.

That, however, is the bray of simpletons. How did we ever get into such a dead-end, "no-win" position?

A Program.

It is time to backtrack, or to move ahead, as you may prefer to call it. As a first step it might be useful to more clearly identify virtue and distinguish it from vice.[3]

Here is one proposal: "Virtue is to assiduously seek what makes us physically and mentally healthy, strong, long-lived, beautiful in a permanent way. Vice is the opposite of virtue: To actively seek sickness, disease, physical and mental decrepitude, weakness, and ugliness is vice."

We must make the virtues more attractive to our young. That way lays our grail. It need not be that difficult, if we use the correct techniques.

It is not enough to preach profit from propriety. We must probe deeper into the psyche of the young, use the appeal of the mysterious.

The ages-old hold of the great religions is founded not only on the proven benefits of adhering to the virtues and practices they preach, but also by the manner of their presentation. Especially their reliance on the mysteries each religion claims as its own.

Acknowledging human inability to reach perfect virtue, they confer upon their adherents forgiveness, and a close-knit, congregation run by authoritarian preachers, who keep their flocks busy forever anxious about their personal salvation.

Using all the techniques described in Appendix A and B, religions and cults have been able to build into the psyches and persona of their penitents, a pervading need for their order and precepts so that even those who, for overpowering reasons leave the fold, do so guiltily, needing something to replace what they've lost.[4]

Today's Program For a Deadly Personality.

We know how the pious priest instructs his peaceful disciples, we now use the obverse side of that coin to form deadly personalities. For a deadly personality is acquired by the same techniques, usually randomly applied without anyone's conscious intention. However, the methods are just as effective, just as binding, to produce either type of personality. Once violent reactions are thoroughly learned when young, as early as three years, strongly ingrained by seven, and ineradicably embedded by thirteen, the main lines of personality are formed. The basic route of where that personality will take the individual is fixed.

What is that route today—for rootless children? One needs a strong stomach to see it and relate it in cold print.

Horrors of violence that used to be only imagined are now daily occurrence. That is the message that is being conveyed to our children. Whatever horror can be imagined is portrayed in convincing dramatic form. Having been seen, talked about, vicariously participated in, no longer is anything is so extreme that it is beyond human perpetration.

Psychiatrist Roderick Anscombe, a teacher at Harvard Medical School reports[5]

> Incest has lost its capacity to shock; studies suggest that one girl in 22 is sexually abused by her father or stepfather before she reaches the age of 18.
>
> A child is beaten unconscious, her arms cut off and left for dead in the desert.
>
> Perhaps it has always been this way and the change is that we know about it. The truth is we are also changing. People are now doing what they had previously thought of doing for one guilty moment before they rejected the possibility of doing it. The exposure given to the molestation of children and the violence against women in the home has turned these private abuses into a public reality.

This behavior has ceased to be extraordinary and becomes a part of everyday life.

> Thus the border between what a person does and what he simply imagines breaks down. Things done personally, actions done in one's presence, events reported in the news media all merge imperceptibly into one. That is reality, but it is not more real than fictional accounts that are no more bizarre, only even more omnipresent, known to others, and accepted by all. We all become monsters hungry for stimulation, like a drug addict we bug out on ever more violence to keep our interest going.

Jaded and unshockable, less intense values lose their meaning to us all. We are no longer mystified or awed. As Dr. Anscombe puts it, "We need secrets, inner sanctums and taboos—otherwise we will be left with nothing but reality."

The pattern of activity that has impelled us to escape magic and mystery has brought us to this impasse of violence with the dark claim that it is really not intended to have that effect. There was no clear target for each event on the path that led us to where we are. It was aimless from the beginning, but it has not been harmless, for what has been harmed has been our entire style of life.

If "aimless" is harmful, presumably we could aim for harmless. . . . or even for the beneficial and therapeutic.

We must be careful, however. Planned economies, and planned societies in general, have not worked so well. We have become rightfully suspicious of central planning. Are there not great hazards in trying to contrive a nondeadly society? Is it not dangerous to control and plan human activity in too detailed a manner?

We examine that question in the next chapter.

Chapter 23

STRATEGIES FOR TYRANNY

"Necessity is the argument of tyrants, it is the creed of slaves."

William Pitt

Mind control is one of the horrors doomsayers warn us against. Their fears are founded on the fact that administrators have many subtle techniques and technologies at their behest.

Managers confess that those powers are available, but they say in extenuation: "There is a crisis of faith in the American System, and a necessity to do something about it."

The Managing of People.

Managers of organizations, public and private, have large discretion in disposing of human and other assets placed under their charge. It is well said that those who have discretion, tend to use that discretion for their own purposes. With all the warnings, one would think that guards have been put up. Well, guards are there, and there is an active claque of government watchers, and corporate warning systems in operation.

Nevertheless, we are on the verge of a strong movement toward corporate mind control by use of the methods used by many cults. Where Werner Erhard and EST left off, other motivational gurus are taking over, to change the way employees think.[2]

As much as 4 billion dollars is estimated to be the amount being spent for better control by corporations of the lives, thoughts, and actions of their people.[3] For more than ten years American management experts have envied the control they saw demonstrated by Japanese companies. The loyalty of the employees, the dedication to solving corporate problems felt by even the lowliest employee, and the quaint singing of company songs every morning in lilting pledges of allegiance to corporate Japan struck envy in the heart of American personnel managers, and chief executive officers.

Traditional Management: Theory X, Adversary Relations.

Traditionally in the United States we have had a managerial style involving adversary relations between workers and management that has been given the name, Theory X. This style of managerial control, relying on reward and punishment, administered in carefully controlled doses, came to be called Theory X when scholars of administration and eminent practitioners started to write about another approach which they imagined might be better.[4]

They objected to the Theory X presumption that people are interested only in their own affairs, not that of the employer. They claimed there was another way to get productive labor out of the employee than to minutely supervise him, instruct him constantly to keep his work up to standards, punish quickly for bad performance.

The defenders of Theory X rested on history and ancient usage. Since before the days of the Pharoahs, it was claimed to be well founded on principles of human behavior and proven by time.

Queried as to why there was so little use in practice of the "reward" part of Theory X, it was explained that reward had to be particularly restricted because of two negative aspects: (A) It caused jealousy among the workers, and (B) It was expensive, and directly attacked the bottom-line of net profit.

As the American version of this approach was effectuated, employers demanded as much control over personnel as could be realized. Unions were discouraged, and when possible, destroyed. Company-controlled unions were substituted, if the semblance of collective bargaining was desired. Company presidents then dealt with union presidents, at favorable terms.

American managers felt that, since they had the responsibility for production and profits, they wanted the power to hire, to fire, and to penalize. They did so, with zest. Labor walked off the job, and from the 1880's on, violence and strikes became synonymous.[5] Literally hundreds of people were killed and injured in violent confrontations between strikers and private guards hired by employers. Property damage in the tens of millions of dollars was estimated.

Angry resentment of men on the job against their employers was a common, almost indigenous condition. Especially was this so in heavy industry, mining, steelmaking, glass and brickmaking, railroad car building. But as long as unemployment rolls were large, workers, even union men, had to submit to harsh employment terms. Dependent on their daily or weekly pay to provide for themselves and their families, an individual worker was without funds to resist, nor could he afford to leave the job.

Later when labor became scarce, workers, especially highly skilled labor, could find jobs easily and leave an employer whose treatment they felt unfair. Workers demanded bonuses for staying in place on the job.

When punishments such as demotion, loss of pay, layoffs, and petty fines were not responded to as hoped by employers, and rewards in the form of bonuses and pay raises became too expensive for management to permit, fringe benefits were offered as bribes. Often they would be deemed attractive by union leaders, who could persuade the members, to accept them in lieu of better pay or shorter hours, while being cheaper for the employer.

When that didn't work, small raises in pay were stretched out over years on the condition of greater productivity. But American productivity in the past twenty years has not kept pace with that of the best of the burgeoning manufacturing industries of the Far East.[6] Not only Japan, but Taiwan, Hong Kong, and Korea seized larger and larger shares of our markets for manufactures for the simple reason that they were able to undersell American products.

America Tries New Methods.

American ingenuity has never been moribund, however, in the face of increasing competition and sluggish productivity growth.[7] As long ago as June, 1903, Frederick Taylor presented his famous paper, "Shop Management," at the Saratoga meeting of the A.S.M.E.[8] which presented in coherent form an attempt at objectively dealing with both men and materials.

Taylor's ideas of "scientific management" as later promoted by himself and others, met with great opposition, much of it because it was presented by "efficiency experts," trained as engineers, primarily interested in time and motion study. There was no equivalent expertise in the human part of the equation.

Theory "Y" the Social Element.

An early acknowledgment of the importance of the people involved in organizations was the reported finding of the Hawthorne Experiments of the Western Electric Company in the 1930's: "That people are important." The experiments continued for a number of years, and the reports on analysis, conclusions, and recommendations spread over several years after that.[9]

There followed many confirming reports and commentaries which declared the importance, not only of the aims, dreams, and qualities of the individual, but also the critical aspects of the social milieu of the work-situation. The reports were widely read, and convinced most of corporate industry of the importance of obtaining and continuing an active interest and cooperation of the people involved in working together. Thus was born Theory "Y," an acknowledgment of the prime importance of the human element in the work situation.

The significance of all this was indelibly emphasized in the late 1930's by new union tactics involving not only primal violence, as before, but actual "sitting-in" and occupying the factories of our largest companies, completely stopping production. This was far more damaging to the corporation than a simple strike which often permitted production to continue, though at higher cost.

Today the importance of the "human" factor in work, worship, and war is undenied. Corporations spend millions trying to reach the inner core of their people's spirit to bring them into a state of personal involvement with the goals and fate of the organization.

Anyone familiar with the history of military discipline and training knows of the storied harsh whippings and punishments given recruits and sailors, as described in the literature. Theory "X" indeed! But the literature also speaks of the dedication of the Spartan hoplites at Thermopylae, the willing self-sacrifice of the Jews of Masada, Russians at Stalingrad, the Kamikaze pilots of the Japanese Navy, and many, many others. . . . all clearly with altruistic devotion to a cause more important than themselves. This is Theory "Y" in full operation.

After Theory "Y."

There followed dozens, if not hundreds of specific programs, allegedly based on a behavioral science which sought to maximize human potential in a form harnessable by leaders and managers. Every few years since then have seen new variations ranging from the inspirational to the kinky. Corporations have tried them all, in a larger or smaller way. While acknowledging the importance of the psychology of the individual, and the social setting in which he was placed, a number of problems and questions were posed.

Encouraging social interaction among workers had many salutary effects in terms of satisfaction and good feelings in that group. There remained, however, the danger that the new groups so formed would combine in opposition to the employer. None wanted to create such a Frankensteinian Monster.

Also, it was discovered, as it was put in Navy terms: A "happy ship" is not necessarily a "taut ship."

That is, the social happiness of the workers did not necessarily include increased, or more efficient production. In fact, on occasion the effect was exactly the reverse. In coping with these problems many experts felt that the type of social-engineering found in Japan, say, in which the worker is inducted into a "family" of workers, with a job guaranteed for life, and with many social amenities on one side, balanced by expectation of lifetime loyalty and selfless dedication to the company was not adapted to the American labor scene. Whereas Sony Corporation employees can seriously commence their working day with a massed singing of the company song, Americans, it was said, are too sophisticated, or perhaps cynical, for that. Also, the obligations on the employer in Japan are enormously greater than in the United States. American executives are not about to commit hari-kiri as did the Japanese, for a costly mistake in management—nor do they want to admit an error by resigning, to remain in debt-servitude for the rest of their professional career, as was done recently by the presidents and chairmen of several Japanese corporations.

Instead a different approach was suggested, from which there are many interesting examples to choose. Pacific Bell, California's largest utility company has undertaken what they call Krone training, as required learning for their 67,000 employees. Motivational gurus have ascended to a higher plane of consciousness of the values of productivity, and intend to drag their disciples up with them. Mysticism is an important part of some of the most successful programs.

The key to the "New Age System" is homogeneity of thought. The theory is that companies whose members agree on fundamental values and norms will be more successful than those who do not.[10]

Programs of this order, which seek to change fundamental attitudes have a variety of names, Breakthrough Learning, Transformational Technologies, Krone training, New Age, and many others. They vary only slightly in their approaches. Some use hypnosis, others use meditation, or encounter groups. Group cohesion, and positive thinking are used by many. Each uses a unique combination of techniques, as preferred by the leading lights of each program.

Attitude Changing, American Style.

Of course, under the name and style of "attitude change," the organized effort to modify personal performance has been known outside of corporate and government circles, in one form or another as long as people have tried to influence other people. The general public has been attracted, from time to time, in cycles of fashions, to try to change their own attitudes, since the inception of the Republic, under various proprietary names and logos.

In the early twenties Emile Coué toured the country preaching his slogan to be used just before falling asleep, and immediately upon waking: "Every day in every way I'm getting better and better!" This was just about as general an approach as could be devised to try to improve one's own performance, emotional attitude, and general success in life. Couéism had great popularity for a few years, then disappeared from the scene, as fads do.

Emphasizing the "importance of attitude" in attaining success has been a part of sales organizations' training programs, since the phrase was discovered. Today in virtually all large corporations, we find that personnel departments and particularly sales organizations have emphasized what they called "attitude." Recently manufacturing supervisors have been faced with declining efficiencies on the assembly line. Thus their attention has been brought anew to attitude change as a possible cure. Today it takes the form of a series of mental exercises. In one recent version, employees:

> ...are taught to think at all times about the "six essentials of organizational health"—expansion, freedom, identity, concentration, order and interaction—and relate them to the demands of the workplace.

Meanwhile, they are asked to examine whether their behaviors are the result of (a) external stimuli, (b) themselves or (c) a "purpose that is beyond self." (The preferred answer is "c.")[11]

In most programs there are many arcane terms providing a secret language for the novitiates to communicate among themselves, keeping outsiders ignorant and distant. "If people speak the same language and approach problems the same way, then, in fact, they'll be coordinated," says management professor Charles O'Reilly of the University of California at Berkeley.[12]

Looking Ahead at "Attitude Change."

Will these methods be successful? Will corporate culture be changed. Will the individuals become coöpted to the company's desires? We do not know, at this point.

What we are sure of is: The effort will cause some change. Much of the change will be in the direction desired, at least temporarily. But some of it will be irrelevant, or even in the opposite direction. Probably it will not be cost-efficient, for many studies show the expenses of change, even when it is beneficial to a corporation, to have been more costly than the benefits obtained were worth.

Additionally, there are complaints that much of the training is harmful, and companies are drawing scorn from outside sources for "brain-washing."

Public utility companies' stockholders and customers are angered by expenses of hundreds of millions of dollars on mind-altering training that must be passed on to the public in their monthly bills.

Many critics oppose the New Age programs on religious grounds, as urging "self-will" rather than God's will. Others complain that it is secular humanism conflicting with the prevailing norms of community.

Defenders of the programs have said, "Companies need to develop a system of beliefs instead of a hierarchy built on carrots and sticks." University researchers, with their penchant for abstracting and categorizing, generally have lauded the move from "Theory X" motivations of punishment and reward, to the newer "Theory Y" motivations attempting to provide "self-realization through work."

That academic rationalization has not been too persuasive to critics, aroused against the use of cult methods of mind control for any purpose.

Companies that have pumped large sums into these programs, however, are unlikely to acknowledge failure.

The issue, while in doubt, has not reached the stage where violence has been resorted to by either side. It has the seeds of violence, nevertheless, if emotions continue to run high.

Chapter 24

STRATEGIES FOR LIBERTY

"Consider your origin; ye were not
formed to live like brutes but to follow
virtue and knowledge."

"The greatest gift . . .
was the freedom of the will."

Dante Alighieri

The Tools of Liberty.

As Tom Paine pointed out, liberty is not handed to anyone[1] it has to be struggled for. Such a struggle calls for not only an attitude of love for liberty, but also the weapons necessary to combat an attempt at despotic action.

We have been called a litigious society, and usually the statement is made in the form of an accusation. There is the obverse side of the coin, however. In a complex social world, it is very difficult to know what is happening that might affect one's health, welfare, or finances, at any given time. Often the awareness of damage does not arrive until after the damage is done. Or there is nothing that can be done by the victim at the time of the injury, and the only recourse available is after the fact, and then perhaps, only in terms of money compensation for the injury.

This appears to have been the motivating force, the dynamics, behind the great upsurge of lawsuits against lawyers, doctors, corporate directors, law enforcement officers, and municipalities in recent years. No longer are people willing to submit under arrogant authority. The force of this moral movement first showed in the expression of anger against the lords of power. Thus the bitter strikes, the bombings, the anarchists from the 1880's to the 1930's. Now they say, "I won't get mad. I'll get even!"

Government and all its agents, as well as professionals, doctors, lawyers, accountants, hospitals and all their employees, have for centuries oper-

215

ated behind walls of secrecy, and immunity. For a combination of reasons, this wall is being broken down. Immunity from responsibility for one's actions is no longer taken for granted. We are reaching for the position that to claim immunity is indecent.

No longer can police officers, in the dead of night so easily trample on the rights of citizens without having to face suit under 42 United States Code, Section 1983, which provides monetary damages for this offense payable by the officer, and his employing municipality. When it costs real money, officer and city official tend to pay attention to the kinds of policies followed, the training and supervision given.

Interestingly the same thing is happening in the corporate field. Not only have consumer-defenders arisen to promote legislation to protect the public from dangerous food, machinery, and polluted environments, but also a new phenomenon is reported: Lawsuit against corporate board members, holding them responsible to shareholders, and even the general public.[2]

At one time, all a director of a large corporation had to do was to "convene once a month, approve whatever the company's CEO wanted, pick up a check, and go off to a convivial round of golf or an elegant meal."[3] Outside board members, like corporate managers are today under pressure from company shareholders. When they come to feel that they have been harmed by what has happened in the boardroom, they sue.

Suits against medical doctors have attained an enormous amount of publicity, with much partisan advertising and publicity being put out, and even more revealing statistical data being unearthed.[4] Without going into the merits of the controversy on either side, the point is that doctors are on notice that patients are willing to sue for money damages for compensation for malpractice and harm done to them. Doctors must diagnose and operate with a thought to the consequence of their actions. No longer can they so easily bury their mistakes. Seen as tools for protection from unwarranted personal violence and deadly force, the revolution in tort law is intriguing.

Patients, clients, shareholders, citizens everywhere have been given new weapons in the decision-law of torts which, while opening us up to the charge of being contentious and quick to sue, is in the last analysis a situation where people who previously had few, if any recourses for hurt, now have remedies. If the remedy is subject to the charge of abuse, the correction is built into the system. We still admire and trust courts and judges more than almost any other institution in our society. After all, a charge of tortious or meretricious acts leading to harm to a patient, still has to be proven in open court.

Thus the strategy of liberty has a new weapon for its arsenal: Money damages for infringement on rights.

It must be understood that this is not to be seen as a source of treasure at the expense of dedicated professionals. No. Proper tort law stands as a bulwark and warning against incompetent or reckless violence against the persons of people who previously had few real remedies.[5]

Naturally, potential defendants race to recreate old immunities, and develop new ones: By-laws to make directors invulnerable to lawsuits, resurrection of sovereign immunity for cities and hospitals, limitation of amount of damages assessable against doctors.[6] But the point has been made: We are reaching for more civilized ways of responding to attacks on us as individuals. It is suggested that civil suit for damages caused by personal violence is certainly less violent than violence in return.

Our Old Defenses May Be Outdated.

In 1912, the quick and fatal response of a grieving father, in the landmark New York case of *People vs. Caruso*[7] opened the door to defenses of "not guilty based on emotional states of the assailant."

The concept opened the door in many other jurisdictions to defenses of, "irresistable impulse," "temporary insanity," and other devices which relieve individuals of responsibility for their actions, which have harmed or killed others.[8]

Our experience with such decisions has not been happy. The list of such cases includes many notorious judgments which have aroused public alarm and media controversy. President Ronald Reagan's assailant was the beneficiary of this type of mercy granted violent assaulters. There are many others on the list.

Of the same order, we have discussed the fact that one declared insane cannot under the present law be executed. If the killer cannot be executed because of his insanity, it is reasonable that he cannot legally be imprisoned.

Somehow that type of "mercy" granted to acknowledged killers seems not so attractive to us any more. Many deride the present law of defense of insanity as being outside the bounds of reality.

Criminals have been defended under theories calling for exculpation not only for the mental disease they suffered at the time, but for being temporarily disturbed by love for a film actress,[9] at the time he shot a number of people; also for young felons who kill old ladies under the influence of television shows depicting scenes of great violence.[10] A college student who killed his girl friend was released because he was "overwrought" at the time.[11]

In San Francisco, enraged because he was not reappointed to a city job he had recently resigned, Dan White took a pistol, extra ammunition, and killed Mayor Moscone and another city official. A substantial part of his defense was that he was disturbed because he had eaten a great deal of "junk-food," just prior to the killings.[12]

Is there a glimmering of a basic strategy for a truer liberty here? The question that seems to be groping its way to the surface of all the controversy and litigation is, "What happened to individual responsibility?"

Compassion is mandated by all the great religions, true enough, but the greatest compassion may be to grant an individual the right, under free will, to be accountable for his own acts.

Precedent Established and Disestablished.

After World War II the Nuremberg Trials were held to make the instigators of the war and terror unleashed in that catastrophe responsible and accountable for their individual crimes.[13] The excuse of "military duty or necessity" was not accepted. The lame excuse, "It was simply the regular procedure," received no approval. This established a precedent that can be followed.

By the same token, we have regularized procedure which has in the past permitted evasions of individual responsibility. This is a precedent that should be disestablished. It should no longer receive our approval. Grant the pragmatic sense of, "If it works, don't fix it!" The reverse is equally on point: "If it doesn't work: Fix it!"

The trials in Argentina of members of the military who caused the torture, death, and "disappearance," of thousands of innocent citizens have underlined the growing world dissatisfaction with violent madmen and malefactors of all kinds who never are held to account.

When violent crimes are concerned, madness is not a reasonable defense in a reasonable society.

The Strategy of Liberty.

The strategy of liberty then takes the simple form: Hold everyone individually accountable.

The details, the tactics, the maneuvers to accomplish such accountability must be left for each case or category. With experience and time devoted to insisting on individual accountability, no doubt a second level of procedural guidelines will develop.

For instance, in the case of corporate or city employees the strategy perhaps could develop an avoidance of holding these corporate bodies liable, in certain cases. We do not want to attract litigants seeking "deep pockets," rather than justice.

Certainly holding a single police officer liable for his actions, as in the cases[14] which join as tort-feasors, the villages employing police officers, and thus bankrupted a municipality may not be the best solution to the problem. That goes past individual liability. In this case, the officer was found wilful and negligent in harming the plaintiff. The call for individual accountability, to prevent a recurrence and for fair money damages is a proper concern of the local community, and the larger society.

The case went on, however, to find that the supervisors of the police department had fostered policies which led to the harm. Here is where they diverged from the principle: For instead of finding those supervisors individually liable, they extended the liability to the entire municipality, thus holding the entire town liable, and granting an award beyond the ability of those citizens to pay.

The fault is not that the award was too high. The error, it appears, was that they went past individual liability, where it truly belonged.[15]

The key target is, "To determine the overall policy required to have a less deadly society." All the evidence adduced appears to lean most strongly toward a policy of invariably reaching for individual accountability for all actions of force, without notable exception.

The Key Problem.

The key problem is the institutional inertia which is the net vector of opposing community interests, and which prevents moving away from the *status quo* of laws and attitudes. This is "constituency politics," which is the way United States politics has worked, leading to long-standing hostility, aggression, and violence between groups. The time has come for a review and a balancing of the interests with a view to moving toward, "idea-based politics," which can break up hyperorthodox and ethnic groups, avoiding some of the problems of violence between constituencies.

It will take creative, persuasive, even dramatic presentations to overwhelm the steady drag of constituency reaction, each toward a built-in vested interest. But it can be done, it is suggested, because there is a "net vector," of the center of everyone's interest. That center is simply the general interest. The major, if not the only, obstacle to promoting the general, core-interest we all have for a less deadly society, is the specific, local, and very temporary interest of those who are accused of violent crime, and their immediate relatives and friends. Generally, we all want less violence in ordinary life. Even a Mr. Hinckley, safe in prison, would want to have maximum protection from violence threatened by a fellow inmate, obsessed with the thought, "Hinckley took away my girl!" or "Hinckley shot my President!"

It is the militant voter and not the indifferent voter that will be satisfied first. It is the vocal community leaders, the vote-controllers, who receive the rewards of politics. Given strong vocal presentation of the logic of the position proposed, it could prevail.

The Simplicity of the Strategy.

All the evidence indicates that the vast majority of people want violent criminals prosecuted effectively. They want the streets made safe. The numerous programs of the 1960's and 1970's that attempted to get at the alleged "root causes of crime"—slums, broken families, unemployment— were, on the whole, failures. The talent, supported though it was by great effort and ample funds, did not find a way to prevent violent crimes. Perhaps that was not the object.

The increasingly violent government reaction of the 1980's appears not to be more successful in controlling drug smuggling and distribution, or assault, or anything else for that matter.[16]

Chapter 25

BRAVE NEW WORLDS IN OUR FUTURE

"You can never plan the future by the past."

Edmund Burke

Byways on the Journey to the Future.

There are many dangerous byways as we journey to the future. There are also some very promising routes. The list of dangers is long, and is the subject of daily comment from every element of opinion: Nuclear confrontation; world-wide irradiation of crops; pollution of air and water; acquired immune deficiency syndrome; tyranny and despotism in government and corporate practices; amoral philosophies countered by overly rigorous or fundamental dogmas; sexual license and teenage pregnancies; drug abuse and abuse by drug enforcement policies, we need not go on, for the list appears endless. Thankfully, that is not the whole story. For, it is true: we are stumbling upon useful truths that can help us reach higher on the scale of social evolution toward less violence and a better way of life.

We now know that people become whatever we make of them. They can be devils or gods, however we define those terms. We have within ourselves that power and the knowledge of how to apply it.

It may be that humans are not, as Freud once claimed, infinitely "polymorphous perverse." Certainly, however, there is a great deal that we can do about changing the nature of our society, and the nature of the individuals that make it up. Whether this will be improvement, or the reverse, must be left for later generations to judge. But we now know the outlines of what seems to us today, would be better: "A less deadly society, with more recourse to peaceful means of dispute resolution."

To reach this new world, however, we must be brave in reaching for, and clear-eyed in implementing, tentative solutions, as realized in specific programs. We should be prompt, too, to discard any program that does not produce both consensus and success.

Some of the proposals written about in prior pages suggest points of view at conflict with the way we now act. Some take positions that at first glance seem to be inconsistent with what most of us believe to be decent respect for the sensibilities of the past. It is submitted, however, that we should listen to them, and consider the implications of each.

To change our present beliefs, and our present practices is not going to be easy, but it can be done—if we really want to do it.

It is important to act only with the informed consent of those concerned, for it is only by this method that we can reach our twin goals: that the democratic process can be preserved, and steady progress achieved. Certainly there will be objections—they must be answered. Certainly there will be backtracking—the near objectives must then be clarified, and a new start made. All of that is simply the way things are with human affairs. Consensus is always difficult—in fact we should suspect we are on the wrong track, if consensus is too easy. Steady progress can be maintained, if when we are stopped in our tracks, we pause a moment to consider the fundamentals that all of us know are true.

The basic credo is: "Early childhood education (ECE), from age three to fifteen, sets the pattern for later behavior."

From this point, it is suggested we tread more tenderly:

The thesis is: "The community is deeply affected by the patterns of behavior of its children, the youths they become, and the adulthood they attain."

Therefore: "The community has the duty and obligation to inquire about the early education of its children."

Continuing: "When the community discovers that a child's early childhood education is deficient or improper, in that violence and crime are what the child is learning, it has an obligation to intervene to correct the omissions or flaws in such education.

Finally: "Techniques and methodologies of cults are acceptable as methods of instruction used by the community. Specifically, mystery, self-discipline, dogma, mass pageantry and celebrations, elite orders, medals and other indicia of rank, honor and prestige—all can be useful.

What can the individual do to advance all this? We leave that to the next chapter.

Chapter 26

WHAT YOU CAN DO ABOUT IT?

"Because we can't do all we would
Does it follow to do nothing's good?"

Arthur Hugh Clough

In our country, all problems have human and political dimensions, which require very careful consideration. Further, in our open society it is not practicable to try to slip something past all the alert community leaders, the press, academia, and the professions. If openness in administration is a difficulty, it is one that must be gracefully borne.

The United States Knows How to Change.

Change may be arduous, but there are certain aspects of our society that can expedite even major changes. This has been proven only recently, as these things go.

To alter a culture which included racial differences and antagonisms to the extent America had before 1954 was seen as difficult, many thought impossible.

It is significant that we have done so, in less than a generation. It would be difficult, if not impossible, to discover a single instance in history where such a major change has occurred, with only peripheral disorder and violence. Look at how we have changed:

In 1954 we still had segregated schools, busses, drinking fountains, restrooms, hotels, and even waiting rooms. Blacks did not vote in elections to any important degree anywhere in the country.

Today, all the above has gone with the wind. Our demographics are completely changed since 1954, in that our largest cities have acquired black political forces which has resulted in the election of many black mayors. *There* is a significant change indeed.

It was done against the express wishes of perhaps a majority of the people, but with the full cooperation of the United States government,

223

especially the Supreme Court, which despite repeated changes in their roster, has consistently insisted on fair and sensitive application of the Constitution to each case that came before it. No other country has such facilities for social change. Can it be used to reduce deadly force in this land?

When certain abuses in institutions for the care of the mentally disturbed came to be known, and brought before the court, federal judges ordered states to correct the abuses or close them.[1] Congress tackled the issue, too. Back in 1975, it appropriated more than $50 million a year to encourage state reform and adopted a "bill of rights" for the retarded, calling for treatment services and decent care.

It may be that federal judges should be more circumspect than to presume to legislate such intervention. It may be that Congress should be either more active or more restrained about participating in state concerns. In any case, the power to act in matters having to do with helpless retarded, deprived, or uncared for children lies with our existing institutions. That would be significant change from the prior state of neglect.

Where Change Is Needed Now.

A child that is being brought up in conditions that are conducive to crime, and violence, with disregard for acquiring the educated skills that can make him a happy, productive adult is as properly a ward of the nation as any helpless retarded, aged, or sick person. The violent child, furthermore, is a time bomb waiting to explode in the face of society, calling for even more attention to his problem, and the problem he will become.

Up to this point it would be easy to obtain national consensus. But the radically innovative programs needed will offend old totems. Thus vested interests displace logic, and ignorance will deny experience. Nevertheless, we must advance.

We must intervene into the lives of children that are not being given the chance to become the best they can. This is not a proposal to invade family privacy. Neither our people nor our institutions would tolerate that. We cannot send law officers to knock on doors and barge into cross-examine parents. We know bureaucracy is notoriously incompetent in such cases, we do not want to burden a reasonable family with State-inspired inspections.

Nor need we look for marginal cases. No, it is only the shriekingly blatant ones that need succor immediately. A child that has been adjudged delinquent ten times before the age of 12 would be a likely target. We have many of them. Their cases clamor for help. Let us take care of these children now, when the need is great, and there is still time to make amends. The court would not be invading the privacy of that child's home. On the contrary, it would be the home that has created a child that is invading the privacy and peace of everyone else. The home, the parents, and the child would be the instigators of society's reaction.

What Kind of Reaction?

What kind of reaction would be suitable in such a case? The welfare of the child demands, above all, that he not be returned to the environment which is turning him into a confirmed violent criminal. Such a child in good conscience must become a continuing ward of society.

The initial step, in our presently constructed system is for that child to receive the concentrated attention of the court, in supervising placement of the child. The need is not for mere housing. The need is for the child to reside permanently in a culturally supportive, stimulating environment that would restructure the value system of the child, building-in the hackneyed ideologies of morality: rejection of violence; rejection of deception and lying; an appreciation for work well done, education, and self-improvement. It would not be amiss if we could orient at least some of these facilities to the Confucian heritage of discipline, family, hard work, and education. But that probably would be too much for most facilities to handle. At least we are not sure we can teach that, now. We need families to do that. We could, no doubt, participate in teaching parents how to create and be such families.

In exceptional cases family structures can be built within these facilities, defining family as any group of people who enjoy each other's company, can function well together, and be productive. Ideally, perhaps a two-parent structure can be simulated. Generally, however, we could be satisfied with the kind of cooperative comradeship that is developed in dormitory schools among compatible groups.

Since funding is always an important element, provisions should be made for the programs to be self-funding to the maximum possible. Without such funding, other interests will tend to siphon away the dollars needed within a facility. Thus the independence of each facility probably will have to be a geographical, functional, and budgetary fact.

What Kind of Projects?

What kind of projects might do this? There are a number of types that have been found reasonably successful. One wonders, however, if recourse should be had to privately controlled agencies, whether religious or social. During the great emergency of the Depression of 1930–1936 when there were many homeless boys wandering the highways of the land, a Civilian Conservation Corps was invented which provided a place for the homeless, the runaways, and the marginally delinquent youth. Minimally funded, in those Depression years, they did much useful work in forestry, roadbuilding, firefighting, and conservation. Often the work they did was worth far more than their cost. To this day there are libraries, roads, and other works projects of the CCC which still serve us well, half a century after having been built.

For older Americans another organization developed at about the same time was the Works Progress Administration. To this day we see many of their good works around the country. In addition the WPA did a vital job in keeping families together, people working and fed.

As delinquent youth were well served by the Civilian Conservation Corps, in the 1930's, today we can be equally creative in forming programs for younger children. These programs probably cannot reproduce a suburban American family environment. But that is not the only route to success. All we may need for a start is:

1. A social milieu where honesty and good deeds are rewarded.

2. Where violence is discouraged without violent reprisal.

3. Where punishment is not more severe than the removal of opportunity to earn special privileges.

4. Where political abuse is avoided in the same ways it was avoided in the Civilian Conservation Corps: By eliminating the opportunity for patronage and profit.

5. Where membership in the projects is made so attractive to children that they come to love it, cling to it, and as they get older, boast about it, its doctrines and ideals.

6. Where there is a fixed upper age limit for children admitted. This could be as little as seven or eight years. By that age, much of a child's

basic personality structure has been formed. Once admitted, perhaps children could stay until age fifteen.

7. Where the cooperation of all churches is solicited, for they are the potential moral backbone of every community. Their help for referrals and enrollment is invaluable. However, it may be recommended that facility management be completely ecumenical, to remove the possible taint of intergroup rivalry and resentment.

8. It is probably important to reserve places in these projects for only the most violent kids. If there has been any failure in bussing children to integrate schools, it has been that bussing has encouraged violent children to dominate the nonviolent, and thus set a violent mood for the new school. War is more addictive than peace, it seems. As a child becomes less violent, he can be "promoted to the better group" that is less violent even within the same facility, to build and retain loyalty to the organization and its ideals.

9. Each project can become attractive to volunteer workers. Working for the homeless and the poor, many volunteers now work without rest to help their charges. For farm laborers, itinerant farm workers, and unwed mothers, volunteers have worked like Trojans. The Peace Corps has attracted dedicated thousands. Perhaps "Kare for Kids," will come to be equally inspiring.

10. Since by the nature of the task, each unit of the system must be quite small, with perhaps not more than twenty children in each, an organizational problem looms. Following standard management tenets, one person must not only be responsible for receipt of directions and instructions and for taking action aimed at successful results, but also, that person must be personally accountable for consequences. Consequences are to be measured in terms of a child's verified record of resolving personal disputes without violence, and with evidence of increasing skill in persuasive ability, compromise in disputes, and willingness to postpone gratification.

As the child reaches the age where he is able to learn specific educational skills, promotion can be based more on these successes. Of course, the accent must always be on recorded successes, so that the child builds a personal history recordbook of his progress. This becomes his personal roll of honor.

Is the Proposal Radical?

As radical as this proposal may seem it is less so than the recent phenomenon we have seen of paid advertisments placed by victims and their families crying out for justice in daily newspapers.[2] Such is the agony of a public repeatedly assaulted and undeservedly punished by violence that has been all but unchecked by government. Each member of the public can do something to help build roadblocks in the path to violence that up to this time has been paved with ineptitude. Leading scientists and futurists reiterate how utterly insane it is to allow a situation where we deliberately and consciously produce the circumstances which build violent personalities in a child, who had no such violent pattern before.

Our Strange Society.

The world loses about 1,000 lives through mini-wars every day. We talk about high ideals, but keep shooting ourselves in the foot. From the moment children are able to walk, they are set down before a television set and programmed for a life of conspicuous consumption with few means to obtain these material goods other than violence taught to them at the same time. The hours spent learning useless things is taken from the time that could have been spent being educated in reading, writing, and arithmetic, not to mention the far more complicated, advanced skills required to produce more than they will consume in the longer life that the science of public health is ready to give them.

What is television programming? Television programming is designed mainly to sell advertising to distributors of material goods. The advertising, itself, depends upon:

1. Attracting a potential customer's attention.
2. Holding the customer long enough to convey a message that will convince the individual that they need the product they sell.

To "attract attention," scenes of danger and violence have been found to be successful, and to provide more profits. Thus cartoons revolve about violent scenes of cartoon characters beating each other up, being thrown off cliffs, and being blown up. Cartoons, too, are cheap to produce. Therefore violent cartoons are selected for children. A rational decision.

Why are the violent cartoons shown on Saturday mornings? Saturday morning is prime time for children's programming. They are the only market that can be attracted to the TV screen at that time. The influence of the messages can concentrate on a homogeneous audience, children, not diluted by the presence of adults. Thus they result in the largest profits. A rational analysis and a rational decision.

Unexpected Consequences.

Thus rational analysis and decision at each level results in a uniquely concentrated cultural message of violence to children at their most impressionable ages.

Certainly there was no intention by any of the highly trained, expert creators of these shows, at any of the subobjective levels, to harm the nation, or the nation's children. No, but each level's decision led inevitably to the next, and on to an utterly unacceptable consequence, the traumatizing of the cultural mix transmitted to the young generation. The creation of children ready, willing and able to accept violence as a necessary part of their world, was the unexpected consequence.

Sequences of innocuous appearing decisions leading in logical order to unexpected, and thoroughly unwanted end-results is not unusual in our free society. One might even say it the general rule, especially when human behavior is either the input, or output.

At the other end of the age-scale, our adult criminal justice system, after eleven years of work, by lawyers, courts, and killers's attorneys have managed to create a system of capital punishment that satisfies no one.

Proponents of capital punishment write stern laws, win convictions and then are dismayed by the expanding gridlock on death row.

Abolitionists—those who would abolish capital punishment—anguish over public opinion and unyielding laws, yet succeed in blocking most executions because of technical errors in the prosecution's procedures.

Victim's families receive no satisfaction, complaining they can obtain neither peace, nor vengeance.

Killers receive no release, nor even certain punishment.

Seekers after justice in the community are left with bitterness at the whole system.

At each level, dedicated, highly trained or concerned individuals try hard. All are frustrated at the end result.

What You Can Do About It.

What can you and I do about it? The answer is so obvious that we all
know it: Think before we act. Visualize the consequences, before we
institutionalize a sequence of decision-making that is fated to end in
disaster.

In the law, judges have two approaches to coming to their weighty
decisions: One is an "Analytical Approach,"[3] relying on preceding
decisions, and reaching for the next logical step. This is similar to the
sequences cited above. Often this method culminates in disastrous *cul-de-
sacs.* Very much as has been seen above in capital punishment.

The other method of decision-making used by judges is called the
"Policy Approach." This method:[4]

> ... is more difficult and more challenging, not only for students but
> also for judges, for lawyers, and for teachers. Instead of neatness and
> symmetry of refinement and logic, we encounter the disorderliness of
> disagreement among those who are best informed, the dissatisfactions
> of guesswork, the discouragements of limitations upon human intellects.
> Instead of relative certainty, we find a high degree of uncertainty and
> even a large proportion of error. The melancholy truth is that error is
> an intrinsic part of the process of trial and error.

Thus the approach that is being proposed by eminent jurists to resolve
grave questions of crime and violence are not without a great background of experience and success.

The infamous decision of Plessy v. Ferguson which quite logically and
indeed inevitably, came to impose the doctrine of "separate but equal,"
on this country, was the result of careful searching for precedent, and
following the sequences of logic that began with the Dred Scott decision
of 1854, and came to its logical, but completely disastrous holding:
"Separate but equal accommodations" should be satisfactory to both
black and white children in school. Well, they were not satisfactory!

It took two generations of struggle before the United States Supreme
Court, reaching for the soul of the people, reversed Plessy, and abandoned logical sequential thinking. Belatedly they realized the end-result
of "separate ... " was disaster for the nation. In 1954 they changed their
route and made the policy-wise conclusion: Separate cannot be equal in
education.

We now see the wisdom of that policy approach.

Thus, the question in the title to this chapter: "What Can You Do

About It?" is answered: Use the courts to develop a well-thought policy approach to assume control over all children who are in danger of being educated into violence and crime. Use the courts and all of public information and opinion to restrict and discourage public condonation, acceptance, or approval of personal violence in any form.

When aroused, our communities have been remarkably successful in limiting the spread of pornography and smut. How much can they do to limit the spread of violence and crime, when equally aroused? We have always been able to join forces to protect our children. We can do so again.

Chapter 27

LAST WARNINGS

*"Blessed is he that readeth
...for the time is at hand."*

Revelation

We bring this book to a close with a last reminder of all the reasoning and impartial research which warns of the consequences we could suffer, should we not change our ways.

Unmanifest Destiny.

It is quite clear by now to most of us that Americans were not chosen by God, necessarily to rule the earth. Our anxiety about the progress of the Russians in war potential, of the Japanese in manufacturing, and of the Chinese in promoting two-pronged success in literacy and nuclear power, indicate that awareness.

The American Dreams of the last century were in part a myth and a mystery of illusion, as the cynics of this century have revealed. But that myth and that mystery germinated the genius that created the most powerful and productive republic in history.

The charge is that genius now lies dormant. We no longer feel powerful and productive. We no longer tingle with feelings of myth and mystery at the strains of the national anthem, or the waving of the flag. We know too much about what is false, and too little of what is true.

Disillusionment.

We are familiar with the deeds of all the people who reside in the inner sanctums of power and production. The knowledge has made us unshockable and jaded. We are disengaged and ennervated. Some of us have been taught to be angry, and vent that anger in mindless violence.

When we return to faith and belief in the great dreams, when we

232

redeem our old taboos and vest our own efforts with value, then we can overcome the lure of violence and crime. It is not too late.

Recourse to Violence.

Violence feeds upon itself. Our cities vie with each other for the title, "Murder City." Gun killings among adults are now an old story, and the example is moving down the age scale. Kids now are "toting guns to school like they used to take lunch."[1] In 1986 322 Detroit children under 17 were shot, 43 of them fatally. Pushing and shoving was old-style, school-boy violence. But even that was rare in disciplined schools. Skylarking and open rebellion finally came into schools with the erosion of the old myths and mysteries of respect to teachers and parents and school. The pushing and shoving was finally tolerated as youthful expression of energy. Of course that was what it was. So are the gunkillings by youth: youthful expressions of energy.

The time has come to suppress or redirect that energy.

Out of Control.

We have let that energy burst out of control because of our beliefs. It is difficult to explain our current beliefs. However they may be described, the description distorts them. Those beliefs, a chiaroscuro pattern of conflicting contemporary values, have made many valuable contributions to our culture.

Because so many of them are in conflict, it is easy to apply them inappropriately. Between defensiveness against contrary ideologies, and the resistance to logical thought and inertia that dogma encourages, we fall into incredible situations where children demonstrate in parades against the American Civil Liberties Union, holding on high, placards marked: "A.C.L.U. KEEP OUT!" and "A CHILD'S LIFE OVER RIGHTS." The A.C.L.U. wanted to "defend" children from searches of lockers and school bags for guns.[2]

One wonders at the twisted logic and ideals of such intrusions. Does the United States Constitution demand a child has the right to secrete guns in his school locker? This is a repudiation of standards of behavior and child-guidance and education entire.

Repudiation of Standards.

We have studiously tried to avoid seeing crime, violence or deadly force in moral terms throughout this book. The crisis of our time is not, as we see it, a crisis of morals. A common belief in morality still prevails. It is what we do with that morality that is the issue. All the prior material has been presented as a problem of uncontrolled violent behavior. For that is all that is needed to remedy the situation described by Deadly Force: The Lure of Violence.

There will be a crisis, however, if we repudiate peaceful, defensive measures to control violent behavior.

Paraphrasing a comment made twenty years ago by a brilliant interpreter of our times, Will Herberg,[3] The real challenge is not the youth who commits violence. The real problem is provided by the youths and adults who shrug their shoulders and say, "Well, so what? What's so bad about violence and deadly force? It's everywhere. We've just got to get used to it."

Our Fear of Indoctrination.

Our country has been notable as never having countenanced a state religion. From 1789 to today, this general attitude has remained with us. It is enshrined in the very First Amendment to our Constitution.

This fear of state religion, however, has gone so far as to deny the very human nature upon which a great nation must rely. It was not the intention of the Founding Fathers, nor of any reasonable person in authority since then, to make every issue adversary in nature. Contention and confrontation are not the theme of the Constitution. They should not be the theme of our daily life. On the contrary, the underlying premise is cooperation of all people, in all positions high and low, to achieve the goals of the Preamble with as little contention and confrontation as practical. In fact, contention and confrontation was specifically abjured. At the risk of being repetitious, we repeat the goals of the Preamble:

> "We the People of the United States, in Order to form a more perfect Union, establish Justice, insure domestic Tranquility, provide for the common defence, promote the general Welfare, and secure the Blessings of Liberty to ourselves and our Posterity . . . "

We must note that one of the words capitalized is, "Tranquility."

Disorder and violence operate against tranquility and undoubtedly are among the things we, as a people, want to avoid as much as possible.

Neither the Constitution nor any other authority or responsible statement has forbade us to use the basic qualities of human nature to help reach a " . . . more perfect Union, establish Justice, . . . promote the general Welfare . . . "

On the contrary, to go against the grain of human nature adds to obstacles, and often may prevent success.

As humans, we are heirs to a phylogeny which insists on mystery and faith to provide stability in our concept of the world. Social relations that depend only upon mere convenience or contract are shallow and meagre compared with relations which are founded on a profound respect for the mysteries of life, love, and death.

As far into the future as we can now visualize, this earnest yearning for communion with something greater than the individual, something admirable and ineffably virtuous, will exist as a valuable tool to attain not only the objectives of the Constitution, but all the other excellent things that a good society can provide.

Why not use this tremendous power within us for a noble purpose?

We Need Not Fear Indoctrination.

The ancient Greek philosophers, the Hebrew prophets, Jesus Christ, and the teachers of Islam are at one at least on this: *The truth by which man lived was something ultimately independent of him, beyond and above him, expressing itself in knowledge of the norms and standards to which he must conform if he was to live a truly human life.*

This idea of truth was challenged by the concept of "relativism." This concept, so shocking to the classical mind, meant that truth was man- and culture-made, varying with psychological and cultural conditioning.

The tradition of the West, that "knowledge is truth," was overturned, and replaced with the creed, "knowledge is power." Power above all, over other men.

Ideological relativism, destroying authority over all normative behavior, whether divinely set, or otherwise, leaves only power and pleasure as the only measures for human conduct.

The belief, the indoctrination, that has swept over us is that there is nothing beyond our desires, nothing beyond our power. Our "values" are ours to make or break, the only criterion being self-satisfaction. That is an indoctrination, an ideology, a cult, is it not? Certainly it is not founded on anything we would call ultimate truth. Thus we need not fear the deed, or the word indoctrination further, for we are already under its spell.

Todays Indoctrination and Creed.

At the present time we find all the techniques and devices of the cults being used to indoctrinate us into, "Glory to Me in the highest, For I, Myself, am the Maker and Master of All," as the dogma runs: "We need be true only to our own desires for pleasure or power. We need meet only the measure of authenticity to ourselves. And I? Yes, I am an Individual, and Only I Count as long as I really believe it with the wholeness of my being."

Thus the worst abominations of a Hitler or a Stalin, of an international terrorist, or a kid who reenacts the murder of an old lady, as he has seen it on television, all meet the demand of authenticity, as well as the finest act of heroism or charity such as saving a comrade on the battlefield, or caring for the sick.

If there is no preference between these two classes of actions, there is no morality, no norms, no life worth calling human. I have no fear that Americans cannot, and do not differentiate between them.

Indoctrination, Mystery, and Revelation.

The ideology of political campaigns attracts devoted workers who labor phenomenal hours for little material reward. Checks and cash flow into the coffers of televangelists. Hare Krishna chanters, with their tinkling bells, spend as many as fifteen hours a day soliciting financial aid from passersby. Single interest movements, from abortion to pro-life, from Anti-AIDS to Anti-gay, draw to themselves dedicated marchers and demonstrators, without pay or emolument, in consecration to their ideals. All seek the emotional food of mystery and commitment.

We do not know if we can use this great emotional, transcendent force in human beings for legimately improving the quality of life. We do not know if we can use it, at least, for reducing deadly force and violence, and thus saving lives.

That is our problem, our plight, and our task.

Appendix A

DETERMINANTS OF BEHAVIOR

Many commentators, scholars, and scientists have studied the role of belief in affecting behavior. The philosopher Charles Sanders Peirce (1830/1914) phrased his understanding of belief as a "rule for action." In that sense, belief is a *determinant* of behavior.

That is, there may be a number of influences, causes, or motivators of behavior, ranging from physiological or hormonally-based emotions, urges, or motivators, on a continuum to vaguely conscious awareness of the source of the incitement to act, on to completely conscious belief in the existence of a tree in one's way, as one acts to avoid it in completing the behavior of walking along a path.

The cognitive factors that are responsible for behavior are the concern of most learning-teaching procedures. This is seen in perhaps its most extreme form in the learning process called "the scientific method."

It is overly simplified to state that the scientific method is the endeavor to obtain new knowledge by a sequential process. It is only a shade more correct to itemize steps in the process, but for lack of space, we offer the following description of the steps in the scientific method:

1. Observing phenomena, effects, or events.

2. Trying to account for them by positing possible causes, explanations or predictions, usually called "theories" or "hypotheses."

3. Empirical research to determine whether to accept or reject the theories.

A limitation of the scientific method of testing theories of prediction, is that logically valid conclusions can be drawn only when the prediction is refuted.

This may be illustrated.

One predicts that if a particular theory is true, then B will occur. That is: If X occurs, then Y will occur. The theorist arranges a physical set-up so that:

X is made to occur. He then observes that Y then occurs.

Can the observer logically claim that the theory is correct? Obviously not, for Y might have occurred even if X had not existed.

BUT if X occurs, and Y is *not* observed to occur . . .

Can the observer then logically claim that the theory was not proved correct? The answer is clearly, "Yes."

Concluding that a theory is true because the prediction is supported is called, "affirming the consequent," and is logically invalid.

Concluding that a theory is not proved true because the prediction is denied by the empirical observation, is a logically valid inference.

However, it would not be logically valid to state that because the prediction is denied by the empirical observation, the theory is not true. We must restrict our statement to merely, "the theory is not proved true."

Another, and more compact way of saying this is that X was not proved necessary and sufficient to cause Y.

In fact, it has not been found possible to identify any X that is rigorously necessary and sufficient to cause any Y.

Thus the scientific method applied to the study of behavior does not claim to uncover any ultimate truths about causation. It has, however, helped to discover many relationships that have been found to be very useful. Especially valuable has been the concept of probability, as applied to relationships between presumed determinants and consequences. Modifying the shorthand expression above, we have, "If X then a certain probability of Y."

Thus, the method of scientific empiricism has been to go the route of probability, and propose useful theories by either of two alternative routes.

A Posteriori: Based on a history of observed sequences of X and Y, that if X is observed then there is a probability of N% one will observe Y, or

A Priori: From an examination of all conceivable possibilities of X and Y occurring: If X occurs, then there is a probability of N% that one will observe Y.

In either of the above cases, empirical verification of the theory must follow, to affirm or deny the theory.

All of the above refers to cognitive factors within our conscious understanding and belief. There is, however, another level of belief that does not rely on what is logically valid or invalid.

This level of belief relies on assumptions that are taken for granted, without recourse to empirical verification. Or, if empirical observations are mentioned, the conclusions are not put to the rigorous logical test of "necessary and sufficient," above described.

A cluster of such assumptions, that helps explain the physical or spiritual world, to the satisfaction of a believer in those assumptions, has been called an "ideology."

There are many ideologies known to the races of man, and each provides the comfort and satisfaction man wants when dealing with so much that mystifies us. Their explanations are often clung to in the face of all contrary physical facts.

An ideology may have some assumptions in common with one or more other ideologies. Insofar as ideologues differ in their assumptions, there are conflicts of belief between the individuals, and potentially other adverse relations, up to and including physical violence. That is why we are so concerned with ideologies here.

Faith in an ideology often is unbreakable, whatever evidence, persuasion, or force may be applied to the truly believing individual. The killing of members, devastation of their places of worship, their sacred relics, their culture, their land has little effect on the core of the most faithful believers. The faith persists, is transmitted to children and converts, and rises again as has happened so often among Christians, of many denominations, in recent years such as Mormons and Mennonites, also among believing Jews, Moslems, Buddhists, even including atheists, agnostics, Santerians, all who have strong convictions. The same has been true of nonreligious ideologues, patriots of various nations, and regions, libertarians, Black Nationalists, Nazis, Aryan Nationalists, and, in fact, innumerable firmly committed ideologues of many different descriptions. Fanatics they have been called by enemies. They call themselves, True Believers, as long as they "Keep the Faith."

Truly these are men and women who have steeled themselves against whatever an unjust world may deliver.

But to outsiders, they are an enigma, their beliefs, which determine much of their behavior, are so incongruous with the world as outsiders "know it," as to appear grotesque.

It is important, however, to realize that modern cultists have not, as has been accused, created a new mental illness. They have not invented an, "information disease." They have simply applied the techniques used for millenia to indoctrinate individuals and groups with belief systems. The ideologies they promote, each different, rest on the same basic genetic endowment all living creatures seem to have to some degree, which is nonpejoratively called, "learning capacity."

Some of the ideologies with which we have been inculcated have been praised as sublime, some have been called depraved. As human beings, especially as children, we are equally susceptible to both.

The course of life from the cradle to the grave has been seen as a continual morality play, a Pilgrim's Progress, as it were, of constantly seeking to believe the sublime, and act on it; whilst avoiding the depraved.

We do not, here, try to single out all the sublime, or even good assumptions. We make a point, however, of one belief which we arbitrarily define as depraved: Deadly Force. That is our only polemic. This book is devoted to the facts related to: how we have come to accept violence as an intrinsic part of life.

What shapes the child? Everything that happens to him, of course, but let us now display the elements which lead to those determinants of behavior which are based on undiscriminate selection of assumptions, beliefs, doctrines, ethos, and full-scale ideologies.

Appendix B

HOW WE BECOME INDOCTRINATED

Indoctrination is a process of inducing a state of mind, consisting of becoming uncritically convinced of the essential truth and validity of a set of principles or assumptions. This state of mind, or belief, is independent of any rational level of logic, or even experience, although logic or experience may be called upon to substantiate the ideology involved.

The process of indoctrination, that is, of acquiring beliefs, commences perhaps simultaneously with birth, with the very first learning to breathe, to cry, to suckle. The edge between genetically induced reactions and actual new learning, as has been said, is diffuse. The separation becomes clearer, as the child develops the clear ability to learn to believe his mother is a source of pleasure in food, cuddling, warmth, and love, and to react to those beliefs by crying at deprivation of his mother's care, and cooing and signs of satisfaction on it being restored.

As the child moves from instinct to identity and develops his own personality[1] he chooses from his social and physical environment a host of beliefs, forming his own personal set of doctrines, most of which is absorbed from other people, particularly those he sees and hears most often.

In short, he acquires the beliefs of those around him, generally accepting that group's ideals, culture, dogma, and ideology.

Quickly it becomes clear to the child how important this idealogy is to the individuals he values most. If the ideology is significant to the person with whom he identifies, it becomes significant to him. When the group ideology is strictly adhered to, and if such orthodox belief and performance reaches beyond the normal, toward a continuous self-monitoring, we have used the descriptive term "hyperorthodox."[2] If the ideology includes a claim of support by spiritual, other-world powers, that becomes part of his doctrine, too. A divine power that allegedly enforces the ideology, and is a part of it, makes a most powerful monitoring tool for continuous internalized enforcement of belief and action. Whatever one calls the feeling of an omniscient presence, either conscience or guilt, the observer is tempted to conclude the result is the same: Discomfort when one is in violation of the precepts of the ideology, comfort when one feels sure one is in compliance.

There is a vast literature about the dysfunctional effects of guilt.[3] There is an equally large literature about the functional aspects of conscience.[4] Since, however, they speak of substantially the same state of mind, it appears that the two words have acquired connotative baggage. Each word, conscience, or guilt represents an ideological approach to the same concept.

In any case, conscience or guilt, both or either, provide a continuous monitoring presence to enforce compliance with ideological constraints. When, in addition there is personal monitoring by parents, elders, siblings, neighbors to assure compliance, the process of indoctrination is strengthened.

Part of the process of social monitoring is strong condemnation by parents, peers, and neighbors of any transgression, with painful mental and physical consequences to the member.

The psychic aspects of being "conscience-stricken" or having "guilt feelings" have been operationally studied for centuries, and have provided countless examples of hyperorthodox performance to a high degree, even unto death, as the saying goes, and it still does.[5]

The specific techniques adapted to developing such high performance, and particularly at hyperorthodox levels, appear to be summarized as:[6]

Obtain Willing Participation.

Create a situation where the individual initiates the contact, with a desire to participate. (It is simplest to do this with a young child, but at all ages, into adult, this is a desirable first step.)

Isolate the Subject.

Produce endless messages of the belief, attitude and behavior wanted and expected. These messages to be conveyed by channels of all sensory reception, hearing, vision, touch, smell, including internal stimuli of hunger and thirst, loneliness, etc., all of which are satisfied best by compliance. The well-documented psychological techniques of reinforcement, in all its manifold varieties, seem to be applicable here. It appears to be helpful to success if the messages can be focused as eminating from, or addressed to, a divine or charismatic figure of infinite power and omniscience, filled with boundless kindness, but a terrible wrath. Not all hyperorthodox organizations use this device, however, especially in developed countries, with relatively sophisticated societies.

Eliminate Competing Messages.

Prevent access to any messages of an import contrary to the desired beliefs, attitudes, and behavior. The greater the inhibition of contrary messages, the greater the impact of the ideologically positive messages will be.

Removal from all sensory stimulation to prevent negative messages has been used by some ideological organizations. Complete sensory deprivation, however, may have consequences undesirable to the ideological or doctrinal objective: insanity, delusions, severe fear reactions, and so on.

Participation.

Active physical participation of the individual aids indoctrination. This refers to personal messages and protestations of faith, belief, and his continued faith and belief, on a round-the-clock daily basis. The practice of the religion and ideology of Islam demands formal prayer five times daily. Some cults demand six to ten or more hours of such devotions daily. Group participation appears to be especially effective.

This can take the form of rites, rituals, processions, dancing, ceremonies, prayers, offerings to the organization or the charismatic figure. There is a certain minimum amount of daily labor at the service of the hyperorthodox organization that is required. The maximum possible amount is not known, but as much as 17 or 18 hours of daily labor, on behalf of the Hare Krishna organization have been noted. It is reliably reported that the cult known as Scientology, and others, have by these techniques been able to substantially change members' personality, awareness, and responsiveness to outside stimuli.[7] Many hyperorthodox organizations demand as much as 55 to 70 hours of devotions weekly.[8] In moments of extreme danger to the organization, even higher levels of output have been obtained. The great effort and time demanded seem not to lessen dedication and compliance—quite to the contrary.

Self-Defense of the Hyperorthodox Society.

Severe punishments, ostracism, and ceremonies of ex-communication, expulsion, and outlawry to be administered to any backsliders with a view to having them return to the fold, and to deter other potential defectors. As a part of this, all other organizations, institutions and strangers to the hyperorthodox groups are denounced as enemies, devils, and malefactors.

Under no circumstances are attacks submitted to within the recesses of the mind of the devout, as long as their belief remains firm. Even when physical submission is mandated by actual force, mental resistance remains, to a degree dependent, it appears, on the depth and extent of the indoctrination. A study of captured Japanese prisoners of war during World War II indicated that while devotion to immediate superiors could be penetrated, faith in the highest officers of the Japanese Army and Navy was extremely resistant, even to intense deprogramming efforts by American psychologists. In fact, one of the largest and most extensive studies was unable to report even a single case in which dedication to the highest almost divine figure of the Mikado was diminished.

As the above has been applied we can point to countless examples of groups and individuals, at almost every level of indoctrination, up to and including the most hyperorthodox, both criminal and noncriminal, that are known to contemporary Americans:

Individuals:	"Son of Sam," the Bronx killer
	Florence Nightingale, founder of the Red Cross
	Most religious leaders, past and present
Small Groups:	The Manson Family, the California cult
	Many ghetto youth gangs,
	Military combat teams
	Terrorist groups
Large Groups:	Hisballah
	The Red Brigades
	Irish Republican Army (IRA)
Nations:	Iran
	(North) Viet Nam

People's Republic of China
Union of Socialist Soviet Republics
Germany under the Nazi regime
Many nations under the emotional .
motivations of war

Unfortunately there is not much respectable research on *how* we become indoctrinated. What there is, however, is more than enough for us to respect the massive effect the process can have on human behavior.

A final note: Indoctrination by no means affects every human action or behavior. Even in the most intensely indoctrinated individual there are congeries of his involuntary and voluntary action that remains relatively unaffected by belief. Much of the action controlled by what physiologists call the autonomic nervous system remains unaffected. However, there is current research that indicates that even such automatically governed aspects can be affected by deeply convinced beliefs and emotions. This is the basis for the recent emphasis on the part of medical science on treating the "whole person." There are research findings indicating that not only are digestive processes, blood pressure, pulse rate, breathing rate, and emotions subject to the current state of belief of the individual, but also reaction to invading disease by bacteria or virus is strongly affected by the subject's mental reactions.

Indoctrination does not, however, ever take over every aspect of a person's mind or body. The fanatic Hisballah terrorist willing to sacrifice his daily conscious thought for months, and his life in an instant, to destroy the United States Marine barracks in Lebanon, no doubt remained for much of his day a normal-appearing individual, loving his family, and his friends, going about many daily tasks, and under many circumstances his confirmed dedication to violence against the object of his hatred remained invisible to people in his vicinity.

However, strong beliefs, by all the available evidence can, and do, act as determinants of behavior.

The prime examples of our concern in this book have been those who have accepted, and live by a creed of criminal and deadly violence that affects a public that has up to now not been able to cope adequately with such indoctrinated individuals.

Of course, the opposite is equally true. We can learn to live by a creed of avoidance of personal violence and peaceful resolution of disputes that will bring us to a new confidence in the liberties and satisfactions of a truly free society.

We must remember! It is not a choice between an indoctrinated and an unindoctrinated society. As we learn, as we mature, all of us become indoctrinated to some degree. The only question is: Shall we be indoctrinated to deadly force, or shall we be indoctrinated against it?

ENDNOTES

CHAPTER 1: THE LURE OF VIOLENCE

1. Stokely Carmichael, "What We Want." in *New York Review of Books,* September 23, 1966.

2. Italy established formal relations with the Red Brigade two decades ago. Lebanon, Lybia, Iran and Syria deal with terrorists at the highest levels of government. The United States National Security Agency and Central Intelligence Agency have from time to time established contacts with terrorists. See Philip Agee, *Inside the Company* (New York: Bantam, 1981); Philip Menason, *The Politics of Protection* (New York: Praeger, 1984).

3. Agee, Ibid.; Menason, Ibid.

4. The Federal Bureau of Investigation reported that in 1986 there were 709 bombings. *New York Times,* February 24, 1986.

5. Hannah Arendt, *Eichman: The Banality of Evil,* (New York: Penguin, 1977).

CHAPTER 2: IRRESISTABLE URGES TO DEADLY FORCE

1. *The Miami Herald,* 5/12/84, p. 16.

2. Mary Parker Follett, "The Giving of Orders," reprinted in Jay Shafritz and Philip H. Whitbeck, eds., *Classics of Organization Theory* (Moore Publishing, 1978).

3. Local governments in many parts of the United States now support pistol ranges as a public service to the community. E.g.: Dade County, Florida.

4. Dale Brooks, *Who's Who In Martial Art* (American Martial Arts Publ., 1985).

5. In the United States there is distributed to children under the age of three, toys that are clear incitements to violence. Following is a quotation from a storybook made in the shape of a truck with the following encouragement to use poison to punish people: "The policeman told the children not to worry. 'I will punish the thief,' he said. We will teach him a lesson with this (poisonous) candy. This time he will get a big belly-ache if he should try to steal again!" (1986, Crest Ind. Corp. Deer Park, NY 11729, item #554).

6. *The Miami Herald,* 9/19/84: *New York Times,* September 4, 1986; July 18, 1986.

7. The phenomenon is described (*Newsweek,* 6/15/87, p. 80) by columnist Meg Greenfield as "The No-Fault Confession."

8. *The Miami Herald* editorial 6/16/84, 6/26/84.

9. *Newsweek,* 6/19/87, "A Trial That Wouldn't End," p. 20ff. *New York Times,* January 1, 2, 3, 4, 5, 6, 7, 7, 9, 10 . . . etc. all in 1986.

10. Frank Vandall, *Police Training For Calls* (Millwood, NY.: Kennekat, 1976); Howard H. Earle, *Police Recruit Training,* (Springfield, Illinois: C C Thomas, 1973); Mason

Williams, *The Law Enforcement Book of Weapons* (Springfield, Illinois: C C Thomas, 1977.

11. Charles W. Bray, *Psychology and Military Proficiency,* (Westport, Conn.: Greenwood, 1984); William D. Henderson, *Why the Viet Cong Fought,* (Westport, Conn.: Greenwood, 1979).

12. *New York Times* March 1, 2, 3, 4, 5, 8, 25, 27, all in 1986.

13. Allen P. Bristow, *The Search For An Effective Police Handgun.* (Greenwood, 1984); many police departments now opt for automatic weapons as sidearms, *New York Times,* May 24, 1986.

14. Mason William, Ibid. The official journal of the International Association of Chiefs of Police, *The Police Chief,* carries many advertisements offering bullet-proof vests for sale.

15. Comment by Miami Police Chief Garland Watkins, and many other police executives.

16. *New York Times,* April 28, 1986.

17. Report of the Dade County Grand Jury, December 1985.

18. Bruno Bettelheim, *The Uses of Enchantment: The Meaning and Importance of Fairy Tales* (Free Press, 1979).

CHAPTER 3: WHAT CAN BE DONE NOW?

1. *Max Weber On Charisma and Institution Building,* S.N. Eisenstadt, ed., (University of Chicago Press, 1968).

2. Nietzsche, Friedrich, *Basic Writings,* Walter Kaufmann, ed. & transl., (Modern Library, 1968); see also the writings of all major theologians.

3. H. H. Scullard, *Festivals and Cermonies of the Roman Republic,* (Cornell University Press, 1981); Ramsay MacMullen, *Soldier and Civilian in the Later Roman Empire,* (Harvard University Press, 1963).

4. E. Roy Calvert, *Capital Punishment in the Twentiety Century,* (Patterson Smith, 1973); John Laurence, *The History of Capital Punishment,* (Citadel Press, 1983).

5. Compact Oxford Dictionary, vol. 1, p. 1359 (Oxford, 1971)

6. Leonard W. Doob, *Patriotism and Nationalism: Their Psychological Foundation* (Greenwood, 1984); James W. Van Hoeven, *Piety and Patriotism* (Erdmans, 1976); George Norlin, *Fascism and Citizenship* (AMS Press, 1934).

7. Kenneth Boa, *Cults, World Religions and You* (Victor Books, 1977); Andros Pavolv, *The Cult Experience* (Greenwood, 1982).

8. Nathan M. Adams, "Irans Ayatollah's of Terror *Readers Digest,* January 1985. For a more substantial background see: David H. Albert, ed., *Tell the American People: Perspectives on the Iranian Revolution* (Mizan Press, 1984).

9. Lester Sumrall, *The Holy War* (Harrison House, 1981) Ramy Nima, *The Wrath of Allah* (Pluto Press, 1983).

10. Dervish cult of Islam. The Shiites, too, with their self-mutilation and bloodletting in memoriam of their founder Hassan. Kashif Al-Gita, *The Shia Origin and Faith,* (Islamic Seminary, 1980); Manazir Ahsan, *Faith and Practice,* (New Era Publ., 1980).

11. Joan Liffring-Zug and John Zug, eds., *The Kalons Heritage: Amish and Mennonite Heritage,* (Penfield, 1983); A. Eastlake, *The Oneida Community,* (AMS Pub., 1900) reprint.

12. Jacob A. Arlow, *Legacy of Sigmund Freud,* (International Univ Press, 1956; Arliner K. Berliner, *Psychoanalysis and Society* (Univ. Pr. of America, 1983).

13. Francis N. Thorpe, *Federal & State Constitutions* (Scholarly Pr., 1968). Geoffrey Marshal, *Constitutional Theory,* (Oxford University Press, 1980) Craig Ducat and Harold W. Chase, *Constitutional Interpretation,* (West Publ., 1983).

14. Marshal, op. cit.

15. See Appendix A and B.

16. Franz Michael and Eugene Knez *Rule by Incarnation: Tibetan Buddhism and Its Role in Society and State* (Westview, 1982); Sidney Lucas, *The Quaker Message* (Pendle Hill, 1983).

CHAPTER 4: BACKGROUND TO DEATH

1. Ruth Benedict, *An Anthropologist at Work: Writings of Ruth Benefict, Margaret Mead* (Greenwood, 1977) H. Russel Bernard *Human Way: Readings in Anthropology* (Macmillan, 1975).

2. Marvin Harris, *Cultural Anthropology,* (Harper & Row, 1983); Adamson E. Hoebel and Thomas Weaver, *Anthropology and the Human Experience,* 5th ed. (McGraw, 1979). Kenelm O. Burridge, *Encountering Aborigines: A Case Study* (Pergamon, 1979).

3. Ralph Linton, *The Science of Man in the World Crisis* (Octagon, 1980); Alfred L. Kroeber, *Anthropology: Culture Patterns and Processes* (Harcourt, Brace and Jovanovich, 1963).

4. See Appendix A and B.

5. Peter Hodge, *The Roman Army* (Longmans, 1977) Henry D. Parker, *Roman Legions* (B&N Imports, 1971) reprint of 1928 edition.

6. Valerius Aurelius Constantinus, the Great, Emperor of Rome (306–337), adopted Christianity and the Sign of the Cross.

7. J. C. Aveling *The Jesuits* (Stein and Day, 1982); Thomas J. Campbell, *Jesuits* (Milford House, 1970) reprint of 1921 edition.

8. Fredericke W. Powicke, *The Christian Life in the Middle Ages* (Greenwood, 1935); Jean LeClerq, et al., *The Spirituality of the Middle Ages* (Winston Press, 1982).

9. Frank Coppa, ed., *Screen and Society: The Impact of Television Upon Aspects of Contemporary Society,* (Nelson-Hall, 1980); Jerry Mander, *Four Arguments for the Elmination of Television* (Morrow, 1978); Bradley S. Greenberg, *Life on Television: Content Analysis of TV Drama* (Ablex Publ., 1980) Jennings Bryant and Daniel Anderson, eds. *Understanding TV: Research in Children's Attention and Comprehension* (Academy Press, 1980); N.S. Biryukov, *Television in the West and its Doctrines* (Progress Publ., 1981) (USSR: Import Publications.)

10. National Endowment for the Arts. *Arts and Cultural Programs on Radio and Television,* Report from the Research Division, 1977.

11. Benedict, op. cit.

12. A.F. Hinrichs, *United Minworkers of America and the Non-union Coal Fields* (AMS Pr., 1923 (reprint)); Harold W. Aurand, *From the Molly Maguires to the United Mine Workers* (Temple University Press, 1971); Barrie O. Pettman, *Current Research in Social Economics* (State Mutual Bk. 1981) B.F. Croke, and J. D. Harris, *Religious Conflict in 4th KCentury Rome* (Sydney University Press, 1982) John Ferguson, *War and Peace in the World's Religions* (Oxford University Press, 1978).

13. Michael Avery and David Rudovsky *Police Misconduct: Law and Litigation* (Clark Boardman, 1986) p. 1.

14. Established hyperorthodox groups include the great religions as well as the newer cults; John Loffland, *Doomsday Cult: A Study of Conversion, Proselytization and Maintenance of Faith* (Irvington, 1981); Mose Durst, *To Bigotry No Sanction: The Reverend Sun Myung Moon and the Unification Church* (Regney-Galway, 1984); Steven Gelberg, *The Hare Krishna Movement* (Garland Publ. 1985) Roland P. Beesley, *Yoga of the Inward Path* (De Vorss, 1978) See also citations for Amish, Mennonite and Oneida communities.

15. See Appendix A and B.

16. Landa F. Jocano, *Slum as a Way of Life: A Study of Coping Behavior in an Urban Environment* (Cellar, 1976); Michael J. Higgins, *Somos Tocayos: Anthropology of Urbanism and Poverty* (University Press of America, 1983).

17. Jocano, op. cit.; Higgins, op. cit.; George D. Spindler and Louise S. Spindler, *Urban Anthropology in the U.S. Four Cases* (Holt, Rinehart and Winston, 1978); Sally E. Merry, *Urban Danger: Life in a Neighborhood of Strangers,* (Temple University Press, 1981); Ulf Hannerz, *Exploring the City: Inquiries Toward an Urban Anthropology,* (Columbia University Press, 1980); Kenneth E. Readm *Other Voices,* (Chandler and Sharp, 1980).

18. Merry, op. cit.; Jocano, op. cit.

19. Merry, op. cit.; Jocano, op. cit.; Hannerz, op. cit.

20. Kristin Helmore and Karen Laing, "Exiles Among Us," reported in *The Cristian Science Monitor,* November 19, 1986.

21. William A. Geller, *Police Misconduct: Scope of the Problem and Remedies* (American Bar Foundation, Report No. 23) (ISBN 0-317-30476-3 2024819 (Books Demand UM); Ernest Hopkins, *Our Lawless Police* (Da Capo, 1931 reprint).

22. Eric Monken, *Police in Urban America,* (Cambridge University Press, 1981); Louis Marchiafava, *The Houston Police* (Rice University Press, 1977); Raymond S. Teske, *Public Perceptions of the Police* (Houston, 1982).

23. Cleo Orange, an ex-convict, having served 14 years in a maximum security prison, at an interview, Spring Term, 1984, at Florida International University, with students in a class studying police in the ghetto of Miami, Florida.

24. Louis A. Ferman, *Poverty in America: A Book of Readings* (University of Michigan Press, 1968); John K. Galbraith, *The Nature of Mass Poverty* (Harvard University Press, 1979); Sergio Cotta, *Why Violence? A Philosophical Interpretation,* Gullace Giovanni, transl., (University Presses, Florida.) ISBN 0-8130-0804-2; Erich Fromm, *Anatomy of Human Destructiveness* (Fawcett, 1978); Erich Fromm, *The Art of Loving* (Harper and Row, 1974); Bruno Bettleheim, *A Home for the Heart* (University of Chicago Press, 1974).

CHAPTER 5: MAN'S DAILY BREAD

1. *Newsweek,* 5/25/87. See also, *The National Law Journal,* 10/2/87.

2. Ernest Beaglehole, *Notes on Hopi Economic Life* (Yale University Press, 1937); Polingaysi Qoyawayma, *No Turning Back* (University of New Mexico, 1977); Tom Bahti, *Southwestern Indian Tribes,* (KC Publications, 1968); R. Bradfield, *The Changing Pattern of Hopi Agriculture,* (State Mutual Books, 1971); Mary-Russel F. Colton, *Hopi Dyes,* (Museum of Northern Arizona, 1978) 2nd ed.

3. J. Hector de Crevecoeur, *Letters From an American Farmer,* (Biblio Distributors, 1982).

4. *The Miami Herald.* 11/23/86.

CHAPTER 6: TOOLS OF DEADLY FORCE

1. Alice Miller, *For Your Own Good; Hidden Cruelty in Child-Rearing and the Roots of Violence* (Farrar, Straus and Giroux, 1983); Alice Miller, *Prisoners of Childhood,* (Basic, 1981).

2. Alice Miller, *The Drama of the Gifted Child,* (Basic, 1983); Robert Sam Anson, *Best Intentions: The Education and Killing of Edmund Perry,* (Random House, 1987).

CHAPTER 7: SOCIAL AND LEGAL ENVIRONMENTS

1. *The Miami Herald,* 10/30/86 recounts the story of Claude Dallas the fugitive killer, on the FBI's most-wanted list and with an outstanding reward of $15,000 for his capture. But the cult of the Old West prevailed. A full-length feature film about his exploits, was made. It was anticipated that A) He would be shortly captured. B) That he would be granted freedom. Both these prophecies came true early in 1987.

2. *The Miami Herald,* 9/1/87 (Associated Press Report); Samuel L. Blumenthal, *NEA: Trojan Horse in American Education,* (Paradigm, 1984); Allan M. West, *The National Education Association: The Power Base for Education,* (Free Press, 1980).

3. *The Miami Herald,* 9/1/87.

4. William M. Bart, and Martin R. Wong, *Psychology of School Learning,* (Irvington, 1974); Richard C. Anderson and Gerald W. Faust, *The Science of Instruction and Learning,* (Harper & Row, 1973); Alex Thomas and Jeff Grimes, eds., *Best Practices in School Psychology,* (National Association of School Psychologists, 1985).

5. Interview with Professor Sidney Mailick, New York University.

6. Abraham H. Maslow, *Motivation and Personality* (Regency, 1971).

7. Rebecca Burlend and Edward Burlend, *A True Picture of Emigration* (Citadel Press, 1974); P. Cafferty and Barry Chiswick, *The Dilemma of American Immigration,* (Transaction Books, 1983); Annual Legal Conference on the Represention of Aliens, 1978–1983, *In Defense of the Alien,* 6 vols., (Center for Migration Studies, 1984).

CHAPTER 8: PHYSICAL ENVIRONMENTS

1. *Design Guidelines for Creating Defensible Space,* (U.S.G.P.O./NILCJ, 1976).

2. Ibid.

3. C. Ray Jeffrey, *Crime Prevention Through Environmental Design* (Sage, 1977); Bill Hillier and Julienne Hanson, *The Social Logic of Space,* (Cambridge University Press, 1984); M. Gottdiener, *The Social Production of Urban Space,* (University of Texas Press, 1985).

4. Clemons Bartollas, *Correctional Treatment, Theory and Practice,* (Prentice-Hall, 1985).

5. Ibid.

6. *Design Guidelines,* op. cit.

7. Martin Wright, *Making Good Prisons: Punishment and Beyond,* (State Mutual Books, 1982); Lawrence S. Travis, et al. *Corrections: An Issues Approach,* (Anderson, 1983).

8. Imre R. Kohn, Karen A. Franck and Arlen Sue Fox, *Defensible Space Modifications for Continuous Row-Houses,* (Institute for Community Design Analysis, 1975).

CHAPTER 9: CHANGING PATTERNS

1. National Center for Health Statistics, cited in *Report to the National Council on Crime and Justice,* (U.S.G.P.O., 1986).

2. U.S. Department of Justice, Bureau of Statistics, *Report to the Nation on Crime and Justice* (U.S.G.P.O., 1985).

3. Ibid.

4. National Institute of Justice, *Incapacitating Criminals: Recent Research Findings,* December, 1986.

5. *The Miami Herald,* 5/12/84, p. 1B.

CHAPTER 10: ADAPTING TO DEADLY FORCE

1. Thorstin Sellen, *The Penalty of Death,* (Sage, 1980); E. Roy Calvert, *Capital Punishment in the Twentieth Century,* (Patterson Smith, 1973).

2. Yonah Alexander, ed., *Behavioral and Quantitative Perspectives on Terrorism,* (Pergamon, 1981); Jonathan Harris, *The New Terrorism: The Politics of Violence* (Messner, 1983)

3. Bowyer J. Bell, *Transnational Terror* (Enterprise, 1975); Louis R. Beres, *Terrorism and Global Security,* (Westview, 1979); Edward F. Mickolus *International Terrorism: Attributes of Terrorist Events* (Inter-University Consortium for Political and Social Research, 1982). David C. Rappaport and Yonah·Alexander, eds., *The Morality of Terrorism: Religious Origins and Ethical Implications* (Pergamon, 1982).

4. Harris, op. cit.; Gil Green, *Terrorism: Is it Revolutionary?* (New Outlook, 1970).

5. Richard B. Lillisch, ed., *Transnational Terrorism: Conventions and Commentary* (Michie, 1982).

6. Betty Friedan, *The Second Stage,* (Summit, 1982).

7. Allen P. Bristow, *The Search for an Effective Police Handgun* (C C Thomas, 1974); Mason Williams, *The Law Enforcement Book of Weapons, Ammunition and Training Procedures* (C C Thomas, 1977).

8. Bristow, op. cit.

9. *Newsweek,* 8/31/87, p. 6, cites a letter to the Academy of Medical Science in Moscow, printed in an official newspaper there. It must be noted that the official newspaper dismissed their sentiments as a "pernicious delusion."

10. Seminars in classroom settings in New York City, Teaneck, New Jersey, and Miami, Florida. Also seminars in community halls in Miami Beach, Florida. All with audience participation, notes taken by the author.

11. Kenneth A. Abbot, *Harmony and Individualism,* (Oriental Bookstore, 1970); Hsaiou-Tung Fei, *Peasant Life in China: A Field Study,* (University Publications of America, reprint of 1939 edition); Maurice Friedman, *The Study of Chinese Society* (Stanford University Press, 1979).

12. See Appendix A and B.

13. Public Broadcasting Network in the South Florida area at 9:15 PM on July 15, 1987. For background, refer to: John P. Brown, *Dervishes: Or Oriental Spiritualism,* (Biblio Distribution Center, 1968); Lucy M. Garnett, *Mysticism and Magic in Turkey: An Account of the Religious Doctrines, Monastic Organization and Ecstatic Powers of the Dervish Orders.* (AMS Press, reprint of 1912 edition).

14. PBS Network, July 15, 1987 (South Florida Region).

15. A small sampling, starting with older works is: Tacitus Aelianus *The Art of Embattling an Army,* (Walter J. Johnson, reprint of 1628 edition) (This is the second part of Tacitus' famous work, detailing Roman practice and theory. Robert Barrett, *The Theoricke and Pratike of Moderne Warres.* (Walter J. Johns, reprint of 1598 edition); Niccolo Macchiavelli, *The Arte of Warre,* (Walter J. Johnson, reprint of 1562 edition); Maurice Saxe, *Reveries, or Memoirs Upon the Art of War,* (Greenwood, reprint of 1757 edition) This notable work by the first marshal of Louis XIV of France is a still a basic text today. Tzu Sun, *The Art of War* (Oxford University Press, 1963). Mark Bothner, *Military Customs and Traditions,* (Greenwood, reprint of 1956 edition).

16. Ernest Dimnet, *What We Live By* (Arden Library, 1976)

CHAPTER 11: KILLERS IN THE STREETS

1. *Newsweek,* April 8, 1985, p. 2; June 29, 1987, p. 10.

2. Stephen P. Klein and Michael Caggiano, *The Prevalence, Predictability and Policy Implications of Recidivism,* (Rand, 1986); Michael Maltz, *Recidivism,* (Academic Press, 1984).

3. Rand Corporation of Santa Monica, California, see Klein, op. cit. as one example of studies made by this major research organization.

4. Klein and Caggiano, op. cit.

5. W.T. Moody, ed., *Nationalism and the Pursuit of National Independence* (Irish Books Media, 1982) Austen Morgan and Bob Purdie, eds., *Ireland: Divided Nation, Divided Class,* (Longwood, 1980); One must note how long ago outsiders have shown keen interest in the "Irish Question." Significantly one notes the following is still in print, and promoted by a publisher that has been accused of having U.S.S.R. connections: Karl Marx and Friedrich Engels, *Ireland and the Irish Question,* (International Publications, 1972). How far foreign support of the Irish violence goes has never been authoritatively determined.

6. Coral L. Daniels, *Encyclopaedia of Superstitions, Folklore and the Occult Sciences,* 3 vols., (Gordon Press, 1971) reprint of 1903 edition.

7. Vincent Bugliosi and Curt Gentry, *Helter Skelter,* Bantam, 1975); Susan Atkins and Bob Slosser, *Child of Satan, Child of God,* (Bridge Publications, 1977)

8. ABC Network, the "Oprah Winfrey Show," aired may 6, 1987 at 4:00 P.M. presented confidants of deadly killers who explained their dubious relationships to the entertainment of tens of millions of enthralled viewers.

CHAPTER 12: IS AMERICAN JUSTICE A CRIME?

1. *New York Times,* May 23, 1985. One year later, *New York Times,* May 23, 1986 the district attorney under political pressure was planning to indict various city officials

for the bombing, fire and deaths that occurred when MOVE was finally besieged. Again, another year later, May 4, 1987, the Public Broadcasting System presented nation-wide a documentary on the attack on MOVE. There was little discussion of the virtually impossible task of dealing with a hyperorthodox group devoted to hatred of its immediate neighbors, in an urban setting, under current doctrinal approaches to the implied religious, ethnic and political issues. Doggedly we return again and again to doctrinal problems we have not resolved.

2. *New York Times,* May 13, 14, 15, 1985.

3. Ibid.

4. James Q. Wilson, ed., *Crime and Public Policy,* (Institute for Contemporary Studies Press, 1983); see also: James Q. Wilson, *Thinking About Crime* (Random, 1977).

5. Jefferson's hope that public media would keep a rein on government is in his Letter to Colonel Edward Carrington, 1/16/1787 in *The Papers of Thomas Jefferson,* Charles T. Cullen, ed., (Princeton University Press, 1982) "The basis of our government being the opinion of the people, the very first object should be to keep that right; and were it left to me to decide whether we should have a government without newspapers, or newspapers without government, I should not hesitate a moment to prefer the latter."

5. 100th Annual Conference, May 4, 1987.

6. Thomas J. Anton, *Federal Aid to Detroit* (Brookings, 1983); James W. Fosset, *Federal Aid to Big Cities: The Politics of Dependence,* (Brookings, 1982); John H. Mollenkopf, *The Contested City,* (Princetone University Press, 1983).

7. Thomas J. Anton, *Federal Aid to Detroit* (Brookings, 1983); John H. Mollenkopf, *The Contested City* (Princeton University Press, 1983).

8. Donald Dahlin C., *Models of Court Management* (Associated Faculty Press, 1985).

9. Ernest Barker, *Political Thought of Plato and Aristotle,* (Dover, 1959).

10. Rene David and John C. Brierley, *Major Legal Systems in the World Today,* 2nd ed., (Free Press, 1978).

11. Ibid.

12. Evan Haines, *The Selection and Tenure of Judges* (Rothman, 1981).

13. In September, 1984 Dade County, Florida opened forty judgeships to the electorate's confusion. With almost eighty candidates from different political parties. The voters' choices ran more to name-familiarity than informed decision-making. The situation is not getting better. For the Fall, 1987 election there were 145 judge's names on the roster, all seeking this electoral office. This county has had seven different office-holders, in less than five years, all with the same name: Gordon. The matter is not resolved much better in most of the counties of the country.

14. *New York Times,* April 21, 1987, I, p. 18; April 27, 1987, II, p. 7; April 30, 1987, II, p. 9.

15. Interviewed on January 3, 1984, reported in *Newsweek,* 1/9/84.

16. Dan J. Lettieri, ed., *Drugs and Suicide* (Sage, annual review); Sidney Cohen, ed., *The Substance Abuse Problems* (Hayworth Press, 1981).

17. *Newsweek,* 10/6/86. Background is available in; Jack Abbott, *In the Belly of the Beast: Letters From Prison;* William Aberg, ed., *A Promise of Morning: Writings from Arizona Prisons* (Blue Moon Press, 1982A).

18. *Newsweek,* 10/6/86.

19. William Wilbanks, *The Myth of a Racist Criminal Justice System* (•••, 1986).

20. Joan Petersilia and Susan Turner, *Guideline-Based Justice: The Implications for Racial Minorities* (Rand, 1985).

CHAPTER 13: SCHOOLS FOR VANDALS

1. Shirley G. Moore and Catherine R. Cooper, eds., *The Young Child: Reviews of Research* (National Association of Child Education, 1982); Susan Isaacs, *The Nursery Years: The Mind of the Child From Birth to Six Years* (Schocken, 1968); Nicholas Hobbes, *The Futures of Children* (Jossey-Bass, 1974).

2. *American Bar Journal.* May, 1987, cover story.

3. *The Miami Herald,* May 10, 1987. Notably this item was in the section called, "Neighbors," on the first page, with the quotation by Miami Beach Police Chief Kenneth Glassman. Other cities demonstrate the same focus on "spot-news."

4. Dade County, Florida, *Report of the Grand Jury,* November, 1986.

5. Jon D. Miller, *The American People and Science Policy* (Pergamon, 1983).

6. *Newsweek,* 9/7/87, p. 60. National Education Association, *Report,* authored by Chairman Lynne V. Cheney, Fall, 1987. See also: Robert Coles, *The Moral Life of Children,* (Atlantic Monthly Press, 1986). This author has made a career out of listening to children. He has been called their spokesman and their poet laureate. Robert Coles, *The Political Life of Children,* (Atlantic Monthly Press, 1986. This book describes the indoctrination of Nicaraguan, and Polish children only ten years old ... *on opposite sides* of the same ideological question.

7. National Education Association, *Report,* authored by Chairman Lynne V. Chency, Fall, 1987.

8. *Newsweek,* 11/23/84.

9. James Q. Wilson, "Raising Kids," in *The Atlantic Monthly,* October 1983.

10. Ibid.

11. Id.

12. Id.

13. Id. citing Merton.

14. Travi Hirschi and Hanan Selvin, *Delinquency Research,* (Free Press, 1973).

15. Ibid.

16. *The Miami Herald,* 8/10/87, p. 9A.

17. John Dewey, *Child and the Curriculum,* (University of Chicago Press, 1956); John Dewey, *Democracy and Education: An Introduction to the Philosophy of Education* (Free Press, 1966).

18. B.F. Skinner. *Contingencies of Reinforcement* (Prentice-Hall, 1969) B.F. Skinner, *Science and Human Behavior.* (Free Press, 1965).

19. James Q. Wilson, (1983).

20. *The Miami Herald,* 7/31/87, p. 24-A *The Christian Science Monitor,* 11/19/86, p. 24ff; Frank G. Bolton, Jr., *The Pregnant Adolescent: Research Related to Clients and Services* (C.C. Thomas, 1980); Paula McGuire, *It Won't Happen to Me: Teenagers Talk About Pregnancy* (Dell, 1983).

21. James L. Hymes, *Behavior and Misbehavior,* (Greenwood, 1979); Rudolph Flesch, *Why Johnny Still Can't Read* (Harper and Row, 1981).

22. *Newsweek,* 9/7/87, p. 61.

23. Jerald Bachman, et al., *Youth in Transition,* (Institute of Social Research, 1971).

24. Lynne Cheney, of the National Education Association, in *Newsweek* 9/1/86, p. 7.

25. *Newsweek*, 5/11/87, p. 48ff; James N. Morgan and Greg Duncan, eds., *Five Thousand American Families: Patterns of Economic Progress*, 10 vols., (Institute of Social Research, 1983); Sidney Weintraub and Richard D. Lambert, eds., *Income Inequality* (American Academy of Political and Social Sciences, 1973); R. Sinha, et al., *Income Distribution, Growth and Basic Needs in India*, (Longwood, 1979); Richard C. Webb, *Government Policy and the Distribution of Income in Peru, 1963-1973* (Harvard University Press, 1977); Allan M. Carter, *The Redistribution of Income in Post-War Britain* (Associated Faculty Press, 1973).

CHAPTER 14: AIMLESS IS NOT HARMLESS

1. Robert Martinson, "What Works? Questions and Answers About Prison Reform," *Public Interest*, 35: pp. 22–54.

2. Yvonne Dilling and Ingrid Rogers, *In Search of Refuge* (Herald Press, 1984); Cynthia Aronson, *El Salvador: A Revolution Confronts the United States* (Institute for Policy Studies, 1982.

3. Samuel D. Warren and Louis D. Brandeis, "The Right to Privacy," in *Harvard Law Review*, Vol. 4 (1890), p. 19; Alan U. Schwartz, *Privacy; The Right to Be Let Alone* (Macmillan, 1962); Alan F. Westin, *Privacy and Freedom*, (Atheneum, 1967).

4. Although the FBI was informed about the plotting of a hate-group calling theNselves, Aryan Nazis, it took no immediate action. However, after they had committed a number of specific crimes arrests were made, April 21–23, 1987.

5. *N.A.A.C.P. v. Alabama*, 357 U.S. 449 (1958).

6. *National Commission on the Causes and Prevention of Violence and D.P. Moynihan* (Braziller, 1970); Daniel Patrick Moynihan, *On Understanding Poverty: Perspectives From the Social Sciences* (Basic, 1969).

7. De Crevecoeur, op. cit.; Daniel Patrick Moynihand, *Coping: On the Practice of Government* (Random, 1973).

CHAPTER 15: WORKERS AND SHIRKERS

1. Fawn Brodie, *Thomas Jefferson: An Intimate Biography* (Norton, 1974).

2. Population Reference Bureau, Inc. reported in *Newsweek* 5/11/87.

3. Nathan Glazer and Daniel P. Moynihan, *Beyond the Melting Pot: The Negroes, Puerto Ricans, Jews, Italians and Irish of New York City*, 2nd ed., revised (MIT Press, 1970); Nathan Glazer and Daniel P. Moynihan, eds. *Ethnicity: Theory and Experience* (Harvard University Press, 1975).

4. Don B. Kates, ed., *Firearms and Violence* (Pacific Institutes Publications, 1983).

5. Ibid.

6. *The Miami Herald*, 10/16/86.

7. 1987 Florida Statutes.

8. *The Miami Herald* 4/13/86 (Associated Press).

9. Brock Yates, *The Decline and Fall of the American Automobile Industry* (Random, 1984).

10. Yates, op. cit.

11. Gayle Kimball, *The Religious Ideas of Harriet Beecher Stowe* (Mellen, 1982); James Fox, *Religion and Morality: Their Nature and Mutual Relations* (Zubal Publisher,

1982, reprint of 1899 edition); Edna McDonagh *Doing the Truth: The Quest for Moral Theology* (University of Notre Dame Press, 1980).

12. Fred Spock, by-lined article in *Newsweek* 6/1/87.

CHAPTER 16: FREEDOM FROM ASSAULT

1. Sally E. Merry, *Urban Danger: Life in a Neighborhood of Strangers* (Temple University Press, 1981) Jacob Fried, *New Town,* (Hapi Press, 1983); Thomas W. Collins, ed., *Cities in a Larger Context,* (University of Georgia Press, 1980).

2. Martin A. Levin, *Urban Politics and the Criminal Courts* (University of Chicago Press, 1979).

3. Department of Justice, Bureau of Justice Statistics, *Special Report,* May, 1987.

4. Bureau of Justice Statistics, *Special Report,* May, 1987; Bureau of Justice Statistics, *Incapacitating Criminals: Recent Research Findings* (U.S.G.P.O., 1987).

5. *Special Report,* May, 1987; *Incapacitating Criminal: Recent Research Findings,* (U.S.G.P.O., 1987).

6. Jacqueline Cohen, *Criminal Justice: An Annual Review of Research* (Chicago University Press, 1983).

7. Alfred Blumstein and Jacqueline Cohen, 1979, "Estimation of Individual Criminal Rates From Arrest Records," *Journal of Criminal Law and Criminal Law,* 70:56–85; Alfred Blumstein and Elizabeth Graddy, 1982, "Prevalence and Recidivism of Index Arrests," *Law and Society Review,* 16:265–90.

8. Jacqueline Cohen, 1983, "Incapacitation as a Strategy for Crime Control: Possibilities and Pitfalls," *Crime and Justice: An Annual Review of Research,* vol. 5, ed., Michael Towry and Norval Morris (University of Chicago Press, 1983).

CHAPTER 17: SAFE HOMES

1. Warren Siegel, *The Criminal Records Book,* Elias Stephen, ed., (Nolo Press, 1983); Committee on National Statistics, National Research Council Surveying Crime, Bettye Penike, ed., (National Academy Press, 1977).

2. Gerald R. Patterson, et al., *Families With Aggressive Children* (Research Press, 1975).

3. Bureau of Justice Statistics, *Special Report: Family Violence.* (U.S.G.P.O., April, 1984).

4. David Finkelhor and Richard J. Gelles, *The Dark Side of Families: Current Family Violence* (Sage, 1983) Donna Hamparian, et al., *The Violent Few,* (Lexington Books, 1978).

5. *New York Times,* September 4, 1986; July 18, 1986.

6. *Newsweek* 2/16/87, p. 21.

7. Gerald R. Patterson, *Families: Applications of Social Learning to Family Life,* (Research Press, 1975); Gerald R. Patterson, *Living With Children: New Methods for Parents and Teachers* (Research Press, 1976); Gerald R. Patterson, *Social Learning Approach to Family Intervention: Coercive Family Processes,* vol. 3, (Castalia Press, 1982).

CHAPTER 18: LAW ABIDING POLICE

1. *New York Times* July 24, 1987. See also: Bob Woodward, *Veil: The Secret Wars of the C.I.A., 1981-1987* (Simon and Schuster, 1987).

2. *Brown v. Mississippi*, 297 U.S. 278 (1936) is one of the leading cases which forbade coerced confessions.

3. Daniel P. Mannix, *A History of Torture* (Dell, 1983); Edward Peters, *Torture* (Basil Blackwell, 1985); John H. Langbein, *Torture and the Law of Proof* (University of Chicago Press, 1977).

4. *Camabridge Ancient History*, vol. 1, p. 514.

5. Eric Monkonnen, *Police in Urban American, 1860-1920* (Cambridge University Press, 1981).

6. *Miranda v. Arizona*, 384 U.S. 436 (1967).

7. *Brewer v. Williams*, 430 U. S. 387 (1977).

8. Langbein, op. cit.

9. *Rochin v California*, 342 U.S. 165 (1952).

10. Interview with Detective Commander Charles Dauner, New York City Police Department.

11. *Schmerber v. California*, 384 U.S. 757 (1966).

12. Heinrich Oppenheimer, *Rationale of Punishment* (Patterson Smith, 1975); Stanley E. Grupp, ed., *Theories of Punishment* (Books Demand UMI, 1971).

13. *Rothman v. The Queen*, 59 C.C.C. 2d 30 (1981). This is a Canadian case, but substantially follows the American Rule. See also: *Sherman v. U.S.* 356 U.S. 369 (1958); *Sorris v. U.S.*, 287 U.S. 435 (1932); *People v. Barrqazsa*, 23 Ca. 3d. 675 (1958).

14. Professor White, "Trickery in Inducing Confessions," 127 *U. Pa. L. Rev.* 581 (1979).

15. *Crooker v. Calif.*, 357 U.S. 433, 437 (1958).

16. James B. Haddad, et al., *Criminal Procedure* (Foundation, 1987).

17. Florida, County of Broward deputy sheriffs shot and killed an 18-year old youth who tried to drive away from the scene of a car-stripping and in the doing, "tried to run over the officer." Reported in *The Miami News* June 28, 1984.

18. Alan Bent and Ralph A. Rossum, *Police, Criminal Justice and the Community* (Harper, 1976); Ernest K. Bramstedt, *Dictatorship and Political Police* (AMS Press, 1945) reprint edition).

19. Woodrow Wilson, "The Study of Administration," *Political Science Quarterly*, vol. 11, no. 1, reprinted in Jam M. Shafritz and Albeert C. Hyde, eds., *Classics of Public Administration*, (Moore Publishing, 1978).

CHAPTER 19: PROTECTION FROM CRIME

1. Eric Monkonnen, *Police in Urban America: 1860-1920* (Cambridge University Press, 1981); Ernest J. Hopkins, *Our Lawless Police* (Da Capo, 1971, reprint of 1931 edition) Josiah Flynt, *Notes of an Itinerant Policeman* (Ayer, 1970, reprint of 1900 edition); Josiah Flynt, *World of Graft* (Ayer, 1970, reprint of 1901 edition). William A. Geller, *Police Misconduct: Scope of the Problems and Remedies* (American Bar Foundation/ Books on Demand UMI, 1969).

2. *Gideon v. Wainwright*, 372 U.S. 335 (1963).

3. *Mapp v. Ohio,* 367 U.S. 643 (1961); *Miranda v. Arizona,* 384 U.S. 436 (1966); are only the tip of the iceberg of such decisions.

4. *In re Gault,* 367 U.S. 85 (1967).

5. Francis A. Allen, *The Decline of the Rehabilitative Ideal: Penal Policy and Social Purpose* (Yale University Press, 1981).

6. Gregg Barak, *In Defense of Whom? A Critique of Criminal Justice Reform* (Anderson, 1980).

7. Ibid. Most of the prosecutors and police officers surveyed in this research agree with this judgment.

8. *Newsweek* 4/27/87, p. 10.

9. Ibid., p. 11.

10. Ibid.

11. Ibid.

12. Raoul Berger, *Death Penalties: The Supreme Court Obstacle Course* (Harvard University Press, 1982) Hugo Bedau, *The Death Penalty in America,* 3rd ed., (Oxford University Press, 1982).

13. Peter Goldman and Tony Fuller, *The Quest for the Presidency* (Bantam, 1985); Kathleen H. Jamieson *Packaging the Presidency* (Oxford University Press, 1984) Richard A. Joslyn, *The Mass Media and Election Campaigns,* (Random, 1984).

14. *The Miami Herald, Sunday Magazine,* 5/24/87, p. 14.

15. Ibid., p. 15.

16. John O'Toole, *The Trouble With Advertising* (Times Books, 1985); Otis Pease, *The Responsibilities of American Advertising* (Ayer, 1978 reprint of 1958 edition) John C. Daly, *Advertising and the Public Interest* (American Enterprise, 1976); N.S. Biryukov, *Television in the West and Its Doctrines* (Imported Publications, 1981). This book is promoted by the U.S.S.R. and provides a Russian impression of the United States.

CHAPTER 20: TO BE A MINORITY

1. Fawn Brodie, op. cit.

2. Stephen Decatur, *The Private Affairs of George Washington* (Da Capo, 1969, reprint of 1933 edition).

3. Ibid.

4. Nicholas Capaldi, *Out of Order: Affirmative Action and the Crisis of Doctrinaire Liberalism* (Prometheus Books, 1985); Thomas Sowell, *Pink and Brown People and Other Controversial Essays* (Hoover Institute Press, 1981).

5. Capaldi, op. cit.; Sowell, op. cit.

6. Shirley F. Heck and C. Ray Williams, *The Complex Roles of the Teacher* (Teachers College, 1984); Terry Herndon, *We the Teachers* (NEA, 1983); Robert Kendall, *White Teacher in a Black School* (Devin, 1980).

7. *The Miami Herald,* 5/10/87, p. 1G, by-lined, Gail Meadows.

8. Harry J. Crockett and Jerome Schulman, eds., *Achievement Among Minority Americans* (Schenkman Books, 1972); Alexander W. Astin, *Minorities in American Higher Education: Recent Trends, Current Prospectgs and Recommendations* (Jossey-Bass, 1982); V.L. Melnick and F.D. Hamilton, *Minorities in Science* (Plenum, 1977).

9. David Reiss, *The Family's Construction of Reality* (Harvard University Press, 1981); Stuart A. Queen, et al. *The Family in Various Cultures,* 5th ed., (Harper and Row, 1985).

10. Susanne MackGregor, *The Politics of Poverty* (Longman, 1982); Louis A. Ferman, et al., eds., *Poverty in America* (University of Michigan Press, 1968).

11. Gerald R. Patterson, et al., *Social Learning Approach to Family Intervention: Coercive Family Process,* vol. 3, (Castalia, 1982).

12. Bill Marshal and Chistina Mae Marshall, *Better Parents — Better Children,* (Hammond, 1979); Saf Lerman, *Parent Awareness: Positive Parenting for the 1980's* (Winston, 1981).

CHAPTER 21: NOT TO BE COUNTED

1. John Galloway, *The Gulf of Tonkin Resolution* (Fairleigh Dickinson University Press, 1970); Gerald Kurland, *The Gulf of Tonkin Incidents,* new edition. (SamHar Press, 1975); John E. Mueller, *Presidents and Public Opinion* (University Press of America, 1985): Douglas Jerrold, *The Lie About the War* (Gordon Press, 1971).

2. Mueller, op. cit.

3. Jerrold, op. cit.

4. Randall B. Ripley and Grace A. Franklin, *Bureaucracy and Policy Implementation* (Dorsey, 1980); Byron Johnson and Robert Ewegen, *The Bureaucratic Syndrome* (Dodd, 1982; Douglas R. Arnold, *Congress and the Bureaucracy* (Yale University Press, 1980); Joel D. Aberbach and Robert D. Putnam, *Bureaucracies and Politicians in Western Democracies* (Harvard University Press, 1982).

5. *Newsweek* 6/11/84, p. 16, "Is He Sane Enough to Die?"

6. Thomas Maeder, *Crime and Madness: The Origins and Evolution of the Insanity Defense* (Free Press, 1976). See also: William J. Winslade and Judith W. Ross, *The Insanity Plea* (Scribner, 1983); Thomas S. Szasz, *Law, Liberty and Psychiatry* (Macmillan. 1968).

7. Szasz, Ibid. See also: C. R. Jeffrey *Attacks on the Insanity Defense* (C.C. Thomas, 1985); Kent S. Miller *Managing Madness* (Free Press, 1976).

8. James C. Giblin, *Fireworks, Picnics and Flags: The Story of the Fourth of July Symbols* (Houghton Mifflin, 1983); Alice Dagliesh, *Fourth of July Story* (Scribner, 1956); Charles P. Graves, *Fourth of July* (Garrard, 1963).

9. Horace Kallen, "Democracy *versus* the Melting Pot," in *The Nation,* 2 parts, 1/25/1915 and 2/18/15, reprinted in *Culture and Democracy in the United States* (Boni and Liverwright, 1923).

10. Ibid.

11. See Appendices A and B.

12. Kallen, 2/18/15, op. cit.

13. Maurice Craft, ed., *Education and Cultural Pluralism* (Taylor and Francies, 1984); Ricardo Garcia, *Education for Cultural Pluralism* (Phi Delta Kappa, 1981); Robert A. Dahl, *Dilemmas of Pluralist Democracy* (Yale University Press, 1982); Nathan Glazer, et al., eds., *Ethnic Pluralism and Public Policy* (Lexington Books, 1984). William A. Kelso, *American Democratic Theory: Pluralism and Its Critics* (Greenwood, 1978).

14. Milton M. Gordon, "Assimilation in America: Theory and Reality," in J. Alan Winter, et al., eds., *Vital Problems for American Society,* (Random, 1968).

CHAPTER 22: A LESS DEADLY SOCIETY

1. Leonard Bernstein, *Six Talks at Harvard,* (Harvard University Press, 1963).

2. Ivan Boesky the Wall Street insidetrader was sentenced, among other items, to pay a fine of $100,000,000. The ramifications were discussed for months. *New York Times* November 13, 15, etc. 1986. See also *Newsweek* December 1, 15, 22, 1986.

3. Jonathan Edwards, *The Nature of True Virtue* (University of Michigan Press, 1960); P.T. Geach, *The Virtues* (Cambridge University Press, 1977). For background: Immanuel Kant, *The Doctdrine of Virtue: Metaphysic of Morals* (University of Pennsylvania Press, 1971).

4. Backsliders of various cults interview by *Newsweek,* 8/5/85, p. 63. See also: Andrew J. Pavlos, *The Cult Experience* (Greenwood, 1982); Dave Hunt, *The Cult Experience* (Harvest House, 1980).

5. Interviewed by *Newsweek,* 5/4/87, p. 8.

6. Ibid.

7. Id.

8. Id.

CHAPTER 23: STRATEGIES FOR TYRANNY

1. Robert Hargrove, *EST: Making Life Work,* (Dell, 1975); Adelaide Bry, *EST* (Avon, 1976).

2. Philip C. Grant, *Employee Motivation: Principles and Practices* (Vantage, 1985); John P. Houston, *Motivation* (Macmilland, 1985); Russel G. Green, et al., *Human Motivation: Physiological, Behavioral and Social Approaches* (Allyn and Bacon, 1984).

3. Stockholders complained to news organizations, reported in *Newsweek,* 5/4/87, p. 36; "Corporate Mind Control." The state of popular interest was reflected in the ABC Network presentation on "20/20," a television show with high ratings, on 9/10/87 with the same name and topic.

4. W. Warner Burke, ed., *Current Issues and Strategies in Organization Development* (Human Science Press, 1977); John R. Schermerhorn, Jr. et al., *Managing Organizational Behavior,* 2nd ed., (Wiley, 1985); F. Luthans and Robert Kreitner, *Organizational Behavior Modification and Beyond,* 2nd ed., (McGraw, 1985).

5. Mary Beard, *The American Labor Movement,* (Ayer, 1969, reprint of 1931 edition); Ray S. Baker, *New Industrial Unrest: Reasons and Remedies* (Ayer, 1971, reprint of 1920 edition); Joseph A. Dacus, *Annals of the Great Strikes in the United States* (Ayer, 1969, reprint of 1877 edition).

6. S. Prakash Seti, et al., *The False Promise of the Japanese Miracle: Illusion and Reality of the Japanese Management System* (Pitman, 1984); Nobuo Noda, *How Japan Absorbed American Management Methods,* (Unip, 1982).

7. Bernard L. Slade and Raj Mohindra, *Winning the Productivity Race* (Lexington Books, 1985); Ralph Barra, *Putting Quality Circles to Work: A Practical Strategy for Boosing Productivity and Profits* (McGraw, 1983).

8. Frederick W. Taylor and Frank B. Gilbreth, *Principles of Scientific Management,* 2nd ed., (Hive, 1911); Donald C. Burnham, *Productivity Improvement* (Columbia University Press, 1973).

9. Elton Mayo, *The Human Problems of An Industrial Civilization,* (Ayer, 1977,

reprint of 1933 edition); T. N. Whitehead, *The Industrial Worker: Human Relations in a Group of Manual Workers*, 2 vols., (Ayer, 1977, reprint of 1938 edition).
10. *Newsweek*, 5/4/87, p. 38.
11. Ibid.
12. Id.

CHAPTER 24: STRATEGIES FOR LIBERTY

1. "Tyranny, like hell, is not easily conquered; ..." in Thomas Paine's, *The American Crisis, No. 1,* originally published, December 23, 1776. Available, *The Writings of Thomas Paine: The Standard Edition,* 4 vols., Moncure D. Conway, ed., (Ams Press, reprint of 1896 edition).

2. *Consumer Class Actions: Legislative Analysis* (American Enterprise, 1977); Herbert G. Newberg, *Newberg on Class Actions,* (Washington State Bar, 1981); Lawrence H. Curtis and Edward D. Tanenhaus, *Management of Mass Tort Litigation,* (Practicing Law Institute, 1981).

3. *Newsweek,* 5/4/87, p. 45. Diane R. Margolis, *The Managers: Corporate Life in America* (Morrow, 1979); Stuart A. Macey, *The Degeneration of the Corporate Managerial System* (American Classical Press, 1980).

4. Patricia M. Danzon, *Medical Malpractice: Theory, Evidence and Public Policy* (Harvard University Press, 1985); Sylvia Law and Stephan Polan, *Pain and Profit: The Politics of Malpractice* (Harper and Row, 1978).

5. Mark Kuperberg, *Law, Economics and Philosophy With Applications to the Law of Torts,* Biblio Distribution Center, 1983); *Consumer Class Actions: Legislative Analysis1,* op. cit.

6. Gamal M. Badr, *State Immunity,* (Kluwer Academic, 1984).

7. *People v. Caruso,* 246 N.Y. 437.

8. Herbert Fingarette and Ann F. Hasse, *Mental Disabilities and Criminal Responsibilities,* (University of California Press, 1979); Susanne Dell, *Murder Into Manslaughter* (Oxford University Press, 1984).

9. *New York* Times, March 18, 1981, and almost daily for months thereafter after John Hinckley, Jr. shot President Ronald Reagan and a number of his entourage.

10. *Florida v. Zamora,* 361 So.2d 776 (1978), 3rd DCA, appealed 372 So.2d 472, certiorari denied. See also *New York Times* May 23, 1978, II, p. 35:1.

11. *New York Times,* September 6, 1986, I, p. 1; September 11, II, p. 1.

12. *New York Times,* November 18, 1978, and almost daily thereafter. White's preliminary hearing was reported in the *New York Times,* January 17, 1979. His one year parole was reported *New York Times,* January 7, 1984, an event which induced a public spirited organization to offer $10,000. reward for the simple information as to where White was residing. See also: Robert Neely, "The Politics of Crime," in *The Atlantic Monthly,* August 1982, p. 31.

13. Robert E. Conot, *Justice At Nuremberg: The First Comprehensive, Dramatic Account of the Trial of the Leaders* (Harper and Row, 1983).

14. The incremental way we grew into the error described can be traced: Monell v. Dep't of Social Services, 436 U.S. 658 (1978); Hutto v. Finney, 437 U.S. 678 (1978); Owen v. City of Independence, 445 U.S.622 (1980); Brandon v. Holt, 105 S.Ct.873 (1985).

15. Hans Jonas, *The Imperative of Responsibility: In Search of An Ethics for the Techno-*

logical Age (University of Chicago Press, 1984); William Horosz, *The Crisis of Responsibility: Man As the Source of Accountability* (University of Oklahoma Press, 1975).

16. The knowledgeable State Prosecutor of Dade County, Florida, stated: "$1.8 billion is not turning away the problem." Reported, *The Miami Herald,* May 5, 1987.

CHAPTER 26: WHAT YOU CAN DO ABOUT IT

1. Willowbrook Hospital in New York City is the most notoriously well-known case, reported in *The New York Times* See also: Billy E. Jones, *Treating the Homeless: Urban Psychiatry's Challenge* (American Psychiatric Press, 1985).

2. Headlined advertisement: "A CRY FOR JUSTICE! I DESERVE JUSTICE! LET ME REST IN PEACE!" The smaller print told the story of a young man who had been slain in a robbery, and the trial of the man arrested for the crime was being overly prolonged. *The Miami Herald,* 5/11/87, p. 2B; Grant H. Morris, *The Mentally Ill and the Right to Treatment* (C C Thomas, 1970).

3. Kenneth Culp Davis, *Administrative Law and Government* (West, 1975), p. 3.

4. Ibid., p. 4.

CHAPTER 27: LAST WARNINGS

1. Unidentified school supervisor quoted in *Newsweek* 5/11/87, p. 74.

2. Photo by Dave Porter and Damon J. Hartley of the Detroit Free Press, published nationally in *Newsweek* 5/11/87, p. 74.

3. Will Herberg, "What Is the Moral Crisis of Our Time?" in *The Intercollegiate Review,* vol. 22, No. 1, Fall 1980.

APPENDIX B

1. Louis Breger, *From Instinct to Identity: The Development of Personality* (Prentice-Hall, 1974); George Butterworth, *Infancy and Epistomology: An Evaluation of Piaget's Theory* (*St. Martin,* 1982); Andrew W. Collins, *Development of Cognition, Affect and Social Relations* (Erlbaum Associates, 1980); Robert M. Kaplan, et al., eds., *Aggression in Children* (Klluwer Academic, 1984); Adrian Pinard, *The Conservation of Conservation: The Child's Acquisition of a Fundamental Concept* (University of Chicago Press, 1981); Jean Piaget, *Construction of Reality in the Child* (Ballantine, 1986).

2. Compact Edition of the Oxford Dictionary of the English Language, vol. 1, p. 1359 (Oxford University Press, 1971).

3. Thomas C. Oden, *Guilt Free* (Abingdon, 1980); William G. Justice, *Guilt: The Source and the Solution* (Tyndale, 1981).

4. Joseph A. Amato, *Guilt and Gratitude: A Study of the Origins of Contemporary Conscience* (Greenwood, 1982); Walter E. Conn, *Conscience Development and Self-Transcendence* (Religious Educational Publications, 1981); Rodney Collin, *The Theory of Conscious Harmony* (Statue Mutual Books, 1981); John Carmody, *Reexamining Conscience* (Winston Press, 1982); Ellery Foster, *The Comming Age of Conscience* (Sandrock and Foster, 1977).

5. A member of the hyperorthodox organization, Hisballah bombed 241 U.S. Marines to death in Lebanon, at the cost of his own life. Yonah Alexander, ed., *Behavioral and Quantitative Perspectives on Terrorism* (Praeger, 1982); Jonathan Harris, *The New Terrorism: Politics of Violence* (Messner, 1983); Christopher Dobson and Ronald Payne, *The Terrorists: Their Weapons, Leaders and Tactics* revised edition (Facts on File, 1982).

6. James E. Mazur, *Learning and Behavior* (Prentice-Hall, 1986); Alan Kazdin, *History of Behavior Modification* (University Park, 1978); Ron Norton, *Parenting* (Prentice-Hall, 1977); Hazel Benton, *Behavior Modification and the Child: An Annotated Bibliography* (Greenwood, 1979); Stephan Chorbver, *From Genesis to Genocide: The Meaning of Human Nature and the Power of Behavior Control* (M.I.T. Press, 1979); Edward W. Craighead, et al., *Behavior Modification*, 2nd ed., (Houghton Mifflin, 1981).

7. Flo Conway and Jim Siegelman, *Snapping: America's Epidemic of Sudden Personality Change* (Doubleday, 1978).

8. James A. Rudin and Marcia R. Rudin, *Prison or Paradise? The New Religious Cults* (Fortress, 1980); Earl Schipper, *Cults in North America* (Baker Books, 1982).

9. Andrew H. Leighton, *The Governing of Men* (Princeton University Press, 1945).

INDEX

265